Reinventing Japan

Reinventing Japan

New Directions in Global Leadership

Martin Fackler and Yoichi Funabashi, Editors

BLOOMSBURY ACADEMIC
NEW YORK • LONDON • OXFORD • NEW DELHI • SYDNEY

BLOOMSBURY ACADEMIC
Bloomsbury Publishing Inc
1385 Broadway, New York, NY 10018, USA
50 Bedford Square, London, WC1B 3DP, UK
29 Earlsfort Terrace, Dublin 2, Ireland

BLOOMSBURY, BLOOMSBURY ACADEMIC and the Diana logo
are trademarks of Bloomsbury Publishing Plc

First published in the United States of America by ABC-CLIO 2018
Paperback edition published by Bloomsbury Academic 2024

Cover photo: Digital handshake. (Peshkova/iStockphoto)
Jacket design by Silverander Communications

Bloomsbury Publishing Inc does not have any control over, or responsibility for,
any third-party websites referred to or in this book. All internet addresses given
in this book were correct at the time of going to press. The author and publisher
regret any inconvenience caused if addresses have changed or sites have
ceased to exist, but can accept no responsibility for any such changes.

A catalog record for this book is available from the Library of Congress.

ISBN: HB: 978-1-4408-6286-1
      PB: 979-8-7651-1830-6
      ePDF: 978-1-4408-6287-8
      eBook: 979-8-2161-3769-6

To find out more about our authors and books visit www.bloomsbury.com
and sign up for our newsletters.

Contents

Preface

Yoichi Funabashi

What is Japan's appeal? Where does its potential lie? What inspirations and ideas can Japan offer to the world? These are some of the questions that launched this project.

To find answers, we invited leading innovators and challengers from wide-ranging fields, and from both within Japan and abroad, to come and share their experiences and opinions. We sifted through their words like prospectors panning for gold, hunting for the precious nuggets of insight into the sources of Japan's appeal, both actual and potential.

The search for relevance is an important one for Japan, because it shows a way for Japan to escape its Lost Decades and find a new future. But this is more than just a quest to end Japan's long years of gentile decline. It can also make Japan part of a much larger international project, to find answers to the host of new problems facing us and our global partners, and to chart a new course for a world that seems to have lost its sense of direction. In other words, both Japan and the world may be seeking the same thing, not just new sources of growth or security but a new set of values.

Obviously, this is not something Japan can do alone. Our challenges are global challenges. The frontiers facing Japan's innovators are also the world's frontiers. Deflation, demographic aging, globalization and its discontents, populism, a changing geopolitical balance—the problems facing both Japan and the world are overlapping, shared, and interlinked.

Japan is no longer a late developer playing catch-up with advanced nations. With no more model to emulate, Japan must stand at the cutting edge of common global challenges and join in forging a new way forward. Japan is a member of the international community, sharing the same goals as other nations: pursuing happiness, building a better society, embracing coexistence, and creating a peaceful world. Japan is also part of the broader current of world history, and as such its endeavors add to the sum of humanity's efforts to improve itself.

Japan can continue to learn from the world while also increasing what it gives back. But what does it have to offer? What are Japan's assets and strengths? Who are the people molding these raw materials into something of greater, more universal value?

It was with these questions in mind that we launched the Why Japan Matters Project in October 2015. We were most fortunate to have Martin Fackler, former Tokyo bureau chief of *The New York Times*, act as project director while serving as a senior researcher and journalist in residence at the Asia Pacific Initiative. Martin led the project and took charge of the English version of this book, which also appeared in Japanese.

Offering him invaluable support was Warren Stanislaus, who served as the project's staff director. Warren joined us at the Asia Pacific Initiative from his previous job at the British Council, where he worked at the forefront of British cultural and public diplomacy.

The project could not have happened without the writers, who are all practitioners and researchers standing at the leading edge of their respective fields. They had the daunting task of synthesizing all that we had learned and forging those nuggets of insight into coherent, comprehensive narratives. They were guided by members of the project's working group, many of whom did not write chapters. Nonetheless, working-group members were involved in the project from the early stages, generously giving their time and wisdom.

Over the past year and a half, the project members gathered at the Asia Pacific Initiative office in Tokyo to hear some 50 speakers talk about Japan's role in the world. As noted above, we invited innovators from various fields who are themselves the embodiments and creators of Japan's appeal and leaders in transmitting Japan's messages to the world. The insights and observations contained in their comments are too numerous to cite. I apologize to these guest speakers and to our readers that only a small portion of those interviews could be recorded in this book.

In May 2016, we also gathered the authors for a day-long study group to begin to hammer out the project's findings. At the time, I made three requests of the authors.

First, I asked them to avoid the already well-known concept of Cool Japan, which has been taken up as a banner by the Japanese government to commercialize the appeal of Japan's popular culture. Of course, the government has the right and responsibility to promote Japan's excellence to the world and to use such concepts in its cultural diplomacy. However, I wanted our project to reflect the Asia Pacific Initiative's principle of complete independence from the government. The Asia Pacific Initiative's founding philosophy is reflected in its motto: Truth, Independence, Humanity. Thus, the project set out to explore fresh new avenues in concert with private-sector actors, including many from outside Japan.

Second, I asked them not to stray into the tired old discourse of Japanese cultural uniqueness, often known as *nihonjinron*. Even as we searched for the sources of Japan's appeal, we would not take the approach that Japan was culturally superior or possessing a unique, timeless essence that informed its strengths. Rather, I wanted to explore the ways in which Japan's frontiers were also the world's frontiers. While Japan's endeavors may have taken unique forms due to specific cultural and historical reasons, they were responses to common problems and reflected common desires and dreams shared by all people. I wanted to help Japan rediscover itself by encouraging the world to discover Japan. If we limit ourselves to claims of cultural uniqueness, we deny the possibility of sharing our values with the world.

Along the same lines, I also asked the project members to refrain from defining Japan's appeal in comparison to other countries, such as by listing their pros and cons. Such a zero-sum approach, particularly one that tries to argue that Japan is better than other countries, can only lead down the rabbit hole of belittling other nations, particularly Japan's regional neighbors. Such an infertile line of inquiry cannot yield creative thinking or leaps of insight.

The Rebuild Japan Initiative Foundation, which became the Asia Pacific Initiative in July 2017, was founded as an independent think tank by myself and some colleagues when we decided to sketch out a plan for rebuilding Japan in the wake of the Great East Japan Earthquake of March 11, 2011. One motivation was our shared conclusion that the nuclear crisis at the Fukushima Daiichi Nuclear Power Plant was a man-made disaster created by a breakdown of governance and failures in risk management and leadership. The Rebuild Japan Initiative Foundation's inaugural research project was the Independent Investigation Commission on the Fukushima Nuclear Accident, the first nongovernmental investigation into the accident and its causes. The commission's findings appeared in Japanese in March 2012, with an English version published by Routledge in 2014 as *The Fukushima Daiichi Nuclear Power Station Disaster: Investigating the Myth and Reality*. The principles that we established in creating this report—Truth, Independence, Humanity—became Asia Pacific Initiative's motto.

In the five years since its original founding as the Rebuild Japan Initiative Foundation, the Asia Pacific Initiative has published several books, including in English: *Japan in Peril? 9 Crisis Scenarios* (2014), *Quiet Deterrence: Building Japan's New National Security Strategy* (2014), *Examining Japan's Lost Decades* (2015), *Anatomy of the Yoshida Testimony: The Fukushima Nuclear Crisis as Seen Through the Yoshida Hearings* (2015), and *The Democratic Party of Japan in Power: Challenges and Failures* (2016). English versions of other projects, on the decline of postwar moderate conservatism and the population implosion in Japan, are being prepared.

The book that you now hold in your hands is the next step in our efforts to articulate a vision for Japan in the 21st century. Our goal is to open new public dialogue and inquiry aimed at finding answers within Japan itself, but without losing sight of the broader global context. In the book, we investigate new ideas and strategies for reviving Japan from its Lost Decades. At the same time, the question of governance hangs in the background. There can be no strategy without governance. Nor can strategy surpass governance—in the case of the state, statecraft. Bearing that somewhere in mind, we have tried to plumb the possibilities of Japan in this book.

Again, I would like to thank the members of the working group and the authors. I would also like to express my deep appreciation to those who spoke at the Asia Pacific Initiative. I thank Martin Fackler and Warren Stanislaus for their dedicated contributions. Tatsuko Masuda and Emi Tsuchiya played large roles in running this project. We also benefited from the help of many gifted interns: Misato Nagawa (Tokyo University), Katsuhiro Maruyama (Waseda University), Kaoruko Kobayashi (Keio University), Miho Genba (Sophia University), Masa Ueda (Sophia University), Ayaka Umehara (International Christian University), and Yuki Makita (University of Tokyo Graduate School). In the final stages, Harry Dempsey provided invaluable help in preparing the English manuscript. So did Elliot Silverberg and Yoshie Akimoto, who carefully fact-checked each chapter.

Each and every one performed wonderfully.

Yoichi Funabashi
November 30, 2016

Introduction: What Can Japan Offer the World?

Lully Miura

Why does Japan matter? This may seem an odd question to pose about an entire nation. Few would ask why Germany or Britain matter, even though Japan has a larger economy than either of those nations. And asking why the United States or China matter would surely just bring puzzled looks.

Yet, this is a question that Japan seems to face these days. Back in the 1980s, Japan mattered because of the perception, captured in books like *Japan as Number One*, that the nation's postwar economic miracle was a challenge to American economic dominance and even capitalism itself. But after the end of the Cold War and the bursting of Japan's spectacular financial bubbles in the late 1980s, the country entered a long period of sluggish growth and eroded confidence known as the Lost Decades. Japan seemed to lose relevance as the epicenters of world growth and innovation shifted to places like Silicon Valley and Shenzhen. Some came to see Japan as an ostrich sticking its head in the sand, willfully ignoring its own decline. Others began calling it an economic and cultural Galapagos, an archipelago increasingly out of synch with a rapidly globalizing world.

However, in recent years, the world's view of Japan has begun to change again. The late 2012 return to office of nationalist-cum-pragmatist Prime Minister Shinzo Abe, and his vows to revive Japan's economy and restore its pride, were an effort to reassert the country's importance. While his Abenomics growth policies have failed to convincingly extricate Japan from deflation or cure its economic malaise, there is no question that the tone of the national conversation has shifted. There is a growing sense that the Lost Decades may not have been as bad as they were made out to be. Some are starting to say that the seeds of a more promising future may have been planted during those gloomy years.

The painful changes of the Lost Decades have yielded new opportunities. The collapse of lifetime employment has made Japanese more willing to take risks and try entrepreneurial careers. The weakening of powerful industries and interest groups has opened cracks for new companies to spring forth. Disruptive new technologies make it easier for innovators to overturn established paradigms and plug into broader global currents. In short, Japan has increasingly seen the appearance of challengers who have been reshaping the status quo, though perhaps at a slower pace—and with less social upheaval—than is the norm in Silicon Valley.

Describing these changes, and the new ideas and directions they offer not only Japan but also the entire world, is one of the goals of this book. Another is finding the Japanese innovations that already contribute to the international community in surprising and profound ways. These are found in wide-ranging fields, from breakthroughs in stem-cell treatments to the mastery of sushi chef Jiro Ono and from working with Silicon Valley to create *Pokémon GO* to pioneering postmodern architecture. In case after case, we have discovered that Japan, in fact, has enormous relevance to the world, especially at a time when the post–World War II order itself is under challenge from rising populism and a shifting geopolitical balance.

Our biggest discovery may be that Japan now seems to stand at a critical juncture. The nation appears ripe for the next phase in its development, when it can offer still more to the world and perhaps help point a way forward for a global community that seems to have lost its compass. Japan has much to bring to this new task. It has built up a storehouse of ideas and innovations, of experiences and lessons, of unique approaches and perspectives accumulated over its history. Some of these are very old and were locked away when Japan began its embrace of Western industrialization and nation building in the 19th century. Others are relatively new, obtained from the bitter lessons of its Lost Decades, which are now being seen in a very different light.

For those decades offer more than just a cautionary tale. Not long ago, economists spoke of the Lost Decades as something unique, the outcome of a "Japanification" that other nations should avoid. Now, Japan's experiences are seen in a more universal light. The challenges of Japan's Lost Decades—aging demographics, deflation, chronic low-to-no growth—are now faced by many wealthy economies, particularly in Europe, but even in still-fast-growing Asia. And as other countries start to grapple with similar problems, there is a growing recognition that Japan did not fare so badly. In fact, Japan was able to maintain a stable, low-growth society that kept employment high and social disruptions low despite its economic troubles, an accomplishment that is all the more respected as other nations face unrest, violence, and the emergence of a new reactionary brand of politics.

"Japan is no longer unique," economic analyst Peter Tasker told the Asia Pacific Initiative when he spoke to us for this project. "Given the burst of the economic bubble and the other conditions Japan faces, one could easily make the argument that Japan has managed to do rather well."[1]

Japan was the first to find ways to deal with problems that many nations now face. This is true not just of deflation and low growth but also of calamities of a more deadly sort. During the devastating 2011 earthquake and tsunami, some coastal communities in northeastern Japan succeeded in protecting the lives of their citizens and keeping casualty rates low. They were also able to bounce back quickly and rebuild. In his chapter in this book, Daniel Aldrich introduces his groundbreaking research into the social infrastructure behind this remarkable resilience to disaster, which has lessons for other nations in an era of climate change and so-called superstorms.

Another finding is that being a Galapagos can actually have its benefits. Increasingly, the world is interested in Japan precisely because it seems to march to its own drummer. Tourists now flock to Tokyo to encounter the unique products, services, and experiences that Japan has to offer. Retailers like Muji, Uniqlo, and Evisu are popular because they offer something novel: original designs, quality craftsmanship, even a different world view. As globalization makes the world seem ever more uniform, these differences, particularly those rooted in Japan's culture and traditions, take on new value by providing refreshing diversity to an increasingly homogenized planet.

This dynamic, which Yoichi Funabashi explores further in his conclusion to this book, holds the key to Japan's potential. In fields such as design, innovation, and even scientific research, Japan has achieved considerable originality and creativity because it has been a Galapagos that did not always embrace global standards. At the same time, as Japanese society does inevitably become more enmeshed in globalization, the rest of the world has discovered Japan's novelty. One result has been the explosion in inbound tourism, which has been driven not just by a cheaper yen but also by the changed global perception of what Japan has to offer.

This ability to provide new products, new ideas, new inspirations—new ways to create value—reflects the richness and depth that Japan brings to the world. In describing this, we need to avoid Orientalizing Japan by presenting it as inscrutably different. Rather, one challenge that

Japan faces in seeking to offer greater value to the world—and thereby mattering more—is its ability to find common ground with other countries. Instead of exoticizing itself, Japan must convey its diversity and depth through narratives of universal significance.

"I think what Japan needs is a storyline," said Shinjiro Koizumi, a rising young member of parliament and son of a former prime minister. "We can no longer be the world's factory like China. So what can we be? We need to make a narrative. We need to live this narrative. Offering this narrative is the task of my generation."[2]

This is also our ultimate goal in this volume. We have set out to identify ways in which Japan matters. We have also taken up the question of how it can matter more. The answers, we learned, lie not only in the freshly original ideas and products that Japan has to offer, though these are numerous—more so than most people realize. They also lie in Japan's ability to present itself, to tell its own stories in ways that broadly resonate with the world's hopes and expectations.

Globalizing the Galapagos

Globalizing Japan's narratives will be a challenge. When people call Japan a Galapagos, the term is usually meant critically, to refer to an inward turn during the Lost Decades seen in data points such as declining numbers of Japanese students studying abroad. And Japan can be quite insular, even in its most globally popular industries.

In recent years, few Japanese products have been as iconic as anime, and few anime studios are as world renowned as Studio Ghibli, creator of *Spirited Away* and *Princess Mononoke*. Under the leadership of Hayao Miyazaki, arguably Japan's best-known anime director, the studio has helped define Japanese popular culture's image abroad.

Yet, to a surprising degree, Studio Ghibli remains a myopic denizen of the Galapagos. According to Toshio Suzuki, a film producer who has worked with Miyazaki for three decades, Studio Ghibli usually thinks only about the domestic market when making a new film. While the studio recently made a film with Wild Bunch, a European film distribution and production services company, most creations are still made solely to please Japanese audiences, with foreign viewers serving as not even an afterthought. He said most of the successes overseas were not due to Studio Ghibli's own efforts but to the work of foreign intermediaries like American animator and director John Lasseter of Pixar Animation Studios and later Walt Disney Animation Studios, who introduced its creations to the West.

"If you were to ask me if we ever considered the international response to a film at the outset, the answer is no—not at first, and not later on, either," Suzuki said. "We never considered it."[3]

In this regard, the Galapagos mentality is a double-edged sword: it can make possible freshly original products and ideas, but it can also lead to a forgetfulness about the outside world. One result is that the Japanese like to stay within their comfort zone. For Ghibli, this has meant the market within Japan's own borders. For others, their comfort zone can be much smaller, limited to even just a single shop.

James Freeman, founder and chief executive officer of Blue Bottle Coffee, praises Japan's baristas for being some of the most skilled and accomplished brewers of coffee in the world. Yet, most seem entirely content to run their own *kissaten*, or small coffee shop, without showing any ambition to open multiple stores, much less expand abroad.

Freeman said that a visit to Tokyo helped inspire him to open the first Blue Bottle in Oakland, California, to re-create the same sort of microroaster experience for Americans. The store took off, helping launch coffee's so-called third wave of more artisanal brews. In 2015, Freeman took Blue Bottle back to Japan, opening its first store in Tokyo to rave reviews and two-hour waits. He now has six shops in Tokyo.

Freeman says that he is still striving to reach the standards of Tokyo's master roasters. But it has taken an American entrepreneur—Freeman himself—to bring Japan's *kissaten* culture to the world.

"What I keep telling everyone is that, whether it's coffee or blue jeans or mozzarella cheese, someone in Tokyo is making it better than anyone else in the world," Freeman told the Asia Pacific Initiative. "But this is the thing: they are doing this amazing work in just one place—Japan. They aren't doing it out in the world."[4]

One Japanese creator who has stepped into the world's spotlight is sculptor Kohei Nawa. He is perhaps best known for his PixCell series, in which he buys animals that have been preserved by taxidermists and then covers their bodies with clear spheres of crystal glass. The idea, he says, is to reconsider the way in which we now see the world via digital images, which are pixelated.

It is the universality of this theme that allows his works to be appreciated overseas, where he sells most of his pieces. Nawa's works have been purchased by New York's Metropolitan Museum of Art and sold at Sotheby's for hundreds of thousands of dollars. He said that as an aspiring artist in Kyoto in the early 2000s, he did not set out to sell his works abroad. Rather, he said he benefited from galleries in Tokyo that had connections abroad and also American curators who scoured Japan looking for new talent and artworks. He said these intermediaries served as bridges between Japanese artists and foreign collectors.

However, Nawa warns that Japan's Galapagos mentality may be getting stronger, especially among younger artists. He said that while his generation, born in the 1960s and 1970s, has embraced the world, those born later have not done so. He said they distrust curators and gallery owners, choosing instead to sell their work directly to a small circle of acquaintances or via their own home pages. He said they show a lack of ambition to go outside their comfort zone.

"The artists in their twenties and thirties really aren't very energetic," Nawa said. "Each generation usually has its prodigies, the ones whom others follow and admire. But there aren't many like that among the younger artists. This has left the European and American curators puzzled. They ask, 'Why are there so few?'"[5]

Globalizing the Galapagos requires an ability to understand what customers outside Japan want. All too often, Japan's successes have been the result of foreigners who promoted Japan to the world and not of Japanese reaching out on their own. While the foreign promoters' efforts are entirely welcome, realizing Japan's full potential requires the Japanese themselves to join these efforts. They must look once more to the outside world, as postwar entrepreneurs like Sony's Akio Morita and carmaker Soichiro Honda once did. This will require a new openness in Japanese society and a willingness to embrace globalization.

It will also require an acceptance of the mavericks who challenge the status quo, as Morita and Honda did in their era. It is the risk takers and the outliers who lead society in new directions and who can unlock the treasures still hidden within Japan's cultural storehouse. However, Japan has a track record of frowning upon those who threaten the established order and its vested interests. In the future, will Japanese society be able to welcome the risk takers, celebrate them, even hold them up as role models? This may prove Japan's ultimate test.

Exploring Japan's Relevance

We believe this is a moment for Japan to step forward and take the lead in upholding the postwar global order. Japan can do more, playing a role commensurate with its size as the world's third-largest economy and its status as Asia's first advanced industrialized democracy. And Japan has much to offer, more than many—both within and outside the nation—realize.

For our project, we brought together some leading thinkers and practitioners in their fields to explore this question of what Japan has to offer the world. We also invited some 50 speakers—corporate CEOs, movie directors, artists, product designers, and other leading figures from Japan and abroad—to come to Asia Pacific Initiative to share their views.

The result is this book, which explores some of the areas in which Japan already offers much and has much more to offer. In their chapters, the authors describe Japan's enormous and often underappreciated contributions to the global commons in a wide range of fields. They also talk about how the world is starting to recognize Japan's importance and the surprising levels of political, economic, and cultural influence that it has already achieved, often under the radar. And they consider Japan's potential to play an even bigger role in the world.

The first three chapters of this book are grouped in a section called "Galapagos Incubator," which explores the unique ecosystems in Japan that allow it to be so creative and prolific.

In the first chapter, Matt Alt asks why Japan's popular culture has become so compelling to the rest of the world. He examines Japan's emergence from its Lost Decades as a new kind of global leader, one whose influence is rooted in anime, blue jeans, and "gross national cool." He describes how this change came not from the top down, via the bureaucratic-led initiatives like Cool Japan, but from the ground up. He focuses on how intense competition to win the fancy of Japan's highly selective and finicky consumers has turned the nation into a hothouse of creation, forcing companies and entrepreneurs to churn out new products from *Pokémon Go* to dozens of varieties of beer. Japan has added to its appeal by presenting an idealized image of itself as a land of Zen minimalism, seen in the no-frills products of retailer Muji and the popularity of Marie Kondo's books on leading an uncluttered life.

The second chapter, by architects Kengo Kuma and Dana Buntrock, examines the influence of Japanese designers in fields from fashion to furniture. The authors seek the sources of Japan's strength in design by taking a deep look at their own field of architecture, which they say Japanese now dominate. They describe how Japanese architects have won almost every major award in recent years, including the Pritzker Prize, architecture's Nobel. They then use their insiders' knowledge to explore architecture's unique ecosystem in Japan: the nexus of political money that funded eye-catching projects, the grueling apprenticeship system that gives young architects enormous freedom and also responsibility, and the intense competition in a highly crowded profession. Driven to

prove themselves, Japan's architects leap on the most minor design projects, including private homes, pieces of furniture, and even dog houses.
Kuma and Buntrock say the field has become a magnet for talent, as the
success of early postwar pioneers like Kenzo Tange established architecture as a path to a global stage.

In the third chapter, Fumiko Kato explores the reasons behind the
explosive increase in foreign tourists coming to Japan over the last five
years. For decades, Japan was a major source of outbound tourism, earning its citizens a reputation as camera-toting shoppers who flooded boutiques in Paris, New York, and Singapore. However, in 2015, for the first
time in 45 years, the net flow reversed when the number of tourists entering Japan surpassed Japanese going abroad. Now it is foreign tourists,
mostly from China, who crowd Japan's poshest department stores and
toniest boutiques. Kato uses surveys and interviews to show that they are
drawn by the high levels of quality and service available at everything
from hair salons to sushi restaurants to ski resorts. She also describes the
impact that this influx is having on Japan, leading to what she calls an
Asianization of Japan.

The next four chapters form a section called "Outliers and Pioneers,"
which look at how Japan has gained enormous creative energy by becoming more open to challengers and mavericks.

In the fourth chapter, Kenji E. Kushida reveals that while the world's
attention has been focused on Silicon Valley and China, Japan has slowly
reinvented itself to become more innovative, as it was during the era of
Sony and Honda after World War II. Using case studies, he describes how
Japan's large firms have turned to outsiders for inspiration and creativity.
He also shows how a vigorous startup ecosystem has begun to take off,
creating a flurry of new companies that are having an impact beyond
Japan's borders. He says these changes are reshaping Japan's society by
making entrepreneurship a much more attractive career path. While these
transformations have been profound, they have taken place at a gradual
pace, reflecting Japan's emphasis on social stability even at the expense of
growth. They are now reaching a critical mass that Kushida says is helping
Japan regain its place as a major global creator of new products and ideas.

The author of chapter 5, Yoshiki Ishikawa, examines how Japan has
become one of the longest-lived nations on earth: if current trends continue, as many as half of Japanese born today will live to a Methuselan age
of 107 years. Ishikawa looks at the secrets of Japan's longevity, including
access to affordable medical treatment, a healthy diet, and innovations in
caring for Japan's growing number of elderly. Ishikawa highlights two
such innovations: medical entrepreneur Shinsuke Muto's development of

in-home medical services to keep patients out of the hospital and Kyoto University professor Shinya Yamanaka's Nobel Prize–winning breakthroughs in so-called pluripotent stem cells and their potential for revolutionary new treatments.

Creating new technologies requires a strong foundation in basic research and science. In the sixth chapter, David Cyranoski explores Japan's rising profile in scientific research, seen in the string of Nobel Prizes won by its scientists. He says Japan has built up a reputation for building large, cutting-edge research facilities and also for producing scientists who demonstrate both mastery of their experimental equipment and a willingness to think outside the box. As examples, he cites the internationally recognized research of Shinya Yamanaka in stem cells, Teruhiko Wakayama in cloning, and Takaaki Kajita in neutrinos. Cyranoski says their breakthroughs were at least partially made possible by the culture of science that developed in Japan starting in the 19th-century Meiji period, when the nation set out to adopt not just the technological achievements of the West but also the scientific mind-set that made those possible. The result, he argues, is a set of unique institutions that shape the practice of science in Japan. One is the so-called laboratory system, derived from the hierarchical prewar German universities, in which a senior professor directs the research of junior faculty and students. In the hands of the right professor, this system offers younger scientists apprenticeship-like training in research methods and also a supportive environment that allows them to take risks by pursuing novel research approaches and ideas.

The seventh chapter, by Chinese author Mao Danqing, looks at how, despite political frictions over history and islands and Japan's own gloomy view of itself as in decline, Chinese interest in Japan has never been higher. This is most evident in the soaring numbers of Chinese traveling to Japan. Mao says the growing interest in Japan coincides with the rise in China's own living standards, which has changed how many Chinese view Japan. He says Japan is now seen as a highly developed society that feels less alien and more familiar to many Chinese than the West's advanced democracies. This growing empathy is apparent in an emerging Chinese view of Japan as a storehouse of Chinese cultural influences, like Buddhist temples, which were erased from their own country during the Maoist era. At the same time, many Chinese admire Japan's prosperous and safe middle-class society, which they see as having pioneered a distinctly Asian version of modernity. He says many Chinese now view Japan as a model of emulation, or at least a guidepost, as their nation tries to repeat Japan's successful emergence as a non-Western economic powerhouse.

The final four chapters take up Japan's role in the world and its potential for showing even more global leadership and are thus entitled "Global Contributor."

In chapter 8, Daniel P. Aldrich delves into the aftermath of the magnitude 9.0 earthquake, tsunami, and nuclear accident that struck northeastern Japan in 2011. Aldrich demonstrates how the ability to recover from disaster and to rebuild was not uniformly shared across the region. He says a handful of communities were able to bounce back and reconstruct within as little as two years, a feat that he attributes to the strength of the social and emotional bonds that tie their members together and create a shared sense of community. He demonstrates that these communal bonds also proved far more effective in saving lives during the actual disaster than more traditional protections, like concrete wave walls. He says these communities' demonstrated resilience to disasters offers lessons to the rest of the world and has already become a model for creating more community-based responses to deadly typhoons and earthquakes in the Philippines and Nepal.

The author of chapter 9, Hiromi Inami, looks at the soft power that Japan has gained from its massive foreign aid programs, which have provided a total of $334.5 billion to 190 countries—a figure surpassed only by the United States. Inami describes Japan as adopting an approach to foreign aid that differs from the United States and other developed-nation donors by focusing more on technical assistance, economic development, and infrastructure. She says this approach comes from Japan's own experience, as the first aid recipient to make the transition to donor. Inami shows that this has led Japan to champion a "customer-oriented" approach that emphasizes building up a nation's capability to be self-reliant instead of depending on the largesse of others—in other words, teaching a nation to fish rather than simply giving it a fish to eat. Inami argues that this approach has won Japan wide admiration in the region and also provides a model for other nations, like South Korea and Thailand, who have followed in making the transition from aid recipient to donor.

In chapter 10, Yuichi Hosoya examines Japan's security and diplomatic posture, which he describes as having reached a turning point. The rise of China, the election of a populist president in the United States, and the reality of Japan's own decline have increased pressure on Japan to shed its passive version of postwar pacifism. Hosoya describes the first appearance of these pressures in the 1990s in the form of calls from within Japan to become a "normal nation" with an assertive foreign policy backed by a full-fledged military. Hosoya also outlines a competing vision of "global civilian power," in which Japan adheres to its postwar pacifism while asserting itself more forcefully by other, "softer" means, such as development aid. He says these two visions may ultimately blend into a new direction for Japan, which will favor nonmilitary solutions while the nation also strengthens its ability to defend itself. Hosoya says Japan's continued emphasis on nonviolent dispute resolution could also become a new norm for a postwar liberal international order that has wearied of inconclusive wars in the Middle East.

The author of chapter 11, Jennifer Lind, takes a close look at former president Barack Obama's historic trip to Hiroshima, and Prime Minister Abe's reciprocal visit to Pearl Harbor, and asks whether this can be a model for Japan's reconciliation with its Asian neighbors. She argues that the visits actually followed decades of profound reconciliation between the United States and Japan and thus were the *result* of a long process of healing and trust building between two former foes, not the *cause*. She describes how the United States and Japan spent decades creating close economic, political, and military bonds, building up the groundwork for one of the most enduring and important alliances of the postwar era. For this reason, she says, Abe and Obama's exchange of visits cannot be seen as a model for creating a breakthrough in Japan's relations with other nations; rather, it should stand as testimony to the years of effort and dedication needed to make such grand gestures possible. She concludes that a similar visit remains a long way off between Japan and South Korea and would not be possible between Japan and China without an extraordinary reordering of regional politics.

Storytelling as Soft Power

The world discovers and adopts Japanese ideas and initiatives. These are then rediscovered back in Japan, where the imprimatur of global acceptance suddenly makes them seem more valuable. This is the process by which Japan learns what it has to offer the world.

This process of discovery, and rediscovery, is hardly unique to Japan. Throughout history, the same dynamic has shaped contact between different cultures and peoples. One lesson of history is that this process relies on those who stand at the borders. They must be ready and willing to seize upon such opportunities for discovery and rediscovery.

Another lesson is that successful interactions rely on the presence of storytellers able to communicate between cultures.

Special Cabinet Advisor Tomohiko Taniguchi, who serves as Prime Minister Abe's foreign policy speech writer, is one such storyteller. His job is to give Abe the words, writing in both English and Japanese, to convey to the world the prime minister's vision and goals. He has had notable successes, including Abe's speech to a joint session of the U.S. Congress in April 2015, which was warmly received.

Never before had a Japanese prime minister addressed both chambers of Congress. And never before has a Japanese prime minister kept a dedicated foreign policy speechwriter. The fact that Abe asked Taniguchi, a former magazine journalist, to fill such a position testifies to the crucial importance of message, and of storytelling, as Japan seeks to assert its relevance in an ever-more-globalizing world.[6]

Innovation depends on the work of outliers and mavericks. Taniguchi is just such an outlier. Japan needs outliers like him to learn its own strengths and possibilities. They can help Japan discover what it has to offer the world. These outliers often stand at the border, where they can help Japan rediscover itself by finding what the world has discovered in Japan.

One definition of soft power might be a nation's ability to shape its own narrative. This volume represents our attempt to find a new narrative for Japan, and in the process, discover the dimensions, and depths, of Japan's soft power.

Notes

1. Peter Tasker, speaking at Asia Pacific Initiative, December 2, 2015.
2. Shinjiro Koizumi, speaking at Asia Pacific Initiative, December 9, 2015.
3. Toshio Suzuki, speaking at Asia Pacific Initiative, November 24, 2015.
4. James Freeman, speaking at Asia Pacific Initiative, March 25, 2016.
5. Kohei Nawa, speaking at Asia Pacific Initiative, March 18, 2016.
6. Tomohiko Taniguchi, speaking at Asia Pacific Initiative, December 4, 2015.

PART 1

Galapagos Incubator

CHAPTER ONE

A Soft Superpower: The Pivot from Manufacturing to Pop Culture

Matt Alt

In the 1980s, Japan's global economic dominance seemed all but assured. Made-in-Japan exports from cars to televisions upended long-established American industries. The 1982 film *Blade Runner* envisioned a crumbling American cityscape lit by the glow of Japanese-language neon. In hard-hit Detroit, laid-off auto workers smashed Japanese cars with sledgehammers. Their anger sprang from fear: that Japan didn't just represent a competitor but their replacement—the future itself.

Such were the anxieties of the United States in which I was raised. However, as we know, the story didn't play out that way, as Japan slid into a nearly 20-year funk. Japan has been beset by challenges: economic stagnation, an aging population, an ongoing nuclear disaster, rising nationalism, and tensions with its neighbors.

By all rights, Japan's image abroad should be quite grim right now. Yet, somehow, it is not. Improbably, incongruously, Japan is viewed as a harmonious, immaculate, safe, high-tech wonderland. Far from a demographic basket case, Japan has become an object of ongoing fascination and appeal: ahead of the rest of us and going somewhere new and completely original.

Japan can appear a bewildering source of whimsical creative energy, where garish popular culture and Zen minimalism swirl and combine to create a postindustrial future of emoji and anime. Silicon Valley designer and business consultant Tom Kelley proclaims Japan "the most creative nation in the world."[1] Britain's *Monocle* magazine calls Tokyo the world's most livable city, offering "a balance of hi-tech efficiency and traditional neighborhood values."[2] Singapore's *Business Times* gushes about "Our Japanese Obsession" with everything from ramen noodles and hot springs to *Ultraman.*[3]

During its so-called Lost Decades, Japan's image underwent a metamorphosis. From a nation whose fortunes were built on heavy industry and hardware, Japan reinvented itself as a purveyor of entertainment and fashion trends. It transformed into a new kind of global leader, and one that has forced observers to speak in a new vocabulary of "soft power" and "gross national cool." One key to Japan's success is the fact that this transformation unfolded organically, percolating from the ground up. At a time when Japan's state-backed manufacturers were slipping into inexorable decline, its new content-producing industries were taking off in workshops and studios far from the corridors of bureaucratic power. In the 1980s, Japanese-produced fashions, foods, video games, and cartoons began to achieve surprising success in the West.

At the time, Japan's growing cultural presence was treated as a sideshow to its ascendance in manufacturing. But as Japan's heavy industries began to falter, global interest in its content began to surge, particularly among young consumers. After the anime and video game booms of the 1980s introduced new audiences to the charms of Japanese popular culture, the 1990s saw a string of international successes: shows such as the *Mighty Morphin Power Rangers*, *Dragonball Z*, and *Sailor Moon*, as well as video game franchises such as *Final Fantasy* and *Pokémon*.

Lana and Lilly Wachowski, cocreators of the hit 1999 film *The Matrix*, cited the anime *Ghost in the Shell* as a direct inspiration and even hired Japanese animators to craft a highly successful direct-to-video prequel called *The Animatrix.*[4] In 2003, Studio Ghibli director Hayao Miyazaki won an Oscar for his animated film *Spirited Away*, and director Quentin Tarantino incorporated an extensive anime sequence into *Kill Bill: Vol. 1*. Rappers such as Lil Wayne and Pharrell Williams pepper Harajuku fashion brand names like A Bathing Ape and Evisu into their songs. English editions of Japanese comic books became so popular that *The New York Times* felt compelled to create a separate best-seller list just for manga works in 2009.

The narrative had changed. Suddenly, it seemed Japan was everywhere cool and trendy people were. The change was so stark that it eluded the Japanese government, which belatedly realized in the 2000s the influence of their nation's pop culture abroad. But it wasn't until 2013 that the government's "Cool Japan" push to promote Japan's soft power became official, as Prime Minister Shinzo Abe announced a ¥10 trillion emergency economic stimulus package that included the creation of the Japan Brand Fund—"an organization to fund and support business activities to cultivate overseas demand for Japan's attractive products and services."[5] It was followed shortly thereafter by the ¥37.5 billion Cool Japan Fund, helmed by former fashion mogul Nobuyuki Ota. The success of these top-down initiatives remains up for debate, as does the very real question of whether authority figures anointing something "cool" actually has the opposite effect. But soft power was officially on the radar of Japan's ruling elite.

These developments beg many questions. Why is the world so fascinated by Japan, viewing it as a cultural superpower despite its decades of economic stagnation? What is the mystique of Japanese products and creations? How does Japan produce these trends and ideas? Can its "coolness" really be harnessed as an economic engine? This chapter analyzes examples of Japanese pop culture that have attained attention abroad to dissect Japan's ongoing attempts to become a cultural powerhouse. Through them, I hope to paint a portrait of modern Japanese cultural influence abroad and perhaps shed some light on its future path.

Japan's "Cultural Greenhouse"

Before unpacking the specific details of how Japanese creators and producers work, let's take a look at how trends start in their native country. Of course, there's no single route to sparking a fad. That said, modern Japanese society has several peculiarities that make it a breeding ground for new trends and ideas, some of which eventually take off abroad, either through deliberate marketing or by being discovered and promoted by foreign tastemakers.

Some are well known, like the concentration of Japanese population into dense urban centers and Japan's high levels of education. But one of the most important features is less well appreciated: Japan is home to some of the world's most finicky and discriminating consumers.

Japan's cities serve as the battlegrounds in an intense competition to win the hearts and minds, and thus the yen, of these consumers. This is seen in the unending efforts of Japan's ubiquitous convenience stores, or *konbini*, to attract and hold shoppers. The major chains like Lawson and 7-Eleven constantly test and introduce new products in a mad rush to gain a competitive edge over rival chains. This makes the shelves of *konbini* and also *depa-chika*—literally "department store basement," usually a floor devoted to dozens of counters selling prepared and packaged foods— incubators of many Japanese trends. Companies fiercely compete for precious shelf space, with the results tallied on a daily basis. Slow-moving products are quickly replaced by new items in a Darwinian survival of the fittest measured by sales. The boom-bust cycles of Japanese fads move at similarly high speeds, meaning that products that were hot one season might be gone the next.

One result is a level of prolific innovation that is simply unseen in other markets. Take Japan's food and beverage makers. In an effort to appeal to every conceivable consumer whim, Kirin produces some 100 varieties of canned and bottled soft drinks; its competitor Suntory has 19 variations in its Boss lineup of canned coffee alone, including Premium Boss The Mild, Boss Silky Drip, and Boss Guts. Even established brands are often refreshed once or twice a year to retain consumers' interest. Beverage companies "have to adapt the product to changing consumer tastes or else the drink will be seen as old-fashioned and consumers will abandon it," Suntory marketing officer Josuke Kimura told the *Financial Times* in 2011.[6]

While there are, of course, longtime best sellers—Coca-Cola and Kirin Lager always get prominent shelf space—retail stores represent dynamic testing grounds where novelty comes to be expected, and then demanded. These environments are greenhouses for creating new products and trends.

Another answer may lie in the still formidable size of Japan's domestic market. Despite its economic troubles, Japan's domestic retail sales still total ¥135 trillion, or $1.23 trillion, a year, a sum that falls behind only China and the United States. Japan's domestic market is large enough that it can seem a world unto itself, giving Japanese companies ample financial incentive to develop unique products and services tailored to Japan's consumers. However, this also has its downside. Japan is large enough that many of its companies have been content to focus on domestic sales, ignoring the potential overseas appeal of their creations. A perfect case in point: the emoji. They were launched in 1999 by domestic cell phone giant DoCoMo as an attempt to deliver graphic elements to then still-primitive phone screens. They quickly took off among young girls, who repurposed the icons to add cute flair to their text messages and e-mails. But by the end of the first decade of the 2000s, most Japanese users had moved on to other things.

It was only after Apple and Google stumbled upon emoji, which were modified for use on iPhones and other global platforms, that they spread outside Japan. So insulated is the Japanese market that many here, including emoji's creator, Shigetaka Kurita, were not even aware of emoji's growing popularity abroad. When President Barack Obama mentioned them in a White House speech in 2015, Kurita said he was taken by surprise. "I suspect most Japanese people's response was, 'What, emoji are popular over there?!'"[7] Emoji may have been born in Japan, but their spread abroad resulted in little economic benefit to their home country.

What Makes Japan "Cool"?

How do foreigners react to these Japanese creations once they leave their own borders? Taken out of their native cultural context, Japanese trends can seem surprising, even perplexing, leading to the proliferation of media stories about "weird" Japan. Even within Japan, there is the recent temptation to lump every new cultural product into the one-size-fits-all category of Cool Japan.

Look a bit more deeply, however, and there are substantial differences in how Japan's creations are perceived, both at home and abroad. As W. David Marx, the author of *Ametora: How Japan Saved American Style*, told me, "When you look at Japanese cultural products, you have to divide them broadly into two types: those for 'elites' and those for average consumers. Things like the books of Haruki Murakami, or Shibuya-kei music, or high-end designer jeans, they're for elites. But things like anime and manga are not for elites; they're for everyone. The lessons you can take from each of these types of products are completely different."[8]

It is important to note here that "elite" doesn't necessarily mean those with more wealth or political power. Rather, Marx is referring to the connoisseurs who might be deeply steeped in a certain trend or subcurrent in the fashion stream and thus willing to pay more. A recent example is the exploding popularity of Japanese denim, long seen as the most American of clothing fabrics. These days, it's Japanese blue jeans that command top dollar overseas, both because of their high quality and the added cultural cachet of being made in Japan. A painstakingly handcrafted pair of blue jeans made by Evisu Genes might fetch $400 in a New York City boutique.

Evisu was founded in 1991 in Osaka by Hidehiko Yamane, former manager of a shop specializing in vintage American jeans, and a die-hard denim aficionado named Mikiharu Tsujita. Paradoxically, "Evisu's trick was to use Oriental design motifs to position its jeans as more authentic than modern American jeans," explained Marx in *Ametora*. "Their jeans told a story of superior Japanese craftsmen working hard to make the things that Americans could no longer make themselves."[9]

Evisu's founders tore apart expensive vintage Levi's to determine what made them so appealing and eschewed the vintage-style denim then on the market for something even more authentic in look and feel. They sourced cotton from Zimbabwe, of all places, had it dyed indigo blue using traditional Japanese techniques, spun it on Japanese looms in Okayama that predate the newer mass-production technologies, and finished off each pair with stylized seagull logos painted by hand. None of this came cheap, and the end product cost many times more than mass-produced jeans.

Evisu's biggest coup may have been its decision to partner with a British distributor who could get their product into luxury boutiques and, perhaps more importantly, the hands of celebrities. David Beckham was an early adopter, followed by American rap stars Jay-Z, Snoop Dogg, and Lil Wayne. By 2006, the Fashion and Style section of *The New York Times* was asking, "Who Pays $600 for Jeans?"—a question it quickly answered by quoting the manager of a New York boutique called Atrium who proclaimed, "We sell through everything we get."[10] Evisu also enjoys a loyal following in Japan, where local denim is also seen as best. "After Japan lost its edge on consumer electronics, semiconductors, and even video gaming consoles, denim gave Japan a new arena for national pride," Marx said.[11]

Yet there is no question that the market for $600 pairs of jeans is a limited one, even in Japan. Evisu is a good example of how elite products are a hard sell to mass-market audiences more motivated by cost than cachet. This highlights a hurdle to the further broadening of Japan's cultural appeal: its "coolest" products are often produced by craftspeople with little ability or even inclination to increase output to grow their market but who instead seem content with offering exclusively to a niche audience.

This elite connoisseurship stands in stark contrast to Japan's much gaudier popular culture. The nation's mass-market aesthetic is seen in the loud, energetic design that informs more prosaic everyday products, such as manga, toys, anime, video games, instant ramen, or the neon-and-LCD festooned architecture of urban areas such as Tokyo's Shibuya, Harajuku, and Shinjuku districts. "The design is kind of bipolar here," said ex-Apple executive James Higa, who frequently visited Japan with Steve Jobs. "You have Ryoan-ji on one side, and you have Hello Kitty on the other side."[12]

Jeans for $600 or $10?

This bifurcation of Japanese products into elite and mainstream is seen in the fashion industry. Here, the polar opposite of Evisu is Uniqlo, which in its home market of Japan is a mass purveyor of low-priced casual wear. While Evisu has 20 outlets in Japan, Uniqlo has 1,861 stores in 18 countries and territories worldwide, including flagships in London, Paris, and New York.[13] If Evisu is for the elite consumer, Uniqlo proudly targets the everyman: a pair of jeans here might set you back only ¥990, or less than $10. While sitting at opposite ends of the spectrum, both fashion companies achieved success abroad. At first glance, there might seem little else to connect a specialty shop like Evisu with a mass-market brand like Uniqlo. But there are intriguing, if indirect, links.

Although Uniqlo's history extends back to the 1940s with the founding of a series of menswear shops in western Japan, its story really begins in 1997, when Uniqlo's parent company, Fast Retailing, took a page from American retailer Gap and began producing their own exclusive lines of clothing. The first urban Uniqlo store opened in Tokyo's Harajuku fashion district in 1998, with an emphasis on fashionable basics at a reasonable cost.

The driver of this change was Uniqlo's second-generation president, Tadashi Yanai, who was every bit as fascinated by American culture as Evisu's Yamane. In an October 2016 interview, Yanai told *The Washington Post* that he was "born and raised in occupied Japan . . . under the great influence of American culture. That was the influence when I was being brought up."[14] But where Evisu focused on replicating vintage mainstream fashions for boutique customers, Yanai chose to bring American-inspired boutique fashions to mainstream consumers.

Uniqlo specializes in Western-style clothing but with a Japanese touch: the highly attentive service that its clerks are trained to provide customers. This Japanese standard of service, known as *omotenashi*, has become a selling point abroad: a sign on the wall of the Uniqlo shop in Manhattan's Soho neighborhood proclaimed itself "A new Tokyo in Soho" and promised that it is "always striving to bring our little bit of Tokyo culture to you."[15] But unlike Japan's boutique producers such as Evisu, Uniqlo offers its Japanese experience at a very affordable price by locating its production in China and other low-cost Asian countries (where there have been disputes about working conditions at factories making clothes for Uniqlo). In essence, Uniqlo tries to balance American-inspired outsourcing of production while maintaining an image of Japanese quality and service.

One notable exception is its line of jeans made with selvedge, a type of denim made using the older, slower weaving techniques of the early 20th century. The fabric is produced by Kaihara, a Japanese company specializing in traditional dyeing and weaving techniques that also supplies selvedge denim to many boutique jeans brands. The difference is that Uniqlo uses the fabric to make its jeans in Bangladesh, allowing for a lower price.

Would Uniqlo be producing selvedge jeans if the path hadn't been forged by elite trailblazers like Evisu? Probably not. And the interaction between the two appears to go the other way as well: faced with Uniqlo's move into vintage-style jeans, Evisu has also been forced to innovate. Evisu's 2016 product lineup includes jeans brightly festooned with motifs of traditional Japanese fabric patterns and Chinese characters—a far cry from the retro American look with which the company began. This unique interplay between boutique retailers like Evisu, craft manufacturers like Kaihara, and mass-market retailers like Uniqlo exemplifies the dynamism in the Japanese fashion industry that has propelled it both domestically and abroad.

Yanai has publicly stated his ambition to overtake Zara, the Spanish company that has grown to become the world's largest clothing retailer and purveyor of the cheap yet stylish casual wear known as fast fashion in the United States.[16] However, so far, his company has failed to win the same mass-market appeal abroad that it enjoys in Japan.

In the United States, Uniqlo's customers are so far limited to urban centers like New York. It does well there: the Soho store sold 2,000 of a single style of fleece jacket in just one day, reported *New York Magazine* in 2010.[17] It also has a store on the swanky Fifth Avenue. But while Uniqlo has established such beachheads in large cities, it has struggled to expand into the shopping malls of suburban and rural United States. Its first attempt, in the early 2000s, was "disastrous," in Yanai's own words, leading to the shuttering of Uniqlo outlets in suburban malls throughout the United States. "People know us in places like New York," lamented Yanai to *Reuters*. "But we're not known in other areas."[18]

So far, Uniqlo has failed to reach beyond its current loyal American consumer base of urban fashion connoisseurs and appeal to average consumers. This is a challenge shared by many Japanese companies. While Japanese producers of elite products in their home market can often find similarly elite audiences abroad, its producers of mass-market fashion have enjoyed less success.

This also holds true with manga. In Japan, it is hard to imagine a more grassroots, mass-market product than manga, which have helped keep the print industry afloat. But the costs of localizing Japanese manga for the American market can make them more expensive than U.S. comic books. There are also cultural hurdles in their stories that can limit their popularity to niche audiences of Japanophile consumers abroad.

In fact, Japanese products tend not to fare well abroad if they appear too Japanese. Many of the most popular cultural products from Japan are not indigenously Japanese in origin but, like Evisu jeans, are adaptations of Western ideas. In the immediate postwar era, Japanese companies strove to create quality copies of Western products for both domestic and foreign sale. Recently, however, the biggest successes tend to be cases where the Japanese do not just imitate the original import but take it a step further. This happens as Japanese companies master the production and then look for ways to improve or innovate in order to win more sales in the domestic market. This can lead to products that not only improve on the original but take a familiar product in some wholly new or even exotic direction.

This pattern holds in many cultural products. Take literature: Haruki Murakami, a perennial candidate for the Nobel Prize in Literature, is popular for writing books in the hard-boiled idiom of the American 1940s but with a uniquely Japanese sensibility. Or animated film: Japan's best-known anime director, Hayao Miyazaki, grew up watching Disney and often favors vaguely European settings for his groundbreaking creations. Another example is Japanese whisky, which has won numerous awards for its fusing of traditional Scottish distilling techniques with local materials, such as *mizunara* wood for barrel aging. Even toilets follow this pattern: Japanese maker Toto is famous for its Washlet toilet seats, which are heated and outfitted with bottom-washing spray nozzles that make paper obsolete and control panels complicated enough to impress a starship captain.

Yet, in the United States, the Washlet remains "a foreign cultural curiosity that has never widely caught on," as *The New York Times* put it in 2015.[19] One reason, according to the paper of record, was the "embarrassment" that American consumers felt when confronted with such high-tech solutions for lowly body functions. It is but one example of a well-designed and highly innovative Japanese idea that has struggled to appeal beyond a connoisseur audience abroad.

The Power of *Pokémon GO*

Video games are one mass-market product that Japan used to dominate. Japanese game consoles like Nintendo's Famicom took off in popularity in the 1980s. A decade later, American companies had all but been displaced from their home market by not only Nintendo but Sega, Sony, Tomy, Bandai, and NEC, turning characters like Super Mario into cultural icons for generations of Americans.

However, Japan's supremacy ended with the coming of the smartphone and free-to-download apps. By 2016, there wasn't a single Japanese title among the top 10 best-selling games in the United States, for either console or smartphone.[20] The biggest reason for this retreat is an increasing divergence between the tastes of consumers in Japan and in other countries, leading to the production of games in Japan with little appeal abroad. As a result, while Japanese developers have enjoyed a great deal of domestic success with free-to-play games, they have often struggled to replicate it overseas.[21] There was, however, one highly notable exception: *Pokémon GO*, released abroad in July 2016 and in Japan shortly thereafter.

Even if you aren't a fan of Japanese popular culture, chances are you're at least passingly familiar with Pokémon, the fictional creatures created by Satoshi Tajiri for Nintendo in 1995. ("Pokémon" is short for the series' original Japanese name, Pocket Monster.) More than 20 years later, Pokémon remains one of Japan's most visible consumer products. Yet despite the ubiquity of its cute characters, the franchise was essentially running on creative fumes until a surprising development in 2016.

That is when Nintendo finally crossed over into smartphones by partnering with a Google spin-off called Niantic Labs to bring its characters to a free gaming app. *Pokémon GO*, as the game came to be called, debuted to instant, explosive success. Within days, it was No. 1 on Apple's app store, sending Nintendo's stock rocketing upward by 53 percent; within two weeks, the game had been downloaded 15 million times.[22] *Pokémon GO* quickly became a social phenomenon and a source of social problems. The game required users to walk around outdoors, staring at their smartphone screens as they "searched" for Pokémon digitally superimposed over the view from the phone's camera. This led to incidents in which engrossed players crowded into normally quiet parks and public spaces, trespassed on private property, or worse. One study in the United States blamed the game for causing more than 110,000 traffic accidents and near misses as both drivers and pedestrians were distracted by the game.[23]

As of August 2016, *Pokémon GO* had been downloaded some 100 million times worldwide and was reportedly generating $10 million a day in revenues from optional in-app purchases.[24] This is soft power turned into hard cash; *Newsweek* magazine even dubbed it "Pokénomics." But how did it happen? What role did Japanese content makers play in making it happen? And is this success replicable?

In 1996, Nintendo released the first two Pokémon games for its Game Boy handheld console. The series was originally launched to little fanfare, as an experimental project aimed at what was assumed to be a limited audience of die-hard game fans. But unlike most video games of the era, which did the vast majority of their sales in the first weeks after going on sale, Pokémon kept selling month after month, fueled by word of mouth among its school-age audience. While the popularity at this stage was purely a grassroots phenomenon, Nintendo quickly sensed its potential, licensing an animated television program, playing cards with the characters, and a series of video game sequels. The canny "media mix" marketing strategy led to sales of some 4 million copies of the game by the end of 1997. By the time it arrived in foreign markets, in September 1998, Pokémon had been honed—or should we say, using the game's own terminology, "evolved"—into a tightly interlocking multimedia franchise that proved as big a hit abroad as it had in its home country. By 1999, Western media outlets were talking about "Pokémania."

Pokémon proved a hugely reliable source of income for many years; in 2014, the Pokémon Company (a joint venture spun off by Nintendo and two other stakeholders in 1998 to manage the franchise) reportedly generated $1.5 billion in annual revenue.[25] Pokémon was ranked the nation's fourth most lucrative character series, rivaling even the venerable Hello Kitty.[26]

This competition played out against the backdrop of a rapid shift in the gaming industry. Consumers were abandoning specialized gaming consoles in favor of smartphones, whose increasing capabilities offered gaming experiences rivaling or even besting those seen on TV screens. At first, Nintendo refused to move into smartphones. In 2013, late president Satoru Iwata told *The Wall Street Journal* that "20 years down the line, we may look back at the decision not to supply Nintendo games to smartphones and think that is the reason why the company is still here."[27]

But change was coming, and just as with emoji, it was delivered by an American tech company. In 2014, Google prepared an elaborate April Fool's joke in which its maps were populated by countless tiny Pocket Monsters. An accompanying video got 18 million views. This attracted the attention of John Hanke, president of Niantic Labs. Niantic had already created a successful "augmented reality" game called *Ingress* that used mobile-mapping technology on smartphones to turn the real world into a virtual playing field.

Ingress's unique approach to gaming earned it many fans in the industry, including, as it turns out, the president of the Pokémon Company in

Japan, Tsunekazu Ishihara. And Nintendo itself had a long interest in getting players off of couches and into the action. Its 2006 Wii console incorporated motion-sensing controllers to allow players to interact with their screens via physical movements. When Hanke pitched the idea of a collaboration that would bring Pokémon hunting into the real world, Nintendo "totally got where we were coming from," Hanke said.[28] The Japanese giant was so enamored, in fact, that it invested $20 million in Niantic, with promises of an additional $10 million to come.[29]

Niantic's augmented reality allows *Pokémon GO* players to freely roam the real world in search of characters that pop up on their smartphone screens. For Pokémon fans, this allowed them to live out the game they had previously only been able to play in their living room. But the game also appealed to new users because it was free to download. This lowered the barrier of entry for casual and first-time gamers, who could jump in without investing in a dedicated game system or software. More serious fans could pay for upgrades to enhance their experience.

The marriage of American technology with Japanese cartoon creatures proved an explosively popular match. While the content "comes from Japan," as Hanke said in a 2016 interview with *VentureBeat*, it was his United States–based company that put it into a game that appealed to non-Japanese consumers.[30]

Pokémon GO's success does represent a "perfect storm": the confluence of an established intellectual property, a new technology, and a massive untapped audience of nostalgic adult gamers who had grown up on Pokémon. In an era where Japan has struggled to appeal to foreign smartphone gamers, *Pokémon GO* represents a striking exception. But it isn't a purely Japanese success, and perhaps that is the lesson to be learned here. An established Japanese company found a foreign partner in whom it could entrust its most lucrative franchise, giving them the budget and freedom to develop a truly borderless product. That much represents strategic thinking. But, as Hanke admitted, a lot of *Pokémon GO*'s success may have been just pure luck: "I don't know how you plan for something as strange as the way it took off virally."[31]

The No-Brand Brand and the God of Tidying

The marketing of Japanese culture abroad can take many forms. Two of the most visible examples today are the retailer Muji, which specializes in low-cost, spartan housewares, and Marie Kondo, whose bestselling book *The Life-Changing Magic of Tidying Up: The Japanese Art of Decluttering and Organizing* earned her a spot on *Time*'s 100 Most

Influential People list in 2015. While one is a major retailer and the other a self-help author, they share one thing in common: they are both selling their own versions of an idealized Japanese lifestyle. The Zen-like simplicity of Muji's sophisticated yet unembellished products has made the retailer a hit with foreign tastemakers. KonMari (as her fans call her, even abroad) has sold some 5 million copies of her book worldwide to people with a desire to declutter not just their homes but also their hectic modern lifestyles.

Muji offers something of a paradox. It is a mass-market retailer that presents itself as the opposite, selling minimalist products that appear to offer an eco-friendly, less-is-better rejection of modern consumer culture. Originally launched in Japan in 1980 as an in-store brand for the Seiyu supermarket chain, Mujirushi Ryohin, as the company is known in Japan, literally means "good products, no brand." In the decades since, it has grown into an independent chain with some 700 stores on three continents. In 2017, the company says it will cross a milestone of actually having more shops overseas than it does in Japan.[32]

The company's stripped-down yet functional products, usually offered in the brown and beige colors of natural wood and untreated paper, have won it many fans abroad. And like a Zen master challenging acolytes with mind-bending riddles, Muji insists that it offers "designs that are not designed" but that bring out an essence already in the object, whether it be a stapler or a sweater.[33] Masaaki Kanai, the chairman of Muji's parent company, can be almost as enigmatic, saying that Muji doesn't actually sell products but rather a lifestyle.[34] Of course, the truth is that Muji's products are the result of a great deal of thought and effort on the part of top Japanese designers like Kenya Hara. But this is the image that Muji seeks to project, of a "no-brand" brand selling "nonproduct" products with "nondesigned" designs—all from a store on Fifth Avenue no less!

"Companies are making more and more things that people don't need in their daily lives," Kanai told the Asia Pacific Initiative. "We try to make things that are just good enough, using the minimum amount of materials, reducing unneeded steps in the process, eliminating unneeded packaging . . . A world without [artificial] color, just the color of the materials themselves. That's Muji."[35]

Muji's carefully crafted minimalist image extends even to its advertising strategy, which relies on word of mouth to attract new customers. As *The New Yorker* put it in a 2015 profile of the company, "Muji, with its lack of logos, represents post-cool . . . Japan, which is, of course, a fetishized version of Japanese culture—serene and neat and proper."[36]

The question is, will this minimalist narrative win customers outside of the elite tastemakers? Muji seeks to be "cool" by refusing to call attention to itself, demanding instead that it be found by consumers who appreciate its purist philosophy. In this, it is a metaphor for Japanese consumer culture as a whole, at least as experienced by fans outside Japan: a connoisseur's choice, available only to those who seek it out. But can Muji's coyness appeal to the far broader swath of non-Japanese consumers who are more concerned with cost than image? The answer remains to be seen; like Uniqlo, Muji is still limited outside Japan to urban flagship stores that appeal to what is essentially a niche consumer market.

Kondo offers another path to an idealized vision of Japanese simplicity. With the subtitle of her book, *The Japanese Art of Decluttering and Organizing*, she is also evoking Japan's image as the home of minimalist rock gardens and ink paintings, in this case to promote a Zen of tidying up. Originally published in 2010 in Japan, where it became a best seller, the book's 2014 English translation proved to be a standout in one of the publishing industry's most popular and competitive genres: self-help books. In the United States, the book and its author quickly became a social phenomenon. Profiles of Kondo proliferated in magazines and newspapers, assisted by her camera-ready, bright demeanor and her knack for turning the simple act of cleaning into a philosophical journey. (For example, she asks readers if their possessions "spark joy" and urges them to thank objects before throwing them away.)

Of course, much of Kondo's success is simply from writing a good book at the right time: her mantra of less consumption, less waste struck a chord among consumers feeling ambivalent about their own materialism. However, her book also faced huge hurdles, particularly in the United States, where the translated works of foreign authors account for only 3 percent of books in print.[37]

Kondo had some help. Her publisher, Penguin Random House, proved adept at marketing the book as more than just a guide to cleaning up. In interviews and articles, they created a narrative of the book as a very Japanese philosophy for living a purer, less burdened existence. According to this narrative, this was no mere book; it was the culmination of a lifetime dedicated to the art of decluttering. In interviews and articles, Kondo is presented as someone who spent her childhood tidying up the classroom bookshelves while schoolmates played outdoors, who learned an ethos of material and spiritual cleanliness through apprenticing at a Shinto shrine, and who at the age of 16 fell unconscious and received a vision from the "god of tidying."[38] This is an extraordinarily exotic background story for a book about cleaning your room. In a 2015 Q&A

session on the Web site Reddit, she admitted that Shinto "influences me, but not as strongly as you might think," while *The New Yorker* revealed that rather than springing fully formed from Kondo's mind, the book was the product of a literary incubator called the Training Course for Creating Best Sellers That Will be Loved for 10 Years run by a Japanese consulting firm.[39]

My point here is not to pick apart Kondo's background but rather to highlight her narrative for what it is: a story crafted to help market a best seller. The narrative of how Kondo became a decluttering guru is every bit as compelling as how Evisu jeans are the product of Japanese craftsmanship, how Uniqlo brings a "little bit of Tokyo" to its foreign stores, or how Muji's products aren't actually designed. It is also proof positive that something Japanese can sell to the American masses, if packaged well.

Kondo's book is an example of how the combination of hard work (including a training course), a fad in her home country (where her book was already a best seller), a powerful foreign partner (her publisher), and a good story line (Kondo's own narrative) can carry a Japanese product a very long way. Like Muji, it is an excellent example of how foreign perceptions of Japan have gravitated toward keywords such as "simplicity" and "functionality." The successes of Muji and Kondo offer differing approaches for exploiting this perception. They are essentially selling experiences as well as products.

Other Japanese retailers have found consumers willing to pay more for experiences than mere products. Hiroshi Aoi, president of the department store operator Marui Group Co., said his company has experimented with "retail experiences" centered on popular characters from anime and film.

In late 2016, Marui's flagship Shinjuku location partnered with the film company Toho to launch a month-long Godzilla Store that sold Godzilla-branded items like keychains and shirts. However, the big draw was not the objects but the experience: customers queued up to have their photo taken with large statues and footprints of the monster. They also played a virtual-reality game in which they tried to avoid getting stepped on by Godzilla and ate at a café featuring Godzilla-themed menu items. Aoi described the initiative as "cocreation with the customer."

"As an economy and culture mature," Aoi said, "values regarding consumption and lifestyle change, with consumers turning away from behaviors such as expressing oneself via fashion towards slightly more inwardly-focused pursuits. What could be called 'personal fulfillment' becomes a 'good': things like foods, dining out, and leisure experiences rise to the forefront."[40]

Beyond Cool Japan

We have explored a range of Japanese products and trends—from blue jeans to smartphone games—that have achieved remarkable success abroad. How did they do it? What do they share in common?

Many of these products, such as clothing or housewares, are commonplace items. What sets them apart is their narrative: they are viewed as somehow uniquely Japanese, the product of a nation that seems able to be both outlandishly garish and elegantly spartan at the same time. In turn, their novelty, and their success, help feed Japan's newly emerging image as a creative superpower. According to a 2015 Pew Research Center survey, 75 percent of Americans now describe the Japanese as inventive people.[41]

However, being Japanese is no guarantee of success. The products that take off overseas represent but a tiny fraction of the attempts to market Japanese cultural content abroad, let alone the nation's total cultural output. Nor does success in Japan necessarily lead to success overseas, as we have seen. With so many games, books, fashions, and foods emerging in Japan on a regular basis, what are the hurdles to marketing them abroad? Why do a few products win acceptance by non-Japanese consumers while most fail or never even get a chance?

The government strategy, perhaps unsurprisingly, has been to throw money at the problem. But three years after the launch of the Cool Japan push, the actual results, if any, remain unclear. One of the biggest concerns is that few of the government funds reach those who actually create the content. "The government money will be funneled into big Japanese corporations and advertising agencies like Dentsu and Hakuhodo," one movie producer told *Time*, and "no real domestic artists will receive the money."[42]

In spite of these criticisms, there has been at least one tangible benefit: increased funds for the expensive task of translating Japanese content into other languages. For video games with extensive text and dialogue, budgets of half a million dollars or more are not unheard of. Even simple content such as comic books can easily run into the tens of thousands of dollars. As part of the Cool Japan strategy, the Ministry of Economy, Trade, and Industry set up the Japanese Content Localization and Promotion (J-LOP) fund, which subsidizes up to 70 percent of the translating costs. Without such public funding, many works would never make it into foreign languages—though translation alone is far from a guarantee of commercial success.

So if language has been removed as a barrier, what is hindering Japanese content producers from taking their ideas abroad? It is certainly not due to a fear of taking risks. Anime, the cornerstone of Cool Japan, is an extremely risky industry. Only 1 in 10 anime productions ever turns a profit, a low enough success rate that banks are reluctant to lend money to even the biggest studios. Instead, studios must rely for funding on groups of investors called "production committees," who provide capital in exchange for a high level of control over production. The rights become shared by other members of the committee, typically television stations, advertising companies, toy companies, and publishing companies. This system funds almost every work of anime produced in Japan. It also consigns the illustrators and other studio workers who actually create the anime to the bottom of the food chain. An animator earns an average yearly salary of just ¥1.1 million, or about $10,000, far below the poverty line. A 2009 Harvard Business School working paper concluded that these "hierarchical forms of industry organization" prevent Japanese studios from sharing in the fruits of success, which has prevented them from growing to anything approaching the size or global influence of a Disney or Pixar.[43]

Japan needs to find better ways to tap the global appeal of its pop culture and spread the benefits to those who actually make Cool Japan a reality. In a digital era in which consumers hunger not for objects but for content and experiences, Japan seems well positioned, given its strength in producing cultural products like manga, anime, and video games. However, it needs a system that incentivizes companies to market overseas, perhaps by allowing them to keep more of their profits. If Japan truly wants to boost its soft power, it will have to change a status quo that robs innovators of ambition and reduces talent to pauperdom.

Notes

1. Tom Kelley, speaking at Asia Pacific Initiative, January 7, 2016.
2. Fiona Wilson, "Most Livable City, 2016: Tokyo," *Monocle*, June 2016.
3. Jamie Ee, "Our Japanese Obsession," *The Business Times*, October 22, 2016.
4. Steve Rose, "Hollywood Is Haunted by *Ghost in the Shell*," *The Guardian*, October 19, 2009.
5. Matt Alt, "Will Cool Japan Finally Heat Up in 2014?" *The Japan Times*, January 9, 2014.
6. Michiyo Nakamoto, "Liquid Experimentation," *Financial Times*, November 10, 2011.

7. Matt Alt, *The Secret Lives of Emoji: How Emoticons Conquered the World* (Seattle, WA: Amazon Digital Services, 2016).

8. W. David Marx, interviewed by author, October 2015.

9. W. David Marx, *Ametora: How Japan Saved American Style* (New York: Basic Books, 2015), p. 216.

10. Guy Trebay, "Who Pays $600 for Jeans?" *The New York Times*, April 21, 2005.

11. Marx, interview, 2015.

12. James Higa, speaking at Asia Pacific Initiative, November 11, 2015.

13. Fast Retailing, "Group Outlets," accessed July 7, 2017, http://www.fast retailing.com/eng/group/shoplist/.

14. Adam Taylor, "Uniqlo: An American Dream for a Japanese Company," *The Washington Post*, October 28, 2016.

15. Dhani Mau, "Uniqlo Aims for Authenticity and Awareness with Remodeled Flagship and New Ads," *Fashionista*, September 3, 2016.

16. Bryant Urstadt, "Uniqlones," *New York Magazine*, May 9, 2010.

17. Ibid.

18. "Uniqlo Yanai Says Revamping US Operations a Top Priority," *Reuters*, May 25, 2016.

19. Steven Kurutz, "The Cult of the Toto Toilet," *The New York Times*, November 18, 2015.

20. Entertainment Software Association, eds., "2017 Sales, Demographic and Usage Data: Essential Facts about the Computer and Video Game Industry," 2017, accessed November 27, 2017, http://www.theesa.com/wp-content/uploads /2017/09/EF2017_Design_FinalDigital.pdf, p. 12.

21. Lauren Klaasse, "Game Over? The End of Japanese Dominance in the American Console Gaming Market," *Post Bubble Culture*, March 14, 2011; Hiroko Tabuchi, "Japanese Playing a New Video Game: Catch Up," *The New York Times*, September 19, 2010.

22. Christopher P. Willis, "Pokénomics: The Secret to the Success of *Pokémon GO*," *Newsweek*, July 28, 2016.

23. John W. Ayers, "*Pokémon GO*—A New Distraction for Drivers and Pedestrians," *JAMA Internal Medicine*, 176 (2016): 1865–1866, doi:10.1001/jamainternmed .2016.6274.

24. Kris Carlon, "*Pokémon GO* Hits 100 Million Installs, Makes $10 Million a Day," *Android Authority*, August 2, 2016, accessed July 7, 2017, www.android authority.com/pokemon-go-100-million-installs-10-million-daily-revenue-706885/.

25. "Top 150 Global Licensors," *License Global*, May 2014, p. T15.

26. John Easum, "A View from the East: Japan," *License Global*, June 16, 2014.

27. Eric Pfanner and Takashi Mochizuki, "Nintendo Opens Door to Smartphone Games," *The Wall Street Journal*, March 17, 2015.

28. Matt Weinberger, "The CEO Behind *Pokémon GO* Explains Why It's Become Such a Phenomenon," *Business Insider*, July 11, 2016.

29. Niantic Inc., "Niantic Inc. Raises $20 Million in Financing from The Pokémon Company, Google and Nintendo," last modified October 15, 2015, https:// nianticlabs.com/blog/niantic-tpc-nintendo/.

30. Dean Takahashi, "*Pokémon GO* Chief Promises Player Battles, Live Events, More Creatures, and Stable Servers," *VentureBeat*, September 17, 2016.

31. Ibid.

32. Tang See Kit, "New Muji Flagship Store in Singapore in the Works," *Channel News Asia*, March 15, 2016.

33. Meg Miller, "How Muji Fuels Explosive Growth without Ads," *Fast Company Design*, November 4, 2016.

34. "MUJI Says It Doesn't Sell Products, It Showcases Lifestyle," *NewsGD.com*, January 17, 2016.

35. Masaaki Kanai, speaking at Asia Pacific Initiative, September 28, 2016.

36. Ibid.

37. Joanna Zgadzaj and Nancy Roberts, "Books in Translation: It's Time for Others to Join the Fight," *Publishing Perspectives*, February 15, 2013.

38. Kate Storey, "Marie Kondo Reveals a Nervous Breakdown Led to Her Joy Method," *Good Housekeeping*, January 15, 2016.

39. Barry Yourgrau, "The Origin Story of Marie Kondo's Decluttering Empire," *The New Yorker*, December 8, 2015.

40. Hiroshi Aoi, speaking at Asia Pacific Initiative, November 21, 2016.

41. Pew Research Center, "Americans, Japanese: Mutual Respect 70 Years after the End of WWII," April 7, 2015.

42. Roland Kelts, "Japan Spends Millions in Order to Be Cool," *Time*, July 1, 2013.

43. Robert Dujarric and Andrei Hagui, "Capitalizing on Innovation: The Case of Japan," Harvard Business School working paper, 2009, accessed July 7, 2017, www.hbs.edu/faculty/Publication%20Files/09-114_02065969-dad8-4f08 -b2ea-8212ba46fb74.pdf.

CHAPTER TWO

Dominating the Pritzkers: Japan's Emergence as a Leader in Design

Kengo Kuma and Dana Buntrock

In the world of design, Japan's leadership role is unquestioned. Nowhere is this more the case than in architecture, where Japanese practitioners attract a celebrity-like following. In New York and London, fans line up to see Tadao Ando or Shigeru Ban in hopes of getting a signature on their sketchbooks, smartphones, or even their shirt sleeves. Iconic structures by Japanese architects, no matter how remote or small, lure a constant stream of unannounced visitors. The sleek glass pavilions of Grace Farms, designed by Kazuyo Sejima and Ryue Nishizawa, drew tens of thousands of lookers upon completion in 2015, despite the fact the site was located in rural Connecticut a 90-minute drive from New York City. Some of this aura even rubs off onto relatively untried Japanese architects, who can draw hundreds, even thousands, to a public lecture—far more than they might attract back home.

Within the profession, Japanese architects have dominated almost every major award. This is true of the Pritzker Prize, sometimes called architecture's equivalent of the Nobel. Seven Japanese-born architects have won Pritzkers since the award was created in 1979—more than from any other nation, including the United States, with a population nearly three times larger than Japan's. And Japan's winners often have the most interesting and atypical backstories. Ando, who won the prize in 1995, was the only laureate not to graduate from college. Sejima, code-signer of Grace Farms, was one of only two women to ever win a Pritzker. She shared the prize in 2010 with Grace Farms collaborator Nishizawa, who at 44 was the youngest laureate ever (Figure 2.1).

And it is not just Japan's top architects who have gained the world's admiration; architectural firms around the world now depend on Japanese talent at all levels. Visit the offices of Renzo Piano, Rem Koolhaas, or the late Zaha Hadid, and chances are you will find Japanese architects working alongside the famous architect, serving as his or her right hand; below them, the staff will also be filled with talented younger Japanese, each assigned important tasks. Indeed, despite the hand-wringing about declining numbers of Japanese students at Western universities and business schools, there has been no shortage of young Japanese architects entering the world's top offices. It would not be an exaggeration to say that without these Japanese architects, most international offices would have trouble maintaining their levels of quality and excellence.

While architects were among the first of Japan's designers to gain worldwide recognition after the war, those in other fields were quick to

Figure 2.1: Grace Farms, which opened in 2015, attracted 50,000 visitors in its first five months. Designed by Kazuyo Sejima and Ryue Nishizawa. Image courtesy of Iwan Baan.

follow. Issey Miyake broke onto the world fashion scene almost four decades ago, challenging consumers and critics alike with clothing featuring whimsical shapes and origami-like folds. Graphic artist Ikko Tanaka won attention in the 1960s and 1970s for his simple yet bold designs for posters and company logos, which were regarded as a marriage of Japanese tradition and a modern industrial sensibility. Eiko Ishioka won a host of awards, including an Oscar, for costumes that appeared in Hollywood films, Broadway musicals, and the 2008 Beijing Olympics.

Then there are the legions of influential Japanese designers who never achieved celebrity status. Many spent careers working within giant manufacturers like Toyota, Sony, and Casio, where they transformed the appearance of our daily lives by designing consumer products from pens and wristwatches to sedans and televisions. The world was reminded of these largely unsung industrial designers in 2015, when Kenji Ekuan, creator of Kikkoman's iconic soy sauce bottles, passed away at age 85.

Japan continues to turn out talent and ideas. The minimalist designs of retailers Muji and Uniqlo have made them into global brands, representing Japan on the world stage today much as Sony and Panasonic did in the 1980s. A new generation of Japanese designers has reached into our homes and wardrobes, from Daisuke Kitagawa's housewares and Hiromichi Konno's furniture to fashion designers led by Rei Kawakubo and Yohji Yamamoto. It is not hard to find articles grouping Japan with Sweden or Italy as one of the world's top design powerhouses.

"Japanese designers are by far the coolest at Paris Fashion Week," *Quartz* magazine said in its coverage of that major fashion event in 2015. "Japan's top designers have dominated."[1] The New York–based fashion blog *Complex* offers a list of the top 50 Japanese clothing brands, making everything from blue jeans to leather jackets, cooing, "I only shop in Tokyo."[2]

"Japan is the most creative nation in the world," says Tom Kelley of the Silicon Valley–based design consultancy Ideo, an author of books on innovation and design.[3] As proof, Kelley points to "State of Create," a poll conducted in 2012 by software giant Adobe Systems that asked 5,000 people in the UK, France, Germany, Japan, and the United States which country they viewed as being the most creative. According to the poll, Japan came out on top, selected by 36 percent of the respondents; they also chose Tokyo as the world's most creative city. (Only Japanese respondents picked another country, the United States, as most creative.)[4]

Japan has also been a source of inspiration for creators elsewhere. James Higa, who used to work at Apple as director of special projects under Steve Jobs, said Japan's clean, minimalist aesthetic lay behind some of the Silicon Valley company's most celebrated products. During their frequent trips together to Japan to meet manufacturers, he and Jobs set aside time to absorb the nation's design sensibility by visiting stores and admiring interiors and product packaging, seeing a kabuki performance or ukiyo-e woodblock exhibit, or making an excursion to Ryoan-ji, the Zen temple in Kyoto famous for its rock garden and raked white gravel. Their enthusiasm was part of a broader rediscovery of Japan, not only of design but also the arts and popular culture.

"I remember a time when Japan was at its height, and we were coming to Sony and Matsushita and everybody in our supply chain," Higa recalled. "The word was, 'Japan, economic animals, horrible at originality and creativity, great at manufacturing, great at industry, everything else that is creative, forget it.' It is kind of ironic that now what the world recognizes about Japan is, 'I think anime is great, I think their architecture is great, I think their fashion is great. The best ballerinas, the best classical musicians, the best artists, they're all Japanese.' . . .These are the original, individual, creative, imaginative types that are being recognized by the Western world. It is completely turned around."[5]

Indeed, pick almost any design-related field these days, and there are Japanese practitioners winning accolades for fastidious quality and path-breaking concepts. This begs the question of why Japanese designers have become such a dominant presence. How did Japan become a leader in design? To find answers, it makes sense to take a deeper look at architecture, the first design-related field where Japanese practitioners broke onto, and then came to dominate, the world stage.

As Higa suggests, the success of Japan's architects lies at least partly in their ability to tap into the nation's rich cultural storehouse. Their comfort with bold lines and unadorned surfaces, their careful use of space, and their perfectionist attention to detail all reflect the sensibility of a people accustomed to living in small houses packed into dense towns and cities that fit into the narrow folds of Japan's mountainous topography.

At the same time, the global prominence of Japanese architecture is very much a postwar phenomenon, rooted in the political and economic realities of a nation emerging from the ashes of defeat in 1945. At one level, architecture offered Japan a perfectly suited means to demonstrate the nation's spectacular postwar recovery and rise to economic power. But at another level, it also became a popular avenue for young Japanese who had talent and entrepreneurial drive, coupled with a desire to eschew the corporate rat race and seek a global stage for their creative ambitions. Architecture became a crowded, competitive profession, one whose energies infused other fields of design in a way unseen in other countries.

Reflecting on how these elements have fostered the fecund creativity propelling Japanese architecture to global prominence, we can discover how the trade has been developed and organized, its strengths and weak points, and perhaps most importantly, whether Japan's preeminence will continue. The coauthors of this chapter offer a detailed view from the inside, drawing from their extensive experience as both working architects and academics.

Architecture's Most Exciting Home

Why do Japan's architects dominate? The answer lies in the creativity and bold beauty of their individual creations, something that springs from each designer's own intensely unique vision. In architecture, the best-known buildings by Japanese designers appeal to us because they stand in stark contrast to the structures that usually surround our daily lives, flouting complicated pleats or luscious curves, sensual uses of materials or soaring, even improbable, spaces. They are sculptural works of genius, each reflecting the unusual creative vision of a single individual.

But such individual creativity does not appear in a vacuum, and the vision and skills of Japan's architects arise from the unique environment that produced them. These are at least partly products of Japan's culture and even its rugged topography, with its narrow valleys and cramped villages that foster a perfectionist attention to detail and frugality of space. Similarly, the prevalence of earthquakes and natural disasters has nurtured an assumption of impermanence that allows a cluttered megalopolis like Tokyo to serve as a surprisingly malleable tableau, where buildings can be speedily razed and rebuilt, yielding an eclectic chaos of architectural styles.

At the same time, many designers credit Japan with a cultural flexibility—a talent for appropriating ideas from the outside world and making them part of Japan's own sensibility. Kelley of Ideo said he thinks Japan's strength is this ability not to cling to the past or fear change but to be willing to mix the old and the new.

"You have to get the balance right about tradition and innovation," Kelley told the Asia Pacific Initiative. "And one of the things I love about Japan is this endless curiosity. It's this willingness to embrace the new. . . . There are some false starts in Japan, but that's okay, it's part of the process of experimentation."[6]

This freedom to range also reflects the lack of bounds that is one of the most important features of the practice of architecture in postwar Japan. For Japan's architects do not limit themselves to just practicing architecture. They design not only buildings but also a whole host of other, less permanent items that might seem unprofitable or even frivolous to their Western counterparts. It is not uncommon for Japanese architects to also dabble in furniture, fabrics, pens, tableware, train interiors, even chocolates. Their main job may be designing structures large enough to seats thousands, but they also proudly create objects small enough to fit in the palm of one's hand. While their building projects might cost hundreds of millions of dollars and take years to complete, they will also take the time to pop out clever trinkets inexpensive enough to be bought on a whim.

This makes architects very much part of the larger world of design in Japan. And as in architecture, Japanese design displays a permeability of boundaries that is perhaps unique in the world. This fluidity is driven by a fierce competition that causes distinctions between architects and other designers to blur within a fast-moving, hotly contested marketplace. Just as Japan's architects freely venture into graphic design or fashion, so have many accomplished designers and artists in other fields, such as Muji's art director Kenya Hara, or Oki Sato, founder of design office Nendo, tried their hand at creating buildings and interiors.

This lack of boundaries helps fuel the intense competition that is one of the defining features of postwar Japanese design. Architecture is an arena for ferocious rivalries, usually between tightly defined communities of architects centered on one or more established figures in the field. These clusters are a major source of the international success of Japanese architects, linking them at an early stage into broader networks of engineers, contractors, and even politicians that enable boldly collaborative projects. At the same time, competition between clusters drives architects and their collaborators to take greater risks. Japan's architects strive to "out-hustle" each other and architects from other nations, seeking ever-greater originality and ingenuity and embracing the latest technologies and most radical artistic trends.

The nuclei of these dynamic clusters are audacious individuals, both established leaders and younger generations seeking to learn from them. Training follows an apprenticeship system that, while demanding enormous dedication and long hours in the office or on the road, gives acolytes the freedom to range broadly in their own creative endeavors, achieving independence at an early stage. Thus, even before one generation of established figures is dominant, another is ready to fill its place, pushing the older generation aside and leading the field of architecture into fresh new directions.

Japanese Architecture Takes Off

One of the first Japanese architects to create such a cluster, and to win international recognition, was Kenzo Tange.

Tange first gained the world's attention with his design for Hiroshima's Peace Park in 1954. The site's political importance was clear; Tange met the challenge of creating a monument to atomic tragedy with a landscape of cultural buildings both expansive and intimate, solemn and heroic. The quality of work is plainly very high. One success, though, will not establish international stature. Building a global reputation requires taking some very risky leaps. Tange did this, and did it successfully, creating a trail that other Japanese architects would follow.

Tange's leap came with the 1964 Olympics, when he designed a gymnasium for swimming and a smaller annex for basketball in Tokyo's Yoyogi neighborhood. For his design, Tange set what seemed to be absurdly ambitious goals, imagining structures with suspended roofs that would be highly challenging for contractors and engineers even. His success turned the structures into not just symbols of the 1964 Games but also a resurgent Japan's soaring aspirations to reclaim a place among the world's leading nations. The Yoyogi National Gymnasium complex also transformed the practice of architecture in Japan by linking technical prowess and artistry, the first step toward the collaborative projects that would come to define the field (Figure 2.2).

To help realize his vision, Tange turned to an exceptionally gifted structural engineer, Yoshikatsu Tsuboi. With Tsuboi's help, Tange tossed away convention; the designs for the Yoyogi venues adopt a completely innovative structural system. Together, the gymnasium and its annex are formed into hyperbolic paraboloids—rounded, saddle-like shapes whose sweeping curves seem to be magically conjured out of straight beams of steel. Only a close and rigorous collaboration between architect and structural engineer could have created such exquisitely artful architecture at technology's cutting edge. One can imagine the two men egging each other toward their magnum opus, surrounded by enthralled and impassioned students and staff.

Such close collaboration between architect and engineer has deep roots in Japan, which historically viewed the two as facets of the same trade. In premodern times, a class of professional carpenters acted as both architect and engineer, charged with designing as well as actually constructing

Figure 2.2: Gymnasium for the 1964 Olympics, designed by Kenzo Tange and Yosikatsu Tsuboi and built by the Shimizu Corporation. Photo by Larry Burrows/ The LIFE Picture Collection/Getty Images.

buildings. Over generations, carpenters passed down these skills from master to apprentice. In the 19th-century Meiji era, when Japan first set out to create a modern education system for architects, it borrowed heavily from the traditions of carpentry. As a result, design and engineering still coexist in the same department at the University of Tokyo, Japan's most prestigious university.

Top Japanese universities gather both architecture and engineering students into what are called labs, where undergraduates are able to work closely with professors on actual building projects, giving them a chance to join other aspiring architects and engineers in gaining real-world experience at an early stage in their careers. Actual classroom instruction at Japanese universities can be disappointingly low in quality due to budget and staffing constraints, but labs offer exciting opportunities for creative cross-fertilization. An architect leading one lab will at times collaborate with an engineer leading another—and at the University of Tokyo, each professional will already be a leader in his or her field. When labs collaborate, as Tange's and Tsuboi's did, exciting and unheard-of innovations can often be the result.

This is an important contrast to universities in the West, where design and engineering are usually treated as different disciplines and are even taught in separate departments. The Western approach can lead to a clear division of labor, in which engineers design the building's bare-bones structure, while architects use aesthetic elements to do little more than clothe it.

It was Tange and Tsuboi who first utilized Japan's blending of design and engineering to push architecture in new directions. From their first joint structure—a small domed library near Hiroshima's Peace Park in 1951—they worked together to create increasingly daring structures. For the main Yoyogi gymnasium, they created a masterpiece that features two evocative pylons towering skyward, holding a roof of supple cables draped between them. Next to it, the smaller basketball arena spirals upward around a single shaft. More than half a century old, the buildings continue to inspire awe.

The Rise of Japanese Design

Bold designs go nowhere unless someone can actually build them. Constructing Tange and Tsuboi's breathtaking creations placed enormous demands on contractors, who had to invent whole new methods to construct them. The main gymnasium's suspended roof was a particular challenge: it was created out of an assembly of rigid plates, ball joints, and cables that moved as it was erected. Even today, building this complex a structure in just 18 months would be a feat. In 1964, it was nothing short of miraculous. Accomplishing this demanded close collaboration not only between Tange and Tsuboi but also between them and the construction companies that actually erected the buildings.

This points to another lesson from the rise of postwar Japanese architecture: the value of technical skill and of designers being close to the actual production of their designs. Tange and Tsuboi benefited from the expertise and technological skills of the Shimizu Corporation, which built the Yoyogi gymnasiums. Japan's postwar architects have been able to strive toward ever-greater complexity and sophistication in part because they had confidence in the skills of the nation's construction industry, which had emerged as a major force in Japan's reconstruction after its wartime defeat.

Just as railroads drove the United States' economic rise, the construction industry powered Japan's postwar economic miracle. Before World War II, cities had been built of wood, in structures that were low, small, fragile, and easily burned down. After 1945, Japan rebuilt its devastated cities in steel and concrete, reflecting Japan's ambition to become an advanced, modern country. Construction companies gained ever-greater skill and competence as public works projects transformed the face of the nation, and that, in turn, created growing demand for new architects and engineers.

Tax revenues funded the postwar reconstruction boom; politicians held the purse strings. This highlights the central role of government in Japanese architecture's postwar emergence. With so much public money flowing into Japan's reconstruction, it was inevitable that the construction industry formed strong ties to politicians; architects were also key players in this nexus. At a crucial point during construction of the Yoyogi gymnasiums, Tange personally visited the finance minister at the time, Kakuei Tanaka, to ask for additional funds to cover the expensive project. Tanaka, who later became a prime minister famous for using public works to win voter patronage, quickly agreed. Just over 50 years later, when faced with an equally exciting opportunity to build a bold stadium for the 2020 Tokyo Olympics, Japan made a far different choice, a point that we will return to below.

While this triad of the construction industry, architects, and politicians has faced criticism, it made postwar Japan's world-class architectural masterpieces possible. The opportunity for architects like Tange and engineers like Tsuboi to collaborate with powerful construction companies, and to do so with generous public funding, led to remarkable advances in architectural design, as Tange's Olympic gymnasiums demonstrate. Such collaboration also gave Japan's construction industry the chance to develop technical skills that became among the world's most advanced. This created a positive feedback loop that allowed other bold visions to become reality. Japan's architects could design with courage and daring, confident that the nation's contractors could build ever-more-complex and demanding structures, which postwar politicians were willing to bankroll.

Tange was the pioneer and the first Japanese architect to win major international prizes, including one of those Pritzkers. Tsuboi, too, won many awards, hobnobbing with international giants in the field like Le Corbusier, Walter Gropius, and Louis Kahn. But they would not be the last. A surprisingly large number of Japanese architects followed in Tange's footsteps. He showed them how to leap to international prominence, using the three-way alliance between architects, contractors, and politicians as a springboard. The powerful blend of daring design and technological innovation that this triad made possible gave other architects who followed an international advantage.

The postwar alliance between construction, architects, and politicians reached its culmination under the leadership of one of Tange's students, Arata Isozaki.

Tange's newfound celebrity attracted many young, impassioned designers. He was blessed with a number of superb students who later became major architects in their own right, including Fumihiko Maki and Kisho

Kurokawa as well as Isozaki. These acolytes competed fiercely with each other, elevating the overall level of design. As Japan itself reached new heights of postwar prosperity, architects were not the only ones in fierce competition: contractors battled contractors, and politicians battled politicians. These passionate rivalries were an engine propelling the rise of the postwar nation and the ambitions of its architects.

Among Tange's elite students, Isozaki stood out. It was not just the excellence of his buildings, though these were also world class. Rather, his greatest legacy was his creation of a whole new approach that would drive architects, both in Japan and abroad, to greater accomplishments. Isozaki succeeded in turning architecture into art.

The Designer as Artist

In the 1970s, when Isozaki launched his revolution, Japan's long period of blistering, double-digit growth rates was winding down. He realized that as Japan became a wealthier, more mature economy, it would seek more than functionality and industrial practicality in its buildings. Taking a clue from the success of Tange's marvelously sweeping gymnasiums, Isozaki set out to prove that the value of architecture lay in its ability to inspire and awe. By turning architecture into art, he hoped to maintain architecture's importance in the dawning post-high-growth era. This revolution was embraced by the public works triad, which saw expensive architectural showpieces as a way to compensate for declining demand.

In his drive to turn architecture into art, Isozaki offered his own eye-catching designs, which are often described as postmodern or even iconoclastic. He also created a new role for himself, as an enabler for other, younger architects to experiment. This pattern, in which an established practitioner serves as a sort of producer, promoting and mentoring younger talent, exists in other design fields in Japan as well.

The apex of Isozaki's efforts in this role as producer was the Kumamoto Artpolis, conceived with Kumamoto's governor at the time, Morihiro Hosokawa, who later became prime minister. The idea was an innovative one: to revive Kumamoto, a remote prefecture on the southwestern island of Kyushu, by inviting the world's most original architects to build structures emphasizing artistry and design over function. Hosokawa and Isozaki, whom Hosokawa asked to lead the project by serving as its commissioner, recognized that although publicly funded architectural landmarks like Tange's Yoyogi gymnasiums could inspire public pride, such projects had rarely been built outside Tokyo. They hoped that by turning Kumamoto into a blank canvas for the creative works of the world's most daring architects, they could reinvent the southwestern prefecture as an international showcase for cutting-edge structures and urban design.

Artpolis's success depended on Isozaki's role as producer; he made the sometimes fanciful designs a reality. Isozaki held the role of commissioner until 1997, when he handed the job to other notable architects, first Tei'ichi Takahashi and then Toyo Ito. As commissioner, Isozaki acted as a go-between linking artist and government, matching exciting architects from around the world to public funding. To push designers ever further, he held competitions, urging them to create bold and often playful designs and rewarding them with prizes and lavish media attention.

Isozaki wooed some of the world's most talented and innovative architects to indulge their most creative fantasies in a far-off corner of Japan. By doing so, he promoted exchanges with Japanese architects, who, benefiting from their unusual alliance with politicians and contractors, further cemented their enduring reputations for audacity. In fact, Japan was entering one of its most prolific periods of architectural experimentation, one that paradoxically began with the collapse of the nation's stock market and real estate bubbles in the early 1990s. When Japan opened the fiscal spigots in an effort to spend its way out of its economic slump, government money once again poured into flashy building projects. The fortunes of Japan's architects perversely rose during the nation's Lost Decades, when some of Japan's best buildings were built.

Isozaki set the tone for this new epoch. His innovations placed Japan's designers on the forefront of a global vanguard treating architecture as art, winning them an international reputation as risk takers with a penchant for radical and experimental work. Isozaki converted architecture from the staid functionality of modernism to something bolder and more whimsical, an approach that then spread from Japan throughout the world. In doing so, he shaped the intellectual trajectories of those who came after him. It is not an overstatement to say that Isozaki shaped the thinking of every major architect in the country today—and many from around the world. This is true not only of those who came immediately after, the so-called "third generation" represented by Ando, Ito, and Itsuko Hasegawa, but also their successors, the "fourth generation" that includes Grace Farms' designer, Sejima; Ban; and one of the authors of this essay, Kengo Kuma. The competition Isozaki encouraged became a template reproduced in each successive generation, driven by rivalries to attempt the ever more ambitious and outrageous.

Perhaps this is what is unique about Japanese architecture and drives its remarkable postwar success. Japan has shown an ability not only to keep producing new generations of talented designers but also to chan-nel them into intensely competitive rivalries that lead to bold and prolific creation. Japanese architecture has seen cycles of explosive innovation in which each new generation strives to push aside its elders and tap Japan's cultural storehouse for creative inspirations to dazzle the world.

This risk taking is made possible by Japan's distinctive system for train-ing new architects in university labs. The labs at top universities offer a distinctive mix of competition and collaboration that pushes aspiring architects to ever-loftier heights. Eager to break in, younger designers vie with each other to take risks while also embracing the support of engi-neers, contractors, and political leaders to make their dreams reality. In the decades that followed wartime defeat, everyone in Japan seemed open to aiming for the impossible, unafraid because they were not alone. They competed not only with each other but with leading architects from other nations, moving more quickly into cutting-edge technologies and radical new forms.

This dynamic of intergenerational competition is not so clear outside Japan. In the United States, there was a flurry of imaginative and influen-tial design during the 1970s. However, younger architects, overshadowed by the established elder generation's greater clout, were unable to drive the profession along provocative new paths. As a result, the United States' burst of architectural creativity proved short-lived, a one-off phenomenon that was not to be repeated.

By contrast, Japan's competitive environment drives younger architects to keep seeking new venues for their work, even in the face of economic chill. During the Lost Decades, young architects like one of the authors of this essay, Kengo Kuma, searched for opportunities in Japan's smaller regional towns and cities, which were the beneficiary of fiscal stimulus aimed at revitalizing depopulating rural areas. The younger architects were also forced to go out into the world beyong Japan in search of work, and the most ambitious embraced any opportunity to speak abroad, no matter how distant, obscure, or poorly paid. The fourth generation grew strong by aggressively engaging in international exchange and building new networks across national borders.

No Detail Too Minor

We have traced the arc of postwar Japanese architecture and its pio-neering practitioners. But what explains the appeal of their designs, espe-cially outside Japan?

The answer at least partly lies in what Kenya Hara, an art director for the retailer Muji, has called Japan's "cultural storehouse." He believes that Japan is just starting to rediscover the cultural traditions that it locked away when the nation embraced Western industrial civilization in the 19th century. Recovery of this older culture, and of Japan's confidence in its traditions, is propelling the nation's growing prominence today. Hara's own product design for Muji is driven by the realization that Japanese minimalism is fundamentally different from that of, say, Denmark or Germany, two countries also noted for clean design. While European minimalism strives for simplicity and easy use, Japan's designers have traditionally sought something different, what Hara called "emptiness." A German designer, he argued, might mold a knife handle to fit a hand, suggesting how it should be held. By contrast, the traditional Japanese knife has a straight, simple hilt that can be held in any number of ways, allowing the user to decide how to grasp it. The knife is an "empty vessel" that buyers "fill" with their own practices and preferences.[7]

Some of these cultural preferences reflect the physical realities of Japan itself. Japan's mountainous topography and crowded urban areas have nurtured a tradition in architecture of maximizing small spaces through an adroit application of design. This leads to the fusion of form and structure mentioned earlier.

When space is at a premium, it is impossible to hide or decorate a pillar by adding walls or attaching other finishes. The pillar itself must be both functional and attractive: a means of holding up the building but also an opportunity to add aesthetic appeal and beauty. This is evident in Japan's traditional wooden houses, where charmingly gnarled, bent tree trunks often conspicuously support walls and ceilings. In this way, the need to make the most effective use of limited space pushes Japanese architects to act not only as engineers but also as interior designers. In the West, those roles are often divided into highly specialized professions isolated from one another; in Japan, the architect must be a jack of all trades, someone able to wear several hats at once.

In Japan, the architect must be shrewd, turning tiny buildings tucked in narrow mountain valleys or on tight city streets into pleasant, even inspirational places. By necessity, rooms must be small but still play a variety of roles, pushing architects to be inventive in dividing and utilizing space. No detail is too minor for the architect's attention, from the look of a drainpipe to the feel of a door handle. Architecture becomes an art of grappling with limits. Japanese architects take pride in using inevitable physical (and financial) limitations to create ingeniously rich, small spaces.

In fact, Japanese architects invest an unusual level of time and energy in working at a very small scale, and not just in buildings. We have noted the lack of boundaries that allows architects to compete in designing even the most mundane objects, such as furniture or fabrics. Or doghouses. In 2012, Hara of Muji offered a playful invitation to architects to venture into his field of industrial design by throwing down an unusual gauntlet: a challenge to create what he termed "extremely sincere" doghouses. He set the tone by offering his own whimsical design, the D-Tunnel (Figure 2.3). Japanese designers know that these smaller, less costly projects can also be the proving ground for rookies. With expensive, showcase building projects, experienced architects have an overwhelming advantage due to their expertise, name recognition, and track record. But designing something as small as a cup or a pen—or a doghouse—becomes a chance for a younger architect to level the playing field. The gravity with which even the tiniest tour de force is treated within the profession also diminishes distinctions between today's esteemed architects and tomorrow's new stars.

For this reason, professional stature is accessible at an unusually early age in Japan. By the same token, even the most mundane objects can be the proud work of a master designer. After a point, such high levels of attention become the norm. This is one reason Japan's architects and

Figure 2.3: D-Tunnel designed by Kenya Hara. Image courtesy of Hiroshi Yoda.

other designers have earned a reputation for perfectionism and discriminating details, a reputation that they have in turn consciously used to further increase their global recognition.

Design as a Profession

By contrast, most architects outside Japan, and especially those in the United States, shun smaller building projects. In part, this is a result of the dynamics of the American market: despite its far larger population, the United States has only a third the number of licensed architects as Japan has. According to the Ministry of Land and Infrastructure, Japan had 360,000 licensed architects in 2015.[8] In the United States during the same year, the number was about 110,000, according to the Bureau of Labor Statistics.[9] Put another way, Japan has one architect for every 350 people, while in the United States, the ratio is almost 10 times larger: one for every 2,900 people.

Facing less competition, American designers can afford to be picky. They will often reject projects that are not profitable enough. For many top architects outside Japan, designing a house would offer too little financial return to be worthy of earnest effort. In Japan, it would be unthinkable to ignore such an opportunity.

Such economic realities have helped shape the trajectory of architecture in the United States. In the 1970s and 1980s, when the trend in architecture was toward modernism, American architects were very active around the world and venerated in Japan. To this day, the United States remains strong in projects that emphasize cost and utility, like office skyscrapers and commercial space. Large multidisciplinary firms, like Skidmore, Owings & Merrill, and Kohn Pedersen Fox, are competitive, but they seem unchanged by time, excelling mostly in work reflecting mid-20th-century ways of thinking. The United States' most influential international offices can appear to be more obsessed with profit than artistry, producing buildings that lack a sense of innovation or curiosity. Younger American architects often appear to have missed architecture's postmodern turn after the 1980s. This limits their international influence and diminishes the United States' leadership in the profession.

By contrast, many Japanese are drawn to architecture precisely because the profession offers them a chance to do something pathbreaking on a global stage. In the first decades after 1945, when postwar Japan was still trying to rebuild and recover its international status, the nation was electrified by the international success of pioneers like Tange and Isozaki.

This gave the field of architecture an enormous cache among young Japanese, which continues to this day. One appeal is the chance for social recognition. Another is financial independence; most architects aspire to one day open their own firm. Entrepreneurial opportunity also attracts ambitious young Japanese to other design-related professions, like fashion or even furniture design, where Japanese practitioners have increasingly won global admiration and assumed a leadership role.

This is a preeminence that China and other Asian countries, which have risen to eclipse Japan in manufacturing industries like electronics, are unlikely to immediately challenge. Chinese architects enjoy the advantages of a seller's market that is far more extreme than even that of the United States. In China, there is just one architect for every 54,000 people, according to Chinese government data.[10] At the same time, China has had a sustained, decades-long boom in construction. There simply have not been enough architects in China to meet demand. As a result, Chinese architects have been able to earn exhilarating commissions close to home without having to seek work abroad or challenge themselves in other ways. At home, they may be designing projects of eye-popping scale, but their global footprint remains modest.

Unlike Japanese students, countless Chinese students do study at architecture schools and universities around the world. But practicing architects from China do not need to go abroad, and so they do not yet stand out on the world stage. Similarly, architects from Taiwan and Korea also study abroad in high numbers but tend to practice their trade at home without making much impact internationally. For the moment, these Chinese and other Asian architects resemble their American counterparts in having little influence beyond their own borders. For now, they seem satisfied by their domestic market and have not followed Japan's best architects in pushing out into the world.

Of course, Chinese and other architects' day may soon come. There is no reason to doubt that both China and South Korea will play an important role in world architecture in the not too distant future. At the office of one of the authors of this essay, Kengo Kuma and Associates, or KKAA, we feel a passion from our Chinese and Korean clients that is no longer common in Japan. They hunger for compelling architecture, buildings that have never been seen before; working with them motivates and stimulates us. During the 1980s and 1990s, we enjoyed clients like this in Japan, but now such opportunities are regrettably rare. Architectural quality in China and Korea is also improving at an amazing pace, fostering the kinds of relationships where people in design and construction support each other, as they did in postwar Japan.

Thinking in Three Dimensions

For the time being, Japanese architects remain dominant, largely due to their unique approach to design and their emphasis on the art of architecture over more prosaic concerns. The profession has been able to transmit these strengths to successive generations, starting with pioneers Tange and Isozaki. How has Japan been able to instill in young architects the less-tangible values and passion that have made Japanese architecture so appealing?

For the last 10 years, we at KKAA have selected our new trainees by presenting them with a one-day design challenge. It starts at 10:00 a.m., when we give applicants 12 hours to complete an assignment by designing a structure based on certain parameters; at 10:00 p.m., we review the results of their effort and I (Kengo Kuma) personally interview them. The same system is used at many architectural offices in Tokyo. However, such a time-consuming system is rare elsewhere in the world, where architectural firms place more emphasis on efficiency.

While Japanese make up about half of our applicants, the rest come from all over the world. Since graduations fall on different dates in different countries, our office is continually giving the test to aspiring architects; we offer it once a week, usually to five or six people at a time. That adds up to about 250 or 300 applicants every year. Once a week, I sit down with applicants late at night to engage in a long conversation about the architectural proposals they created over the past 12 hours. Only a few will be offered an opportunity to join the office.

Despite the time and effort that it takes, the great strength of this hiring approach is that it allows us to look for applicants who are capable of something surprising. During that 12-hour test, anything goes. Aspirants can use models, computer graphics, hand-drawn sketches, or animation. Anything.

A number of observations have emerged from this experience. One is that every Japanese applicant chooses to build models to test and explain his or her design. Not only do they use models more, but the quality and precision of their model building is superior. One might think that Japan and Asia follow similar trends, but that's not the case; Chinese and Korean applicants do not seem to favor models nearly as much. They and applicants from other countries often choose to use drawings instead, which they create with computer software.

Applicants from Japan have a defter hand with models because architectural programs at Japanese universities make heavy use of models in their instruction. Japanese students become used to working in three dimensions. There is a reason for this emphasis on building models by hand. When you use your hands, information travels back and forth between the fingers and the brain, giving the designer a tactile feel for the structure that is taking shape. You can create a very solid, concrete mental image of an architectural space not yet built. And if you do this for a long time, you become good at design.

It is not the same if a designer is merely good at drawing. Working in two dimensions simply does not offer a full understanding of what will take form in three-dimensional space. Designers who only draw seem to have a harder time building an accurate physical model of their proposals. In a tight spot where furniture or plumbing fixtures are involved, our staff must produce an accurately scaled, highly detailed rendering of how everything will fit. Japanese candidates seem as if they can shrink themselves down to the size of an ant and walk around within the reality of their models. They grasp the actuality of how spaces will be used, an understanding that is reflected in their work.

Applicants from overseas just don't have that sense. Their drawings frequently omit smaller details, such as placement of furniture or plumbing fixtures. While eloquent in communicating their concepts or architectural philosophies, they produce drawings that overlook the important details of daily life, which can determine a structure's success or failure. To be blunt, applicants like that just do not have a lot to offer, in architecture or any other design field. No matter how lovely their drawings or their words, a person who lacks an authentic vision of the realities of daily life simply cannot be a skilled designer. And they will not be of much use in an architectural office like KKAA.

The importance of models in Japan has its own history. People often assume that all architects are good at drawing, but that is not the case. In fact, Tange was said to have been self-conscious of his poor drawing skills, and as a result left few sketches behind. Rather, he relied extensively on models, which he used to convey ideas to engineers, contractors, and politicians. If one of his staff designers came to him without a model, Tange would simply refuse to respond. Two-dimensional images were not enough to bring a show of interest; he needed a three-dimensional representation to stir his imagination.

Of course, there are strong economic motives for relying on drawings and computer renderings, which are so much faster and cheaper to produce. But the choices we make have an impact on our designs. The sculptural forms so loved by Japanese architects are rooted in the way their projects begin, as models.

Compared with counterparts overseas, Japanese architects have long been only lightly concerned with economic efficiency in their work.

Instead, most have chosen to focus painstakingly on tiny details that few may even notice, much less appreciate. Similarly, we are willing to spend late nights in the office sifting through applicants in order to hire someone special. Those whom we hire are rewarded with apprenticeships offering low pay, long office hours, whimsical and enigmatic demands— and an unparalleled opportunity to ignore expectations in favor of innovative creativity.

From the first day, every new hire has an opportunity to make a mark, expressing his or her own unique approaches to projects large and small. The fierce competition that exists between architects, and that exists between architects and other designers, is also found inside each successful firm. In the early stages of a project, staff jockey for attention and impact, offering multiple models of their proposals; with a little luck, they can quickly emerge as team leaders even with limited experience. A new hire may work on a speculative master plan one day, have sole responsibility for a clever but short-lived installation a few weeks later, and end the month fleshing out the details of an eye-catching element in a larger building. Rookie apprentices join in meetings with clients and trips to the construction site. They also travel with me to cities around Japan and around the world. They quickly develop pluck and skill.

There is one notable problem with Japan's intensive apprenticeship system: by the age of 35 or 40, most are quite comfortable starting their own offices, further intensifying the battle for work that drives each architect to propose designs that are ever more eye-catching. But as large numbers of these ambitious and experienced architects strike out on their own, the country is at a turning point, its appetite for such innovation dwindling.

An Uncertain Future

One of the clearest recent signs of this declining appetite was Prime Minister Shinzo Abe's cancelation in 2015 of Iraqi-British architect Zaha Hadid's design of a new National Olympic Stadium for the 2020 Games in Tokyo. She won the contract three years earlier with a spectacularly curvaceous structure that would have been a rousing centerpiece to the Summer Olympics' return to Tokyo after more than half a century. With a pair of 70-meter-tall arches, a retractable roof, and seating capacity for up to 80,000, the stadium's mammoth proportions would have proclaimed Japan's place in the world. But the proposed stadium came with an outsized and ever-increasing price tag: by the time the prime minister canceled it, the projected cost had ballooned to more than ¥250 billion, three times the price of the Olympic stadium in London.[11]

Postwar Japan once used visionary construction projects to make bold national statements. Indeed, Hadid's design was consistent with this history, echoing Tange's or Isozaki's soaring aspirations. However, the times had changed; her design came under immediate criticism from architects and citizens' groups for being extravagant and oversized, an opprobrium that only grew with the proposed stadium's price. At its root, this criticism was part of a backlash against the postwar alliance between architects, contractors, and politicians, which many in Japan now felt funded costly avant-garde architecture that the nation did not want and could no longer afford.

In December 2015, after reopening bidding on the project, the Japan Sports Council chose KKAA's more modest design of a smaller, wooden stadium with a price tag of about ¥150 billion.[12] The episode sent a warning to the nation's and the world's architects. Unlike Kakuei Tanaka a half century earlier, Japan had openly refused to spend whatever it takes to build a lasting monument. More than anything else so far, this decision seemed to mark the end of a postwar era that had been so generous to architects. Replacing Hadid's spectacular design with KKAA's more modestly scaled one shocked architects around the world because it so neatly repudiated what Japan had come to stand for: cosmopolitan and audacious designs built in spite of technical challenges or budget overruns.

Reigniting the Network

Is it possible that Japan's competition-driven creative dynamic is now coming to an end? There are strong architects in the next generation, born in the 1960s and 1970s, but each stands alone, lacking the collaborative network of public clients, political backers, and contractors that their elders enjoyed. This has made it harder for their visions to actually get constructed. Often, today's younger architects are better known for their unbuilt concepts than actual structures, or for contributing subtle architectural distinctions rather than bold departures. There is little sense of a strong collective identity or ambition. While the rich networks and dynamic clusters that drove Japan's architectural excellence have not disappeared, it is less clear whether they have enough momentum to create a new vanguard.

The fierce rivalries that once propelled architects to ever-greater heights have begun to wane. So has Japanese architects' curiosity about the outside world. Oddly enough, at a time when international exchange is easier and cheaper than ever, the next generation of Japanese architects is increasingly isolated from global discourse, content to stay home. They

Figure 2.4: Nest We Grow, Grand Prize winner at the 2014 LIXIL International Student Architectural Competition hosted by LIXIL JS Foundation. Designed by students from the University of California, Berkeley, in collaboration with Kengo Kuma and Associates, Masato Araya, and the Tomonari Yashiro Laboratory at the University of Tokyo. Image courtesy of Shinkenchiku-sha.

seem to feel less compelled to make the leap that others made before them.

Many of Japan's most talented young designers still do go abroad. However, it is increasingly less clear if their presence outside their country remains a sign of success or instead has become a symptom of emerging failure. A generation ago, Japan's young architects went overseas to absorb the world's best ideas and practices and bring them home again. Today, the world still welcomes young Japanese architects because of their skill and novel ideas. What is less clear is if these young architects are welcome when they return to Japan, which seems to have lost interest in the world outside its borders. These days, many opt to just stay overseas. The few who do try to return often find difficulties fitting back in, with no clear avenue to utilize their experiences.

Intense, richly rewarded competition drove architects and, in time, their colleagues in other, allied design fields to achieve international renown (Figure 2.4). What will spark the next ember? The days of politicians, contractors, and architects existing in a tight alliance is passing. Instead of moaning over the loss, architects should find new allies so that Japan's innovative cycles of exciting architecture will not be extinguished.

Notes

1. Marc Bain, "Japanese Designers Are by Far the Coolest at Paris Fashion Week," *Quartz*, March 10, 2015.

2. James Harris, "The 50 Greatest Japanese Brands of All Time," *Complex Style*, January 16, 2013.

3. Tom Kelley, speaking at Asia Pacific Initiative, January 7, 2016.

4. "State of Create Study: Global Benchmark Study on Attitudes and Beliefs about Creativity at Work, School and Home," Adobe Systems, April 2012, pp. 18-21, accessed November 27, 2017, www.adobe.com/aboutadobe/pressroom /pdfs/Adobe_State_of_Create_Global_Benchmark_Study.pdf.

5. James Higa, speaking at Asia Pacific Initiative, November 11, 2015.

6. Kelley, 2016.

7. Kenya Hara, speaking at Asia Pacific Initiative, January 18, 2016.

8. Japan Federation of Architects and Building Engineers Associations, "Architect Registration Status for FY2015," March 31, 2016, accessed November 17, 2017, www.kenchikushikai.or.jp/touroku/meibo/tourokusu20160331.pdf.

9. United States Bureau of Labor Statistics, "Occupational Outlook Handbook: Architects," accessed December 17, 2015, www.bls.gov/ooh/architecture-and-engi neering/architects.htm.

10. "Chinese Ministry of Housing and Urban-Rural Development," accessed July 10, 2017, http://www.mohurd.gov.cn. For a slightly older look, see Charles Q. L. Xue, *Building a Revolution: Chinese Architecture Since 1980* (Hong Kong: Hong Kong University Press, 2006), p. 159.

11. Anne Quito, "Japan Has Scrapped Zaha Hadid's Ostentatious Design for Its New National Stadium," *Quartz*, July 18, 2015.

12. "Japan OKs 150 Billion Yen Contract for New Tokyo Stadium," *Associated Press*, September 30, 2016.

CHAPTER THREE

Asia's Rediscovery of Japan: The Boom in Inbound Tourism

Fumiko Kato

A profound transformation is taking place in Japan, one that is best captured by the revolution in the nation's tourism industry.

For decades, Japan was a source of outbound tourism, a nation whose legions of camera-toting travelers descended upon the world's toniest shopping districts, from Fifth Avenue and Champs-Élysées to Singapore's Orchard Road. However, that has all been turned on its head. In 2015, for the first time in 45 years, the net flow of tourism reversed: the number of Japanese going abroad was surpassed by the number of visitors entering Japan, mostly from Asia. Chinese tourists now flood Tokyo's poshest department stores in Ginza and Shinjuku in such numbers, and spend so freely, that a new word has been coined to describe their behavior: *bakugai*, or "explosive buying."

The recent surge in foreign visits to Japan has been truly remarkable. According to the official Japan National Tourism Organization, the number of overseas tourists coming to Japan hit a record 19.74 million in 2015, a 47.1 percent increase from the year before.[1] That is almost two and a half times larger than the 8.61 million visitors a half decade earlier, in 2010. So dramatic has been the increase that the Japanese government has scrapped its original goal of attracting 20 million foreign tourists by 2020, the year of the Tokyo Olympics, in order to double that target to 40 million.

The explosion in inbound tourism has catapulted Japan into the upper echelon of global tourist destinations and brought the promise of economic revitalization to a nation whose domestic growth rates may have peaked. But the effects go beyond that. Many in Japan are starting to reconceptualize their nation as a destination for foreign tourists and to come up with ways to provide for and satisfy these new masses of visitors.

The fact that most of these tourists come from neighboring nations and regions has also led to what might be called an Asianization of Japan. By far, the largest number of foreign tourists to Japan in 2015 came from mainland China: 4.99 million, more than double the year before. This was followed by South Korea (4 million), Taiwan (3.68 million), and Hong Kong (1.52 million). If we add in Thailand, 800,000 of whose citizens visited Japan, then eastern Asia accounted for a full three-quarters of all foreign tourists to Japan. By contrast, the biggest non-Asian source of visitors was the United States: the number of Americans visiting Japan surged by 15.9 percent to 1.03 million, the first time that figure has topped 1 million, the organization said.

Several reasons are given for these dramatic increases. One is the emergence of a growing middle class in China and elsewhere in Asia that has the money and the appetite for travel. Steep declines in the value of the Japanese yen since 2012 have also helped make Japan, once one of the world's most expensive destinations, much more affordable. Compared to cities like Hong Kong, New York, or even Beijing, Tokyo can now seem a downright bargain at times. Also contributing have been government measures to increase tourism, such as easing or waiving visa restrictions. Improved access, including the opening of a third terminal at Tokyo's Haneda Airport to a far larger number of international flights, has also provided a boost.

This unprecedented boom in inbound tourism has presented Japan with more than just the need to build additional hotel rooms, duty-free shops, and English- and Chinese-language signage. It has also led to what might be called a rediscovery of Japan, not only by the foreigners who come but also among the Japanese themselves. The influx is pushing Japan to reconsider what is appealing or valuable within itself by forcing the nation to see itself through the eyes of non-Japanese visitors. It is also creating new encounters and new connections with Asian neighbors that are challenging the very identity of Japan, a nation that has long tilted toward the West. Perhaps most importantly, these encounters have become a chance for Japan to rethink what it has to offer the region and the world, as measured by its ability to attract visitors to its shores.

Linking Japan to Asia

Shinichi Inoue has been on a mission to link Japan more closely to the rest of Asia. He has found success by pioneering a very straightforward way to do this: by dramatically lowering the cost of travel to Japan.

Inoue is president of Peach Aviation, a low-cost carrier, or LCC, that has been a leader in increasing inbound tourism from Asia to Japan. For decades, travel to and from Japan was a monopoly of full-service carriers like the national champion Japan Airlines, founded right after World War II. Peach did not even start carrying passengers until 2012, after years of deregulation and Japan Airlines' high-profile bankruptcy finally opened slots at Japanese airports to new competitors. While Peach was one of the first, it has been joined by a slew of low-cost carriers, including Jetstar, AirAsia, and Vanilla Air.

Among these new LCCs, Peach has emerged as one of the few known to be profitable. It also offers the largest number of seats to international destinations.

Inoue was the director of the Beijing office of All-Nippon Airways when that airline tapped him to head a new LCC business venture with the Hong Kong investment company First Eastern Investment Group. Inoue said he leapt at the opportunity.

Under Inoue, Peach has quickly established itself as the benchmark for other LCCs in the region through its combination of quality service and visible branding: a distinctive purple coloring makes its fleet of 19 Airbus 320-200s an easily recognizable presence on the crowded tarmacs of Asia's airports. The pricing has also been right. A seat on a Peach flight from its hub at Kansai International Airport, which serves the cities of Osaka and Kyoto, to Seoul's Incheon International Airport costs an average of ¥38,100, half of what a full-service carrier charges, Inoue says. A flight to Hong Kong is an even bigger bargain, costing ¥21,980 on average, a third the regular fare.

Inoue says this has made Peach an increasingly popular airline for Chinese and other Asian tourists coming into Japan. In 2015, Peach carried almost 2 million foreign visitors into Japan, surpassing for the first time the number of Japanese passengers that it carried abroad, Inoue said.

He said many of these non-Japanese passengers are wealthy Asians who are repeat travelers to Japan. Most want to save on the cost of travel so they can spend money in Japan. Inoue said that unlike Western tourists, who tend to stay longer in Japan to experience its culture and history, many Asian visitors come for short visits that are heavily focused on shopping and consumption. The biggest spenders are the Chinese, who on average spend about ¥280,000 per person during a visit.

This has been a huge economic boon to cities in Japan's western Kansai region, like Osaka, which was hit hard by Japan's long bout of deflation in the 1990s and 2000s. But Inoue said the benefits go beyond money. He said the Chinese and other visitors are helping Japan regain confidence by demonstrating the appeal that Japan holds in the rest of Asia. These are encounters that Inoue hopes to encourage, as expressed in Peach's mission statement: "To serve as a bridge for Asia to deepen its exchange of people, goods, and things. To be an airline that nurtures love between people."

"In Asia, Japan has various historical conflicts with its neighboring countries," Inoue told Asia Pacific Initiative. "I had long felt that something needed to be done to change this. I want to build a future-oriented relationship between Japan and Asia, and I felt I should contribute by facilitating communication and exchange among young people. Young people don't have much money, but I was certain that they would make use of an LCC."[2]

Reviving Regional Economies

Many economists and policy makers now see tourism as essential for lifting Japan's regional economies, which have been hit hardest by years of deflation and depopulation. Some hope that inbound tourism can be the silver bullet that eases the growing inequalities between Japan's rural regions and its thriving urban centers like Tokyo and Nagoya, the hub of its auto industry.

Prime Minister Shinzo Abe has designated tourism as a major pillar of his program for resuscitating economic growth, especially in Japan's regions. In April 2016, the Land Ministry, which is in charge of tourism, announced a new set of deregulation measures and subsidies aimed at encouraging construction of new hotels for foreign tourists outside the three major cities of Tokyo, Osaka, and Nagoya. The ministry said it will instruct local governments to ease restrictions on the size of structures (usually a limit on the ratio of a building's total floor area to the size of the plot of land on which it sits) to allow construction of taller hotels with more rooms.

The government will also offer subsidies to help older hotels or more traditional style *ryokan* inns attract foreign customers by making such changes as converting older squat toilets into Western-style seated ones or creating Web sites in foreign languages. The ministry will also fund projects to turn unused homes and school buildings into lodging to expand capacity.

Similar deregulation has already resulted in a rush of new hotel construction in Tokyo and Osaka.

The government is responding to increasingly dire shortages of vacant hotel rooms caused by the boom in inbound tourism. According to a report in April 2016 by the real estate firm Savills, the occupancy rate of hotels in Japan reached 83.7 percent in 2015 and has been above 80 percent since 2013. (By contrast, the occupancy rate of hotels in the United States was 64.4 percent.) To meet the growing demand, construction is planned or under way to add 45,000 hotel rooms across Japan. Much of this new expansion is taking place outside Tokyo to accommodate an increase in inbound tourists visiting regional destinations, Savills said.[3]

This influx of foreign visitors into the Japanese hinterlands has spurred a rediscovery within Japan of the charms of its own rural areas. One result has been a new appreciation of the scenery, traditions, cuisine, and arts and crafts of these areas, which were long ignored as backwaters. As foreign tourists show interest in these long overlooked areas, many Japanese are also reexamining them in order to identify new attractions and other resources for further increasing tourism, with mixed success.

This has helped bring a new awareness within Japan of its own diversity, which is actually a source of appeal to inbound visitors. There has been a new realization that foreign tourists are not just drawn by the stock images of Japan, such as Mount Fuji, cherry blossoms, and geisha. Rather, many use foreign Web sites and blogs completely unknown to Japanese to find the nooks and crannies that most Japanese had missed: the small *onsen* inn not overrun by busloads of domestic tourists, the pottery village with a distinct glaze or style of kiln, the cramped but delicious ramen shop tucked away in a residential neighborhood. The discovery of what actually attracts foreign interest has been eye-opening for many Japanese, leading to a self-awareness about the diversity and appeals of their own nation.

David Atkinson, a British former financial analyst who recently wrote a book calling on Japan to be a "tourism-focused country," says that this is precisely the sort of self-discovery that Japan needs. He said that tourism is a global growth industry and one that Japan has only just begun to tap. He said Japan could become a world-class tourist destination by making better use of its charms and appeals. One of these is its remarkable diversity in offerings, something that remains underappreciated at home.[4]

One underutilized asset is Japan's remarkable range of climates and topography, spread across an archipelago that extends from the edge of Siberia to the tropics. At Hokkaido's northernmost point, Cape Soya, the Russian island of Sakhalin is visible, and the winters become so frigid that the surrounding sea gets locked in ice. Japan's southernmost point is Hateruma, a sun-drenched island in the Ryukyus near Taiwan that is surrounded by coral and renowned for producing sugar cane and fiery *awamori* spirits. Hateruma shares the same latitude as monsoonal India.

The geographical diversity has offered Japan novel ways to market itself to tourists, particularly from Asia. One of the most successful efforts has been to present Japan as a winter sports wonderland whose ski slopes, skating rings, and sledding hills are within easy reach of travelers from warmer climates like Taiwan and Southeast Asia. This strategy has been particularly effective for Hokkaido, whose tall mountains, rolling farmlands, and heavy snowfall offer an environment similar to northern Europe or North America. Hokkaido has become a hugely popular destination for Taiwanese, Hong Kongers, and increasingly mainland Chinese tourists, not just in winter but all year round.

Asianizing Snow Country

These winter charms have helped Japan turn one of its biggest backwaters, the once remote and impoverished rural regions along its backside facing the Sea of Japan, into a draw for overseas tourists. This region has long been known as Snow Country because the snow-laden clouds blowing in from Siberia must dump their loads before crossing Japan's mountainous interior. It is not uncommon for places like Niigata or western Hokkaido to get three or more meters of snow. Photos of cars driving through white chasms of snowpack that tower overhead have long served to reinforce the area's image as a remote and even forbidding part of Japan.

Now, those same images are the centerpiece of a marketing campaign aimed at attracting visitors from tropical Southeast Asia, where there is no snow. On July 1, 2015, Southeast Asia's first snow theme park, Snow Town, opened in a shopping mall in Bangkok. It has a plaza surrounded by streets modeled after Otaru in Hokkaido, and an artificial snow machine is used to create snowfall. A Japanese winter scene is re-created there, one in which visitors can even play in the snow. It also has many restaurants, including the first Thai branches of Japanese steak and other chain restaurants.

One of the advisors who helped launch this snow plaza was Tatsumi Ichinomoto, president of MacEarth, a Yabu, Japan-based operator of ski resorts.

With 32 ski slopes in Japan, MacEarth is Asia's largest such operator. Ichinomoto hopes Thai patrons who enjoy Snow Town will decide to try the real thing by making a trip to one of Japan's ski slopes. Even if not all of them do go, he said he himself has already learned a lot by watching the Thai patrons at Snow Town and how they find appeal in things that Japanese might avoid, like the chilly air blasting out from the snow machine itself.

"The area around the part of the machine where snow blows out is so cold that most Japanese people would not go near it," Ichinomoto said. "But Thai people like to gather there. They say 'Just once in my life, I wish to go to Japan and enjoy the winter scenery and play in the snow.' When I tell them I'm from Japan, they ask me to send them snow by express mail."[5]

For Ichinomoto, the desire to attract Asian tourists to Japan's ski slopes stems from a personal desire to contribute to the economic revival of his hometown. Ichinomoto grew up in the mountains of Hachi Kogen, in western Japan's Hyogo Prefecture, where Yabu is located. This is a very rural region that has little to offer tourists except mountains, snow, and the ski resort that is the area's economic mainstay.

Ichinomoto's dream extends to other parts of Japan, where he is helping develop ski resorts in hopes of one day rivaling the best ski slopes of Europe. At Norikuradake, a ski mountain located on the border of Nagano and Gifu prefectures, he is lobbying the government to have the area designated as a special zone for resort development by international collaboration, which would give it some regulatory and tax benefits. He is also trying to find financial support and investment money for improvements such as building a European-style tramway to the ski area's top, at 3,000 meters.

There are challenges, such as the fact that Japan's ski resorts tend to be much smaller than those in Europe or North America. Japan's largest ski resort, Niseko United in Hokkaido, is 480 hectares, less than half the average size of the major ski resorts in Europe. However, most of Japan's more than 500 ski resorts are blessed with one thing: ample amounts of natural snow.[6]

Still, Japan's ski industry has been in a long, slow decline for the past 20 years. Many of its resorts were built during the late 1980s bubble economy, when skiing enjoyed a boom in popularity. From a peak of some 18 million mostly domestic skiers, the number of visitors each year to Japan's ski slopes has declined to about half of that figure now, leaving many slopes feeling empty and their lodging and facilities looking increasingly dilapidated.[7]

Japan's ski resorts see a new opportunity in the current boom in Asian visitors. Aware that many of these tourists may never have skiied before, resorts and tour operators are trying to entice them by offering packages that also include nonskiing options. In the winter of 2016, the Japanese travel agency JTB launched Experience Japan package tours that offered skiers a side trip to a farm to pick strawberries.[8] Package tours also play up the fact that skiers can soak in a natural *onsen* hot spring, or enjoy gourmet meals.

Harunobu Kiyonaga, the general manager of the Norn Minakami Ski Resort in Gunma Prefecture north of Tokyo, wants to attract Asian tourists who have never skied before. To do this, he has asked travel companies to bill trips to Japanese ski slopes as chances to "play in the snow," a suggestion that many have followed. He said this makes the trip seem a lot less intimidating to first-timers, who might decide to give skiing a try once they actually see others doing it.

"When people spend some time playing in snow at ski resorts, they see skiers gliding down the slopes and it looks like a lot of fun," Kiyonaga said. "That makes them want to try skiing themselves the next time they visit Japan."[9]

Not all foreign tourists need convincing about the pleasures of skiing. Two countries in the Asia Pacific region that already have large numbers of avid, experienced skiers are Australia and New Zealand. In recent years, some Japanese ski resorts have become so popular among antipodean skiers that they are experiencing an economic renaissance.

While Hokkaido is more than a 10-hour flight from Australia, most of the travel is north-south, without the exhausting changes in time zones that travelers experience going to North America or Europe. At the same time, Hokkaido's top resorts like Niseko offer high-quality snow, including fresh, soft powder. Hokkaido's reputation for winter sports goes back to the 1972 Winter Olympics, held near the city of Sapporo.

Perhaps most importantly, Hokkaido's winter ski season falls during summer in the southern hemisphere, allowing snow lovers in Australia and New Zealand to enjoy skiing when their own countries' slopes are closed for the season.

The influx of skiers from Australia and New Zealand has had a particularly large impact at Niseko, a resort in southern Hokkaido. Australians have reshaped the local economy; Australian developers build and operate luxury condominiums; and Australian entrepreneurs have started travel agencies, guide services, and even steak restaurants. With the types of food offered and the widespread use of English, visitors to Niseko might be forgiven for feeling that they have left Japan and suddenly reappeared in some Western country.

The Foreigners' Gaze

In some cases, the discovery of a place by foreign tourists has led to its rediscovery by Japanese, who learn to see its appeals through fresh eyes. One such place is the Seto Inland Sea, whose island-studded waters offer one of the most picturesque landscapes in all Japan.

Overseas visitors have remarked on the sea's beauty since the first Westerners began arriving. In the early 19th century, German scientist and traveler Philipp Franz von Siebold praised its scenic views. Thomas Cook and Ulysses Grant also toured the region. These visitors praised as beautifully exotic the scenes that must have struck the local Japanese as dully mundane: peasants planting seedlings in terraced rice paddies, fishers plying the waters in wooden boats, and the graceful curves of the tiled roofs on farmhouses and temples.

However, the foreigners' interest changed how the Japanese themselves viewed the region. As local populations fell under the "tourist gaze" of these foreign visitors, they sought to satisfy the visitors' desire for an authentic experience.[10] One result was a predictable commoditization of the area's heritage. However, the local response went beyond simply a reactive desire to fulfill foreigners' expectations. Japanese also began to cast their own gaze on the scenery, rediscovering it but also reshaping it into something very different.

Many of the Japanese who gazed at the Seto Inland Sea did not seek to simply preserve it as an authentic scenery of an older, vanishing Japan. Some saw it as an appropriately scenic canvas to become a global hub for the visual arts. In recent years, several world-class art museums, galleries, and exhibition halls have appeared along the inland sea, including the Ohara Museum of Art in Okayama, the Isamu Noguchi Garden Museum in Takamatsu, the Marugame Genichiro-Inokuma Museum of Contemporary Art, and the Toyo Ito Museum of Architecture. These undertakings have proven enormously attractive to new generations of Western tourists.

Among these, the island of Naoshima has achieved particular acclaim for its Benesse Art Site, the Chichu Art Museum, and the Art House

Project. Naoshima stands as a dramatic success story, a once-poor rural fishing area that was able to leverage its scenic advantages into a new tourism resource. Naoshima is frequently featured in the travel guide-book *Lonely Planet* and leading international travel magazines as one of Japan's top attractions. Neighboring areas have also been able to leverage off of Naoshima's success. Every three years, nearby islands like Teshima and Inujima and the city of Takamatsu host the Setouchi International Art Festival, also known as the Setouchi Triennale, which attracts more than a million visitors from across Japan and the world.

As the number of international visitors to Japan increases, there have been other instances of these tourists discovering attractions, which only then receive domestic attention. One recent example was the Ashikaga Flower Park, which few Japanese had heard of until it was listed as one of CNN Travel's top nine dream vacation destinations in 2014.[11] The park in the city of Ashikaga, north of Tokyo, has more than 350 wisteria trees, including one more than 140 years old, creating almost magical scenery that few Japanese had bothered to visit.

Some Japanese have set out to find those sites of natural beauty that have yet to attract the foreigners' gaze. Some of these are very remote, possessing an inaccessibility that may add to their future appeal. Kenya Hara, an internationally recognized art director for the retailer Muji, says the next boom in foreign ecotourism to Japan may be driven by a discovery of its many spectacular peninsulas, where the Japanese archipelago's jagged mountains jut into the sea to form dramatic vistas. However, most remain hard to reach, leading Hara to propose linking them to each other and to Tokyo via a seaplane service that could cater to well-heeled foreign and Japanese travelers. The peninsulas would also offer a ruggedly natural setting for high-end inns and resorts, which could also be developed.

"Peninsulas jut into the ocean, and that makes them have by far the most attractive and intriguing scenic qualities," Hara said. "I predict that Japanese peninsula tours will become valuable tourism resources. I'm looking forward to new airlines that only fly between peninsula regions."[12]

Natural scenery is not the only thing that captures the foreign tourists' interest. In fact, sometimes their collective gaze falls upon things that seem surprising commonplace, even unattractive to many Japanese. The Japan Tourism Agency has found that on Twitter, the most common subject of posts by foreign travelers to Japan is the Shibuya Scramble Crossing, an extremely busy intersection in Tokyo that is crossed by 500,000 people per day. What might be viewed by many Japanese residents as just another tiresome encounter with urban crowds has become one of Tokyo's most iconic scenes in the eyes of overseas visitors. The intersection, where waves of pedestrians pour forth each green light to cross in every possible direction, is widely recognized around the world, appearing in Hollywood films like *Lost in Translation*.

Selling Beauty to Asia

One of the growth trends in the global tourism industry is so-called beauty tourism, in which travelers visit beauty salons and spas. While South Korea has been a player in this market, Japan has become another popular destination among women in Asia. According to a 2016 report by the Hot Pepper Beauty Academy, a Japanese research group that studies beauty trends, women from China, Taiwan, South Korea, and Hong Kong who had visited Japan overwhelmingly responded that they view Japan as the country that they most admire for beauty services. According to this survey, 64 percent said they admired Japan in this way, versus 57 percent who said this about South Korea and 26 percent about France. (Respondents could name more than one country.)

In the report, the Hot Pepper Beauty Academy concluded that there is an observable shift in spending by Asian tourists in Japan toward purchasing services including visits to hair and nail salons and beauty-treatment clinics. "In 2016, demand from inbound tourism will be very important for the beauty industry," the report concluded.[13]

An increasing number of young Asian women are seeking out ordinary Japanese beauty parlors that were originally established for local customers. They do this to have their hair done in styles that are popular in Japan, and take a refreshing break for a few hours that many seem to find enjoyable and relaxing.

But why Japan? What is it about Japanese beauty services that attracts growing numbers of Asian women?

Surveys show that part of the appeal is the quality of the experience at Japanese salons, which take pride in pampering customers with services from free consultations to stress-relieving scalp massages and hot towels to freshen up the face. But the answer may also lie in the growing popularity of Japanese popular culture abroad, especially in Asia.

In 2016, the Japanese travel agency HIS started offering a beauty services tour called the Kawaii Plan.[14] While *kawaii* means "cute" in Japanese, the term is increasingly used overseas to describe the childlike characters, self-consciously adorable facial expressions, and playful colors that are a central aesthetic of Japan's popular culture. The tour's aim is to attract young women by offering the opportunity to experience not just trendy Japanese nail salons and beauty parlors but also an immersion into Japanese youth culture itself.

For a long time, young women in Japan looked to Europe and the United States for guidance on beauty products and clothing fashions. During the 1980s, Japanese women flocked to Paris and Los Angeles to buy everything from cosmetics to handbags. However, one thing that we did not hear much about was Japanese women having their hair cut at beauty salons in those countries. There must have been a reluctance to having one's hair cut or permed in a foreign country where they didn't speak the language, or where most customers and beauticians were not Asian.

This is one of the big differences with the current boom in inbound Asian tourists into Japan. These new visitors appear to feel far less of a barrier to trying Japanese beauty clinics and hair and nail salons.

Yoko Saito, senior researcher at the Hot Pepper Beauty Academy, says, "Asian women see Japanese women as having an appearance similar to their own. They have similar physiques and hair types. And yet young Japanese women are skilled at makeup, and their hairstyles are fashionable. Asian women find them to be cute and sophisticated. I think that stimulates their desire to make use of Japanese beauty services."[15]

Add to this the appeal of Japanese popular culture and you get a large and growing demand for Japanese beauty products and services, Saito said. This popularity appears in the sales figures of Japanese makers of beauty products such as Shiseido, which says that more than half—53 percent— of its 2015 revenues of ¥777.7 billion came from abroad. But the appeal of Japanese beauty services has also become a major lure for inbound tourists from Asia. This trend is evident on social networks, where Asian women visiting Japan often write that they have gone to Japan to transform themselves into a "cute, fashionable, and sophisticated me," Saito said.

They share selfies and videos of their new hairstyles and makeup online, which "contributes to Japan's improved image as a worldwide leader in beauty services," Saito said. She said the popularity of services like hairstyling and beauty clinics has also led to an increase in repeaters: tourists, mostly from neighboring Asian countries, who make multiple trips to Japan. In fact, the prevalence of repeaters has been one of the features of Japan's current inbound tourism boom: for instance, among visitors from Taiwan and Hong Kong, 80 percent have visited Japan two or more times.[16]

The number of Asian customers has risen so dramatically that Forcise, a company operating 26 beauty parlors and nail salons in Osaka and

Tokyo, began offering English language training to its staff in 2013. The company said that at first it asked non-Japanese speakers to point at pictures of hairstyles but soon realized that this was not enough. With other beauty parlors facing similar challenges, Forcise launched a specialized English-language school that uses textbooks the company created especially for beauticians.[17]

Other beauty-related businesses have also profited from Asia's interest in Japanese popular culture. One is Ita Color's Yellow, a nail salon in Tokyo's pop culture mecca of Akihabara that specializes in so-called *ita* art. *Ita* is a genre of Japanese popular culture that refers to things emblazoned with brightly colored images from anime and manga. The term comes from the Japanese word *itai*, or "ouch," a reference to the use of garish colors and designs that "hurt" the eye. Ita Color's Yellow specializes in *itanails*, painting finger and toe nails with highly detailed images of popular cartoon characters.

The salon said that it now gets many customers from Asia, including repeaters who come for its finely detailed designs. But the popularity of *itanails* has also made its way to the West. The American singer Katy Perry helped ignite interest when, during a 2012 trip to Japan, she tweeted photos of nails painted with characters from the American cartoon *Daria* that she had had done at a Tokyo salon. "Katy Perry Gets 'Daria' Nail Art, Our Minds Explode," proclaimed a posting on MTV's social media accounts.[18]

But the appeal is not limited to pop culture. Ita Color's Yellow said that some of the most popular designs among foreign customers feature traditional Japanese themes, such as sushi, kabuki, and Mount Fuji.

The WASPA, a beauty spa in Tokyo's Ginza shopping district, has also tried to tap the surge in inbound tourism by highlighting traditional Japanese culture. On entering, the customer encounters a peaceful, elegant space decorated with a golden *byobu* screen, a tea kettle, and a statue of a bodhisattva. The spa menu includes Aotake Therapy, featuring *aotake*, or green bamboo, that has been blessed for health and longevity by Buddhist priests at Daigo-ji Temple in Kyoto, and Mount Fuji Hot Stone Therapy, in which spa-goers sit in a sauna-like room heated with lava stones brought from the slopes of Mount Fuji. To welcome customers, WASPA provides matcha tea and seasonal sweets in a traditional tea ceremony room decorated with fresh flowers and incense.

Japan's Top Draw

The Japan Tourism Agency conducts regular surveys of inbound tourists in which it asks visitors from overseas to rank what they look forward to most during their trip to Japan. The second- and third-ranked answers tend to reflect the national differences that we discussed above: Chinese tourists say shopping, Westerners say culture and history, and Southeast Asians may say snow or seasons. However, the top reply is the same in every survey, regardless of the nationality of the visitor: food.[19]

Japan has long enjoyed global recognition for its healthy, sophisticated cuisine. More recently, Japan's top chefs have also begun to earn an international celebrity status similar to their counterparts in Paris and New York. One is sushi master Jiro Ono, whose Sukiyabashi Jiro restaurant draws foodies from around the planet. Ono gained global fame after appearing in David Gelb's 2011 documentary film *Jiro Dreams of Sushi*, which profiled Ono and his tiny restaurant in a Tokyo subway station. According to Ono, Japanese cuisine has several draws. One is its dedication to simplicity and purity, in which fewer ingredients are used and their original flavors highlighted instead of being hidden behind heavy sauces or within elaborate mash-ups. Another is the emphasis placed on the quality of the ingredients, whether it's raw fish or a perfectly shaped pear.[20]

So it is understandable that tourists would prioritize an opportunity to eat authentic Japanese food and to learn more about the cuisine at its place of origin. However, the fact that very few Japanese restaurants have English menus or English-speaking staff has presented foreign visitors with formidable linguistic challenges.

Now, some companies are using the power of digital technology to eliminate such barriers. One is Pocket Concierge, which gives users the ability to reserve a table, order food, and pay the bill all by means of an English-language Web site that is accessible via a smartphone application. Pocket Concierge's president, Kei Tokado, says his company has partnered with some 410 restaurants, including Michelin three-starred Ryugin and Kanda, to offer greater accessibility to non-Japanese-speaking customers. He said that as of June 2016, Pocket Concierge had approximately 120,000 users and adds 1,000 new members from overseas every month. He said about 20 to 30 percent of those new members actually use Pocket Concierge to make reservations.

Tokado's interest in dining comes from his own background. While growing up, he helped his parents run their Japanese restaurant outside Tokyo. As an adult, he followed in their footsteps, working as a chef for eight years and then as a restaurant consultant before founding Pocket Concierge in 2011.

He says this has given him a personal interest in promoting Japanese food both at home and abroad. He says that language is not the only barrier to accessing Japan's cuisine. Japanese high cuisine remains a closed, insular world, largely because of a grueling apprenticeship system that takes years to complete. Having spent so much time and effort to establish themselves, few of Japan's top chefs ever work abroad, much less open restaurants outside Japan. Likewise, their recipes and other know-how are transmitted to their own apprentices, who can guard them like trade secrets.

"In Japan, there is a preconception that recipes are meant to be kept secret," said Tokado, who says the country is falling out of step with global trends toward "open-sourcing" of cuisine. "I would like to run a business that creates more opportunities for Japanese chefs to thrive on the world stage."[21]

Within Japan, the chefs don't seem to need much help. In 2010, Tokyo became the city with the most three-Michelin-star restaurants in the entire world, topping even the French guidebook's own home city of Paris. In the press conference where this announcement was made, the director general in charge of the Michelin Guide at the time, Jean-Luc Naret, said, "Tokyo is the culinary capital of the world."[22]

In Michelin's 2015 guides, Tokyo boasted 226 restaurants that had earned stars, keeping its sizable lead over Paris, which had 95 starred restaurants. Tokyo's success may be due partly to its size: the city has 160,000 restaurants, versus 15,000 in Paris and 200,000 in all of France.[23]

"When it comes to the number of restaurants and their quality, I know of few cities that rival Tokyo," said Bernard Delmas, chairman of Michelin Japan. "The high quality of the restaurants in Tokyo is a result of the fierce competition they are faced with."[24]

Not just the skill of the chefs but the quality of ingredients is also propelling the popularity of Japanese cuisine. Hisato Hamada runs a business that helps restaurants overseas buy Japan's famed Wagyu beef directly from Japanese producers. He said that Japanese beef has become enormously popular despite the cost.

"Kobe beef is the most expensive beef in the world," Hamada said. Out of the some 3,000 cows that are bred each year to make Kobe beef, about 10 percent are now exported to meet growing global demand.[25]

Is Japan Ready?

Japan's inbound tourism boom has brought benefits but also a host of new problems and challenges. The most obvious may be the question of whether Japan is actually ready to welcome the 40 million foreign visitors per year that the government hopes will arrive by 2020. To put that figure in perspective, that would be a fivefold increase over the number of foreign tourists in 2010.[26]

Concerns are being raised that Japan simply does not have the infrastructure to support this many arrivals. We have seen that Japan's hotel occupancy rates are now among the highest in the world. There are also reports of foreign tourists overwhelming top attractions such as Kyoto's Kinkaku-ji, or Golden Pavilion, which has seen rising complaints of noise, littering, and trampled grass.

Overcrowded and overbooked hotels risk degrading the experience for foreign tourists coming to Japan. In July 2016, the influential American travel magazine *Travel and Leisure* removed the ancient Japanese capital of Kyoto from its perch as the world's top tourist city, lowering it to No. 6. (Charleston, South Carolina, replaced it on top.)[27]

"While the reasons for the fall were not explained, city officials suggested that the huge crowds of foreign and Japanese tourists visiting its popular temples, shrines and gardens as well as its major downtown shopping districts, might be the cause," said an article in *The Japan Times* about the downgrade. "The result of the recent tourism boom has been often long lines in shops and restaurants, as well as traffic gridlock." The article listed other ills that might also be tarnishing Kyoto's luster: complaints about price gouging that have appeared on English-language travel Web sites; hotel occupancy rates of greater than 90 percent that have driven up prices or made rooms impossible to find at all; and a shortage of foreign-language information for non-Japanese visitors.[28]

Another problem has been Japan's inability to keep up with new developments in the tourism industry, particularly those driven by digital technologies and services. While the so-called sharing economy has taken off in other developed nations, it has been slow to come to Japan, largely because of regulations. For instance, the ride-sharing giant Uber remains restricted here by laws protecting the taxi industry.

One exception has been Airbnb, which has finally begun to get traction. With 11,500 listings as of January 2016, Tokyo still trails far behind other major cities, like Paris with 66,000. However, Japan has emerged as one of Airbnb's biggest growth markets, with listings increasing more than 400 percent in 2015. During the same period, the number of overseas tourists using Airbnb in Japan rose even more dramatically, by 600 percent, the service's highest growth rate in the world.[29]

That growth has brought a backlash from Japan's hotel industry, which feels threatened by the new service. Pressured by the hotel industry, and by neighborhood groups objecting to a sudden increase in foreigners on their streets, the government proposed new guidelines in early 2016 that would restrict home sharing, called *minpaku* in Japanese, to stays of a week or longer. That would effectively make most Airbnb rentals illegal.

In June, the hotel industry's largest lobbying group, the All Japan Ryokan Hotel Association, called for new regulations to block most private home-owners from offering short-stay accommodations. The proposals also call for requiring those who rent out rooms to register as business operators and observe safety laws such as installing fire escapes.

However, officials have also leaned the other way, encouraging home-sharing services like Airbnb as a means to boost tourism. In April, the government eased restrictions in selected neighborhoods in Tokyo and Osaka to create "special economic zones" where individuals can more easily obtain a license to operate *minpaku* accommodations. The government has asked other municipalities to follow suit by revising local ordinances, but some have resisted. Kyoto, one of Japan's top tourist destinations, has kept most home sharing illegal, citing not just noise complaints but also owners who allow dangerous overcrowding in rooms.

At the root of this tug-of-war over home sharing is the Inns and Hotels Act, which dates back to the turbulent years after defeat in World War II, when regulations were needed to maintain minimum standards of cleanliness and sanitation. In today's Japan, policy makers must be careful not to allow such an outdated law to become an excuse for protecting vested interests at the expense of innovation. Japan ignores the preferences of foreign tourists at its own risk. They can always take their money elsewhere if restrictions here grow too onerous.

Tapping Japan's Potential

Tourism is one of the world's great growth markets. The World Tourism and Travel Council, a global industry group, estimated that in 2016 the global tourism industry was worth $7.2 trillion, more than the entire Japanese economy.[30] While Japan's inbound tourism has grown, the council's statistics make it clear that Japan has room to expand further. According to the council, in 2014, travel and tourism generated ¥36.3 trillion, or about 7.5 percent of Japan's gross domestic product, or GDP. While the revenue figure was enough to make Japan the world's fourth-largest tourism market in overall size, the nation was ranked a mere 117th out of 184 nations in terms of the size of tourism's contribution to national GDP. Japan came in low even among developed countries: tourism contributed 8.9 percent of Germany's GDP and 15.2 percent of Spain's.[31]

But tourism has more to offer Japan than jobs and revenues, though these are important. It promises to raise Japan's visibility and build positive feelings about the nation, especially within Asia, which could in turn boost Japan's regional influence, or soft power. Many in Japan have begun to recognize that a vibrant inbound tourism industry is a means of raising national prestige. This includes the Japanese government. In announcing its goal of 40 million overseas tourists by 2020, the government has said it wants Japan to become a "major tourism nation," just as it once set targets in hard industries like automobiles and electronics.[32]

The boom in inbound tourists from Asia also offers a means to bridge the still-yawning gaps that separate Japan from the region on such emotionally sensitive issues as history. As more Japanese come in contact with Asian visitors, and rely on those visitors for their livelihoods, they are more likely to see themselves and other Asians as standing on an equal footing and in need of coexistence. Under the gaze of these Asian tourists, Japanese will also become more aware of themselves as others in the region regard them. This could break down barriers between Japan and the region and contribute to a new Asianization in which Japan becomes more comfortable with viewing itself as part of Asia.

Notes

1. Japan National Tourist Organization, "2015 Foreign Visitors & Japan Departures," accessed July 10, 2017, www.jnto.go.jp/eng/ttp/sta/PDF/E2015.pdf.

2. Shinichi Inoue, speaking at Asia Pacific Initiative, April 22, 2016.

3. Savills World Research, "Spotlight Japan Hospitality," April 2016.

4. David Atkinson, *Shin Kanko Rikkokuron* (Tokyo: Toyo Keizai Shinposha, 2015), p. 57.

5. Tatsumi Ichinomoto, interviewed by author, June 24, 2016.

6. Japan-Guide.com, "Skiing and Snowboarding," accessed July 10, 2017, www.japan-guide.com/e/e2262.html.

7. Japan Tourism Agency, "Snoorizooto chiiki no genjo," January 30, 2015.

8. PR Times, "JTB honichi kojin kankokyaku muke package tour 'Experience Japan' no kono fuyu no ichioshi honichi ryoko shohin," November 10, 2015.

9. Harunobu Kiyonaga, interviewed by author, June 6, 2016.

10. John Urry, *The Tourist Gaze: Leisure and Travel in Contemporary Societies* (Thousand Oaks, CA: Sage Publications, 1990).

11. CNN Travel Staff, "Dream Destinations for 2014," January 9, 2014.

12. Kenya Hara, speaking at Asia Pacific Initiative, January 18, 2016.

13. Hot Pepper Beauty Academy, "Survey on Inbound Beauty Services," posted August 2015, http://hba.beauty.hotpepper.jp/check/6044/.

14. Recruit Holdings, "2016 Trade Predictions," December 15, 2015.

15. Yoko Saito, interviewed by author, June 28, 2016.

16. Japan Tourism Agency, "Survey of Consumption Trends by Foreigners Visiting Japan," updated March 17, 2017, http://www.mlit.go.jp/kankocho/en/siryou/toukei/syouhityousa.html.

17. "Salon List," *Forcise*, accessed July 10, 2017, http://forcise.info/salon/#nail.

18. Chrissy Mahlmeister, "Katy Perry Gets 'Daria' Nail Art, Our Minds Explode," *MTV News*, September 24, 2012.

19. Japan Tourism Agency, "Survey of Consumption."

20. Jiro Ono and Yoshikazu Ono, *Sushi Jiro Gastronomy* (San Francisco, CA: VIZ Media, 2016).

21. Kei Tokado, interviewed by author, June 27, 2016.

22. Tokyo MX, "Michelin Guide Tokyo 2010: 'Tokyo wa sekai no bishoku no shuto,'" posted on November 17, 2009, https://www.youtube.com/watch?v=5zUn EhLX9xU.

23. "Tokyo, championne des tables étoilées," *Le Monde*, posted November 29, 2011, http://www.lemonde.fr/gastronomie/article/2011/11/29/tokyo-championne -des-tables-etoilees_1610595_1383316.html?xtmc=160_000_tokyo_restaurant &xtcr=3.

24. Bernard Delmas, speaking at Asia Pacific Initiative, February 23, 2016.

25. Hisato Hamada, speaking at Asia Pacific Initiative, June 3, 2016.

26. Japan National Tourism Organization, "2010 Foreign Visitors & Japanese Departures," accessed July 10, 2017, https://www.jnto.go.jp/eng/ttp/sta/PDF /E2010.pdf.

27. Melanie Lieberman, "The World's Best Cities," *Travel and Leisure*, 2016, accessed July 10, 2017, www.travelandleisure.com/worlds-best/cities#intro.

28. Eric Johnston, "Travel Survey Bumps Kyoto from World's Top Tourist Spot," *The Japan Times*, July 7, 2016.

29. Alexander Martin and Eric Pfanner, "Japan Slowly Opens Doors to Sharing Economy," *The Wall Street Journal*, February 9, 2016.

30. World Travel & Tourism Council, "Economic Impact Analysis," accessed July 10, 2017, www.wttc.org/research/economic-research/economic-impact -analysis//.

31. "World Travel & Tourism Council's Economic Impact Reports for Japan (2015), Spain (2015), and Germany (2016)," accessed July 10, 2017, https://www .wttc.org/research/economic-research/economic-impact-analysis/country-reports/.

32. "Kanko rikkoku suishin kakuryo kaigi," Prime Minister of Japan and His Cabinet, accessed July 10, 2017, http://www.kantei.go.jp/jp/singi/kankorikkoku/.

PART 2

Outliers and Pioneers

CHAPTER FOUR

Departing from Silicon Valley: Japan's New Startup Ecosystem

Kenji E. Kushida

Few nations have suffered as dramatic a reversal of economic expectations as Japan. From a surging industrial power in the 1980s that appeared poised to take over global manufacturing and software, Japan had within a decade morphed into a cautionary tale of failure and stagnation. Japanese corporate champions like Toyota and Sharp once upended entire industries, but by the early 2000s, the epicenter of global innovation had shifted back across the Pacific Ocean to Silicon Valley and its model of venture capitalism. Japan appeared unable to keep up, choosing as a society to preserve companies and jobs at the expense of fostering new waves of entrepreneurs and disruptive startups.

However, this picture misses the gradual but dramatic changes that have actually taken place within Japan. As this chapter reveals, while the world's attention was diverted elsewhere, Japan has been developing in significant ways that matter for global competition. Once written off as hidebound and insular, many of Japan's large firms have quietly invented new approaches to innovation that are keeping them highly competitive. They have done this by looking outside their corporate borders to embrace the startups that they once shunned as threats, partnering with the new-comers to harness their ideas and creative energies.

As will be described below, some of these partnerships are taking place with Silicon Valley–based companies. But many are also happening within Japan, a development made possible by the emergence of a small but vigorous new startup ecosystem. This flurry of entrepreneurship has been visible in the proliferation of young Japanese companies that are already having an impact outside Japan, not only in information technology but also in science-based innovation. They are forming partnerships with Japan's large companies, allowing some to quickly become significant players in their industries. These newcomers have also benefited from an influx of young talent, as the unraveling of Japan's once-vaunted lifetime employment system has led more graduates of elite universities to view startups and entrepreneurship as attractive career choices. This new ecosystem is also attracting previously underutilized sources of talent, such as women, who were often stymied in Japan's male-dominated big companies.

While these changes have taken place gradually, reflecting Japan's emphasis on social stability, they have brought an invigorating new diversity to Japan's economy. As they do, they are having a transformative effect that will enable this still very wealthy, technologically sophisticated, and highly educated nation to find new ways to remain a major player in the global economy.

Japan's Quiet Reform

The common perception has been that Japan fell into stasis and stagnation during the 1990s and 2000s, a period that has come to be called the Lost Decades. However, a more careful look shows that Japan was in fact adjusting to changes in itself and the global economy, though in a gradual and incremental manner.

Nuanced observers saw processes of change that followed Japan's established patterns of institutional reform, with government and industry taking steps to slowly transform themselves.[1] Large companies reduced headcount by attrition and early retirement incentives, avoiding mass lay-offs. Similarly, Japan's laws and accounting practices were changed gradually to give companies time to adapt to new standards of governance, which have, over time, made corporate Japan more transparent and responsive to shareholders.

At the same time, deregulation opened previously protected sectors, such as finance, to foreign firms, bringing in new competition and also new sources of jobs.[2] Other changes included the creation of a stock exchange for smaller firms and startups; corporate code revisions that enabled new forms of executive compensation, such as stock options; and the restructuring of national universities into independent legal entities in order to push them to innovate. Legal and regulatory reforms also made it easier for companies to transform themselves by absorbing rivals, spinning off businesses, and creating holding companies.

The Japanese economic model that emerged by the early 2000s was more open and diverse and less cohesive than the so-called Japan Inc. of the 1980s.[3] It also embraced a form of change that allowed the coexistence of old, new, and hybrid organizational forms and business practices.[4] Whole swaths of Japan's economy, like regional banks and small manufacturing companies, have remained largely unchanged, keeping the old business models that they have used for decades. However, other industries, like information technology, have seen dramatically new types of companies appear as a product of Japan's flourishing new startup ecosystem. In many of Japan's large firms, the old and new coexist as companies have drastically altered some parts of their business while keeping other parts largely intact.

This diversity of responses helps account for one of the most perplexing features of Japan since the 1990s and 2000s—the nation's shape-changer-like ability to mirror the expectations of the observer. If one sought examples of companies and entire industries resisting change, one could easily find them, leading to conclusions that Japan was stagnant. Yet, looking at a different segment of the economy, one could just as easily find examples of dynamic change and the appearance of new firms, practices, and forms of competition. Widely differing interpretations of the Lost Decades were possible because Japan allowed change and stasis to coexist.

This chapter focuses on the new and hybrid areas that are gaining enough critical mass to make Japan more relevant to global competition than images of a nation mired in deflationary stagnation would suggest. We will first look at the emerging startup ecosystem, which is more easily observable as a center of dynamism, before examining some notable large-firm innovations.

Japan's New Startup Ecosystem

While still small when compared to Silicon Valley, a startup ecosystem has emerged in Japan since the mid-2000s that is clearly more vibrant and dynamic than many observers realize. This development was partly fueled by the appearance of new technologies like the smartphone and cloud computing, which drastically lowered the cost of creating new businesses. But the new ecosystem has also been aided by the removal of numerous social and economic impediments to entrepreneurship, a change that was a by-product of Japan's overall economic transformation. A nurturing environment for startups seems to have taken root, with new business creation gaining momentum. Success has bred success, as wave after wave of new startups build upon the progress of the previous ones, finding it easier to form partnerships with large firms, attract top university graduates, and tap the creative and financial energy of Silicon Valley across the Pacific Ocean.

Many of these new startups are science- and technology-based—that is, they seek to turn some invention or laboratory discovery into a new business. One reason for the prevalence of such firms is the relatively high levels of spending on research and development, or R&D, by the Japanese government and universities. When measured in actual dollars spent, Japan is now third in the world in government expenditures on R&D, behind only the United States and more recently China (Table 4.1). Similarly, Japan also ranks third in spending on higher education, including research universities (Table 4.2).[5]

One of the most dramatic changes at Japanese universities and public research institutes in recent years has been the creation of incubators and programs of study in entrepreneurship. As universities have sought to plug into the startup ecosystem, one result has been a flurry of new companies that spring from academia. An example is Spiber, which was founded by two university researchers in 2007 to manufacture synthetic spider silk. As any high school biology teacher knows, spider silk is light and flexible but can be stronger than steel when pulled in the right

Table 4.1   Government Expenditures on R&D (billions of U.S. dollars)

Year	2005		2010		2013	
Country	Amount	% GDP	Amount	% GDP	Amount	% GDP
Japan	128,695	3.31	140,607	3.25	162,347	3.47
United States	328,128	2.51	410,093	2.74	456,977	2.74
China	86,828	1.32	213,460	1.73	333,522	2.01
Germany	64,299	2.42	87,883	2.71	102,573	2.83
United Kingdom	34,081	1.63	38,166	1.69	41,743	1.66
France	39,236	2.04	50,765	2.18	57,987	2.24
South Korea	30,618	2.63	52,173	3.47	68,051	4.15

Source: OECD

Table 4.2   Government Expenditures on Higher Education (billions of U.S. dollars)

Year	2005	2010	2013
Japan	18,849	18,099	20,807
United States	51,725	60,374	61,227
China	9,449	18,053	22,874
Germany	12,218	15,996	17,157
United Kingdom	9,262	10,322	10,437
France	8,646	10,955	11,225
Korea	3,208	5,646	6,298

Source: OECD

direction. Spiber has found a way to produce this silk, without the spiders, by decoding the genes that spiders use to create fibroin, a protein that is the main component of their silk. The genetic code was actually cracked at a laboratory at Keio University in early 2007 by Kazuhide Sekiyama and Junichi Sugahara, who went on to launch the company later that year.

In 2012, the company entered into an alliance with Kojima Industries, a supplier of auto parts to Toyota, and together they set up a factory for large-scale production of spider-silk thread. One of its first major products was unveiled in 2015, when Spiber announced it was working with U.S. outdoor apparel giant The North Face to create a new parka using the fibroin proteins of spider silk, which make it tough, warm, and lightweight. According to Spiber, the parka's outer shell has the "natural color of the Golden Orb spider," giving it an "almost unearthly glow."[6]

Another such startup is Healios, a biotech firm that spun out of RIKEN, Japan's largest publicly funded research institute. Healios has commercialized one of the first actual treatments using so-called induced pluripotent stem cells, or iPS cells, which can grow into any kind of tissue. While these cells have been widely regarded as a promising new field in medicine, researchers have been slow to find actual ways to use them. An ophthalmologist at RIKEN, Masayo Takahashi, had successfully developed a method to slow age-related loss of vision by transplanting retinal tissue that had been grown from iPS cells. The breakthrough eventually earned Takahashi a spot on a *Nature* magazine list of 10 scientists whose work mattered to the world; however, the method that Takahashi pioneered at RIKEN cost an estimated $1 million per treatment, too expensive for widespread use.[7]

That drew the interest of Tadahisa Kagimoto, a medical doctor and serial entrepreneur. As a medical student, Kagimoto had visited Silicon Valley, where he was fascinated by the biotech startups. Staying at a friend's dormitory room at Stanford University, he set out to learn about startups, not only how they raised money but also how they selected the most promising technologies on which to place their bets. "I could understand Silicon Valley's startup ecosystem, so I wanted to do a biotech startup in Japan," Kagimoto told *Beacon Reports* in an October 2015 interview.[8]

In 2011, Kagimoto founded Healios to license the technology from RIKEN and Takahashi in order to develop a lower-cost way to create the iPS cells used in her therapy. Receiving support from the RIKEN Venture System, an effort by the lab to support spin-offs, Healios successfully obtained ¥3 billion (about $27 million) in funding from a group of Japanese firms involved in biopharmaceutical research that included Sumitomo Dainippon Pharma and Nikon. In June 2015, Healios listed on the Tokyo Stock Exchange Mothers market, which caters to high-growth and emerging companies. The company is now seen as a leader in a new generation of biotech startups in Japan.

Entrepreneur as Hero

As providers of stable, well-paying jobs, large firms have traditionally soaked up much of Japan's best talent. However, attitudes toward employment began to change as big companies ended the lifetime job guarantees that were once a centerpiece of Japan's postwar social contract. The old certitudes seemed to crumble during the Lost Decades, when former pillars of the financial system like the Long Term Credit Bank and Yamaichi Securities went bankrupt and industrial giants like Sanyo and Sharp were taken over by rival Japanese and even foreign firms. In an era when big companies can and do go bankrupt, lifetime employment guarantees have become a thing of the past.

This has led to dramatic changes in attitudes on elite university campuses, where students who once flocked to government or big corporate employers are now more willing to consider the greater risks and returns of the startup world. As in the United States, entrepreneurs have increasingly become celebrated figures on campus, where they are held up as models for emulation. Top Japanese universities now offer classes in entrepreneurship, and some, like the University of Tokyo and Waseda University, have created their own incubators on campus where students can try their hand at starting companies, with university support that can include funding. Many of Japan's most successful new entrepreneurs are products of these universities. A look at the Japanese startups receiving the most venture capital funds reveals that almost all the founders were graduates of elite higher education (see Table 4.5).

Employees at big corporations are also increasingly willing to strike out midcareer and start their own companies. One example is UPQ, a consumer electronics startup founded in 2015 that immediately made headlines in Japan by rolling out 24 sleekly designed products in its first two months, including a smartphone, a keyboard made of glass, and a backpack with a built-in battery for charging mobile devices. The entrepreneur, Yuko Nakazawa, was a twentysomething former cell-phone designer at Casio, who had her epiphany after her employer sold off its handset business to rival NEC. If a big company could just drop out of an entire line of business, then maybe she could do better by striking out on her own?

"I realized that I could make something interesting without a large company," she told the Web site *Tech in Asia* in 2015. "I didn't even know the word startup then, but I knew I wanted to build more products from scratch."[9]

Silicon Valley firms entering Japan have also become a training ground for future entrepreneurs. Wantedly, which operates a job recruiting service via social networking, was founded by Akiko Naka, a Kyoto University graduate who had worked at Goldman Sachs and then Facebook. Naka joined Facebook's Japan operation when it was still essentially a startup with only six people. The success of her business lies in her realization that when many younger Japanese select a job, they place at least as much emphasis on career fulfillment as they do on compensation. Wantedly, which she founded in 2010, makes a point of not allowing prospective employers to include salaries in job postings, asking them instead to appeal to job seekers' potential for feeling passionate about the job. The recruiting service has taken off, as not just startups but also major Japanese firms have increased midcareer hires, creating a highly dynamic job market in Japan's information technology sector. Wantedly was quickly adopted by more than 1,000 companies and 10 million users, making the company profitable early on.

More recently, some entrepreneurs have come from Japan's elite central government ministries and agencies, leaving highly prestigious, stable jobs to seek their fortune in the startup world. One is Yasuyuki Hamada, formerly a researcher at the Ministry of Agriculture, Forestry, and Fisheries, who left to found a startup called Agri Info Design in 2014. The company provides a smartphone application that uses global positioning satellites to help farmers drive tractors in straight lines while working their fields. This has been a boon for farmers in developing countries, allowing them to fit more rows of crops onto their plots without the high fees of automated tractor services. The company has won several startup pitch contests, including the New Economy Summit 2016.

Startup ecosystems require more than just a steady inflow of talent to thrive. Fledgling companies also require the ability to sell their products and services—and in some cases, even themselves—to bigger, more established firms. Japan's large companies were historically hesitant to do business with newcomers, an insularity that served as an impediment to startups. But as its own global position has eroded, corporate Japan has changed its attitude toward newcomers, showing a willingness to do business with them. Wantedly achieved profitability by attracting big companies to use its recruiting service. Another example is Preferred Networks, founded in 2014 by a University of Tokyo computer scientist, which found success by partnering with big firms like Toyota and robot producer FANUC to develop so-called deep-learning software that enables production-line robots to learn new movements and tasks by themselves, without operators having to reprogram them.

One measure of corporate Japan's greater openness to startups is an increase in the number of mergers and acquisitions, which rose from 1,707 in 2010 to 2,285 in 2014. A growing proportion of these acquisitions are purchases of startups by larger companies.[10] Even Silicon Valley firms are beginning to buy Japanese startups. In 2013, Google bought Japanese robotics company SCHAFT, which had been founded by University of Tokyo researchers to produce walking robots. SCHAFT won attention by entering a robotics competition held by the U.S. Department of Defense's Defense Advanced Research Projects Agency, or DARPA, and dominating the trial round. (Google pulled SCHAFT out of the final round of competition, in line with its philosophical opposition to receiving funding from the U.S. military.)[11] As one of the first purchases of a Japanese technology startup by a major Silicon Valley firm, the move seemed to blaze the way for more acquisitions of Japanese startups by big American companies.

Enter (Independent) Venture Capital

Another sign of Japan's burgeoning startup ecosystem has been the emergence of a thriving venture capital industry (Table 4.3). While its size remains far smaller than that of the United States, the amounts are

Table 4.3   Venture Capital Investment Amounts (billions of U.S. dollars)

Financial Year	2010	2015
Japan	1.29	1.11
EU	4.26	5.91
Germany	0.97	0.87
France	0.80	0.84
UK	0.79	0.62
Israel	0.41	0.65
South Korea	0.96	1.78
U.S. Total	23.52	59.70
Silicon Valley	9.39	27.76

Source: Venture Enterprise Center, GVCA, BVCA, AFIC, IVC Research Center, KVCA (UK's data is as of 2014)

actually greater than other advanced industrialized countries, such as France, Germany, and the United Kingdom.

The most important qualitative shift in Japan's venture capital industry has been the rise of independent venture capital funds. Historically, Japan's small companies have funded themselves with loans from big banks, a strategy that incentivized entrepreneurs to seek stable cash flows to repay those loans instead of pursuing high returns. Starting in the late 1990s, however, disruptions to Japan's financial industry prompted banks to pull back from small business lending, pushing entrepreneurs to seek other means of funding. Venture capital investors have increasingly stepped into the gap. By 2015, independent venture capital funds—that is, those not affiliated with a big financial company or government entity—accounted for 35 percent of investments in new businesses, replacing banks and other established financial institutions, which provided just 18 percent.[12] Some examples of homegrown independent venture capital funds that have won growing attention in Japan include World Innovation Lab, Globis Capital Partners, and B Dash Ventures.

An important driver of Japan's venture capital growth was the creation in 1999 of two stock exchanges for small companies and startups, Mothers and JASDAQ. Both provide a means for startups to raise money and for investors to take a stake by buying shares. Moreover, both are very accessible to small firms: the cost of listing on Japan's small-cap markets is far lower than on other Asian markets, and the companies that list in Japan tend to be much smaller than those that list on the U.S. NASDAQ (Table 4.4).[13]

Table 4.4   Amounts Raised in IPO, Small-Cap Markets in Japan, United States (millions of U.S. dollars)

	Average		Median	
	Japan (Mothers/JQ)	U.S. NASDAQ	Japan (Mothers/JQ)	U.S. NASDAQ
2015	7.6	116.0	3.5	75.0
2014	8.7	121.6	5.7	65.0

Source: Tokyo Stock Exchange, NASDAQ

The government has also taken a role in nurturing the startup ecosystem. The Innovation Network Corporation of Japan was established in 2009 with a 15-year lifespan, and ¥300 billion yen in funds to invest in startups. Most of this money comes from the government, though 26 corporations, including Toyota, Canon, and members of the Mitsubishi group, chipped in ¥14 billion. The government has guaranteed another ¥1.8 trillion in loans, giving the corporation more than ¥2 trillion to invest. While some analysts may view this as government crowding out private investors, the corporation has not only bankrolled startups but also tried to support private-sector venture capital funds.

Table 4.5 shows the Japanese startups that raised the most venture capital funding, based on publicly available news and data sources. It also shows their founders' backgrounds. While many of these firms may not exist five years from now, as would be expected in a healthy startup ecosystem, the list offers a useful window into where the professional venture capitalists have been placing their largest bets. One observation we can make is that the Japanese startups receiving the most venture capital investment are spread across a broad range of sectors. They range from synthetic silk producer Spiber to Quantum Biosystems, a commercial DNA sequencer, to Foodison, a distributor of fresh fish.

Maturing Startup Ecosystem

One sign of a maturing startup ecosystem has been the appearance of university-based venture capital funds, such as the University of Tokyo Edge Capital, or UTEC, and Miyako Capital affiliated with Kyoto University, which have sought to spin out technologies from these universities into high-growth companies. Established in 2004 with approximately $300 million, UTEC had 65 portfolio companies at the end of 2015, of which nine had launched initial public offerings and eight had been bought by larger companies.[14]

Table 4.5 Major Venture Capital Fundraising by Japanese Startups, 2015

Company	Amount Raised (billion yen)	Description	Founder	Education
Spiber	10.54	New-generation biomaterial development	Kazuhide Sekiyama	Keio University
Metaps	4.89	Marketing tools and consulting service in mobile business	Katsuaki Sato	Waseda University
Freee	4.49	Cloud-based accounting software	Daisuke Sasaki	Hitotshbashi University
Raksul	3.99	Commercial printing service	Yasukane Matsumoto	Keio University
Megakaryon	2.54	Producing platelet products from iPS cells	Genjiro Miwa	University of Tokyo, Harvard University
Quantum Biosystems	2.4	Commercial DNA sequencer	Toshihiko Honkura	University of Tokyo, Columbia University
Plus One Marketing	2.13	Mobility hardware products made by Japan	Kaoru Masuda	Waseda University
Preferred Networks	1.9	Industrial IoT applications with AI	Toru Nishikawa, Daisuke Okanohara	University of Tokyo, University of Tokyo
AXELSPACE	1.89	Commercial microsatellite imaging and data service	Yuya Nakamura	University of Tokyo
Treasure Data	1.77	Cloud data management platform	Hiro Yoshikawa	Waseda University
GLM	1.69	EV Development/providing EV platform	Hiroyasu Koma	Kyoto University
Origami	1.59	Mobile payment service	Yoshiki Yasui	Waseda University, University of Sydney

(continued)

Table 4.5 (*continued*)

Company	Amount Raised (billion yen)	Description	Founder	Education
iPS PORTAL	1.53	Instruments to analyze and measure iPS cells	Syosaku Murayama	Doshisya University
seven dreamers	1.52	R&D of carbon tool and medical equipment	Shin Sakane	University of Delaware
Money Design	1.5	Financial portfolio design with AI	Mamoru Taniya, Tomoyoshi Hirose	University of Tokyo, Yokohama National University
CYFUSE	1.41	3D tissue-engineering technology	Koji Kuchiishi	Keio University
from scratch	1.29	Next-generation marketing platform	Yasuhiro Abe	Nihon University
SmartNews	1.19	News discovery app	Ken Suzuki	Keio University, University of Tokyo
Ptmind	1.1	Data analysis and monitoring	Zheng Yuan, Takashi Ando	Nihon University, Rikkyo University
Money Forward	1.03	Online application for personal accounting	Yosuke Tsuji	Kyoto University, University of Pennsylvania
AnyPerk	1.02	Integrated perks and rewards platform	Taro Fukuyama	Keio University
FOODiSON	1.01	Fresh fish distribution platform	Tohru Yamamoto	Hokkaido University
JOMDD	1.01	Medical device incubator	Takahiro Uchida	Fukushima Medical University, Harvard University
Retty	1.0	Social gourmet site	Kazuya Takeda	Aoyama Gakuin Univeristy
LOCONDO	1.0	Shoes and fashion e-commerce service, buy first and then choose	Yusuke Tanaka	Hitotsubashi University, UC Berkeley

Source: Japan Venture Research Co.

Another sign has been the proliferation of startup pitch contests and major events celebrating startups. These events can draw audiences that number in the thousands, and they often receive national news coverage. Such events help legitimize and popularize Japan's burgeoning startup culture. One of the most visible is the annual New Economy Summit, which was begun in 2013 by the Japan Association of New Economy and Japan's largest listed online commerce company, Rakuten. The summit has invited prominent Silicon Valley entrepreneurs, including Oracle's Larry Ellison and also the founders of Dropbox, Lyft, and Box.com. Another is the Infinity Ventures Summit, launched in Kyoto in 2009, which is a hub for investors, entrepreneurs, and large firms to meet. In 2015, the Ministry of Economy, Trade, and Industry started hosting the NEDO Technology Commercialization Program, a pitch contest that allows aspiring entrepreneurs of technology-based startups from around Japan to make their case directly to venture capital investors.

Other members of the startup ecosystem, such as accounting and law firms, have also begun orchestrating startup-focused events and promotions. For example, Tohmatsu Venture Support, a subsidiary of accounting firm Deloitte Tohmatsu, has been supporting weekly "morning pitch" events at 7:00 a.m. in Tokyo since 2011 and has begun organizing similar events in other major cities as well. One aim of the events is to provide services to early-stage startups free of charge in order to foster a vibrant startup ecosystem from which the organizer can also benefit. Deloitte Tohmatsu has also set up a Silicon Valley branch to help Japanese startups expand there.

Japan's growing presence in Silicon Valley is testimony to the development of its domestic startup ecosystem. While there is no comprehensive database of Japanese startups in Silicon Valley, ties between the Japanese startup ecosystem and Silicon Valley are strengthening (Table 4.6).[15] Japanese entrepreneurs, financiers, and government officials have also become visible at the programs at top accelerators, such as Y Combinator and 500 Startups.

Bulldozers and Drones

Large companies face obvious challenges in making the breakthrough innovations of Silicon Valley. By their very nature, these established players are slower and more bureaucratic than startups. They also carry far higher costs and require larger revenues to justify moving into new lines of business. Unlike new firms, big companies face such constraints as the so-called innovator's dilemma, in which they favor maintaining ties to

Table 4.6   Silicon Valley Startup Ecosystem Characteristics Compared to Japan in mid-1990s, Japan in 2016

Silicon Valley Startup Ecosystem Characteristic	Japan in the Mid-1990s: Impediments	Japan in 2016: Changes that Facilitate Startup Ecosystem
Financial System: Venture Capital	Bank-centered financial intermediation; most funding via loans by banks and other financial institutions	Financial disintermediation with growth of VC industry, rise of independent VCs; financing via small-cap equity markets
Labor Market: Fluid, Diverse, Highly Skilled	Long-term employment with seniority ties creating illiquid labor markets; best and brightest locked into large firms for entire career	Increasing labor mobility, especially in IT sector and with foreign firms; lower prestige and opportunity with large firms
Industry-University-Government Ties	Numerous formal regulatory constraints	Active efforts by universities, private venture capital, and government to spin out successful startups with university technology
"Open" Innovation with Large Firms and Small Firm Symbiosis	Closed innovation with large firms in-house R&D and uninterested in business with startups	Firms more interested in open innovation, participation in VC funds, business with startups
Social System Encouraging Entrepreneurship	Entrepreneurship seen as low prestige vis-à-vis large firms and government	Rising attractiveness of entrepreneurship as large firms enter competitive crises, increases cases of successful startups
Professional Services Ecosystem	Small size of professional ecosystem	Law firms and accounting firms setting up startup-focused practice areas to foster and benefit from growing startup ecosystem

current customers and suppliers instead of jettisoning these to foray into something new and untried. Thus, they often fall behind when new, game-changing technologies appear.[16]

Japan's large firms can be particularly slow in adapting. One reason is that moves out of old technologies often require reductions in personnel. However, social prohibitions against layoffs limit Japanese companies to gradual means such as attrition, which can take years. Corporate Japan has preferred to spin off unprofitable business lines into new companies, which are often joint ventures with former competitors. NEC, Hitachi, and Mitsubishi Electric did this in 2010 by merging their semiconductor operations into an independent new firm, Renesas Electronics. But this approach doesn't work for every business line.

Facing such constraints, many large Japanese firms have chosen a different tack: working with smaller startups to create a hybrid model of innovation. Construction equipment giant Komatsu has used this strategy to move aggressively into Internet connectivity, artificial intelligence, and three-dimensional modeling to improve the performance of its bulldozers and dump trucks. Komatsu obtained many of these technologies from startups, using an open-innovation approach that is unusual for one of Japan's big manufacturers, whose long-held preference has been to develop in house.

While the recent push by Google, Apple, and Tesla into autonomously driven vehicles has left car makers scrambling to catch up, Tokyo-based Komatsu got ahead of Silicon Valley in 2008 by commercializing the first fully automated dump trucks. Komatsu, a global firm with almost 50,000 employees, was also a pioneer in linking its equipment to the Web long before most people ever heard of the Internet of Things. In the early 2000s, Komatsu developed a system called Komtrax that constantly gathers detailed information from all the Komatsu-made machinery operating around the world. These data are used to alert customers if parts require maintenance or replacement, remotely turn off machinery if lease payments are late, or even issue alerts if fuel levels start dropping in unused machinery, a warning sign of illegal siphoning.

Komatsu's goal is to more fully automate its construction machinery. Doing this requires not only artificial intelligence but new ways to increase the equipment's so-called situational awareness: the ability of automated machines to "see" what is around them so they can move efficiently while avoiding collisions. Komatsu has installed sensors and GPS devices that allow machines to map the terrain and determine their own position. But coordinating a busy construction site requires getting an overall picture of where the machines are in relation to each other. Komatsu has concluded that obtaining that level of situational awareness requires having eyes in the sky in the form of drones flying above construction sites.

Komatsu has recognized that working on its own to develop such technology would be prohibitively expensive and fall far outside the company's expertise. So instead, it has chosen to partner with Skycatch, a San Francisco–based startup that specializes in using drones in three-dimensional terrain modeling. Skycatch has technology that combines drones and high-speed data processing to create accurate three-dimensional maps of construction sites in real time. These can be transmitted to both the automated machinery and also to human clients to allow remote monitoring.

"We've understood the potential of automated drone technology early on, and Skycatch's product gives us incredible insights into what's happening with our equipment on the ground," Komatsu Rental's then-president, Akinori Onodera, said in announcing the tie-up in early 2015. "We now have the fastest, most comprehensive aerial data solution out there."[17]

The partnership with Skycatch is just one way that Komatsu is trying to tap the creative energy of Silicon Valley's startup culture. The company has begun investing in local venture capital funds and has sent employees to do research at the region's two top universities, Stanford University and the University of California, Berkeley. It has also begun to adapt its own culture to Silicon Valley's freer ways of doing things. To create a new system that would allow its automated machines to communicate with each other, Komatsu has adopted a so-called open-platform approach that will allow other companies to access data and also connect their non-Komatsu machinery to the network. Komatsu hopes this Silicon Valley–style open approach will allow its new system to win acceptance beyond just its own customer base as a new industry standard.

Robot Motorcycles

In 2015, as research and development into self-driving automobiles grabbed headlines, Yamaha Motors developed the Motobot, the first humanoid robot capable of driving a motorcycle (Figure 4.1). As with Komatsu, Yamaha, a half-century-old maker of motorcycles and outboard motors with 53,000 employees, was able to accomplish this by harnessing Silicon Valley.

The company decided that building such a robot would be a means of showcasing the technology behind its motorcycles, which face stiff competition from lower-cost competitors. At the same time, Yamaha's

Figure 4.1: Yamaha's Motobot. Image courtesy of Yamaha Motor Company.

management realized that developing the robot internally would be difficult and costly. Instead, it decided to draw from the vast technological expertise of Silicon Valley. To lead the effort, it tapped Hiroshi Saijo, a robotics engineer with two decades of experience at Yamaha in Japan.

In 2014, Saijo relocated to the Bay Area, where he started off by borrowing space in a Silicon Valley incubator called Plug and Play. However, Saijo quickly realized that operating under the control of slow-moving corporate headquarters back in Japan hindered his small field office from making inroads in fast-paced Silicon Valley. He decided that Yamaha needed an entity with more autonomy. The result, a year later, was the launch of the Yamaha Motor Ventures & Laboratory Silicon Valley. Saijo, who serves as the new unit's chief executive officer, convinced Yamaha's top management to give his unit the freedom to pursue business opportunities even if they disrupted Yamaha's existing businesses. Saijo was allowed to make snap investment decisions, such as when his unit took just 10 days to buy a stake in a mobile Wi-Fi grid startup based in Vietnam.

In late 2014, Saijo contacted SRI International, the Silicon Valley research institute that won accolades for developing the Siri voice-recognition software used by Apple. By coincidence, SRI's robotics department had just proposed a similar autonomous driving system to DARPA in aircraft to help human pilots. Using that technology, SRI helped Yamaha roll out the first Motobot prototype in just 10 months, far faster and at a much lower cost than the Japanese firm had initially expected. SRI provided the automation expertise, while Yamaha engineers created a light-weight robot that could fit on a motorcycle.

While Yamaha admits that there is no immediate commercial market for a humanoid robotic driver, it says the technology can be used in performance testing of new motorcycles. The successful development was also a major morale booster for a company that many worried was becoming a technological has-been.

"Before we proved the concept, several smart people were not sure whether this was possible," Saijo said during a demonstration of the Motobot in January 2016. "Now the conversation has changed to what the future might hold."[18]

Honda Comes to Silicon Valley

Honda has gone further than most big Japanese firms in its efforts to tap Silicon Valley and embrace an open innovation approach.

Honda began its push into Silicon Valley back in 2000, when it opened computer science research offices. Five years later, it was one of the first big Japanese manufacturers to establish its own corporate venture capital investment arm. But its biggest move to promote partnerships with startups came in 2011, when Honda decided to create an open innovation lab, the Honda Silicon Valley Lab, later renamed Honda R&D Innovations.

To head the lab and Honda's other Silicon Valley operations, the carmaker made an unusual pick: Naoki Sugimoto, who was not a life-long employee of Honda but actually started his career at a Japanese job-placement company called Recruit. He left to get an MBA in 1996 from the University of California, Berkeley, and then founded his own technology company that he sold to Recruit in 2001. After spending several years as a consultant and venture capital investor, he joined Honda in 2005.

By bringing an outsider's perspective on Honda's operations, and an insider's knowledge of Silicon Valley, Sugimoto was able to give the lab an unusually open orientation. To attract startups, Sugimoto said he had to push through several changes at Honda, including battling with the company's legal department to rewrite the Japanese automaker's standard nondisclosure agreement to allow a less restrained flow of information. He also convinced Honda to drop some onerous conditions that it had imposed on partner companies, such as carrying several million dollars' worth of insurance.[19]

Under Sugimoto's leadership, the Honda Silicon Valley Lab has become the launchpad for some unique initiatives. One is the Honda Xcelerator, begun in 2015. It seeks to attract startups by offering funding for prototyping and also access to test vehicles, workspace, and mentors from within Honda itself. In effect, Honda is offering startups the resources to develop, test, and refine their products and services in a joint development–type arrangement. Significantly, however, Honda does not try to monopolize the new technologies. Startups are free to sell products and services developed in the Honda Xcelerator to other companies, including rival automakers. Honda is betting that codevelopment will still give it a leg up by allowing Honda to be the first to see the new technologies and incorporate them into new products. More importantly, Honda has concluded that this open approach will prove more attractive to the startups themselves, allowing Honda to lure those with the best ideas and potentially transformative technologies.

Another of the lab's major initiatives has been the Honda Developer Studio, established in 2014. The studio—an actual workspace in Mountain View, California—offers the same open approach as Honda Xcelerator but aimed at software developers. The studio provides space and support to developers making apps for Google's Android Auto platform, used in the "infotainment" systems of Honda's automobiles. The aim is to speed up production of apps by putting developers in direct contact with Honda engineers and research and development teams. Developers get advice on the Android Auto system as well as issues like driver safety and privacy, and are allowed to test and refine their products in an actual Honda test vehicle. Numerous developers are partnering with Honda, including Silicon Valley startup Drivemode, which provides a driver-friendly interface and functionality for Android phones.

Bridging Startups and Corporate Giants

Out of Japan's long stagnation, a new corporate ecosystem has appeared, one that differs from Silicon Valley's by incorporating big firms as partners and innovators, and not simply targets for disruption. In fact, there is a growing recognition that many large Japanese companies may actually be sitting on a gold mine of untapped technologies and product ideas, as well as having talented employees who might feel stymied within rigid corporate structures. In recent years, new companies and investment funds have appeared to help unleash this enormous potential, of which the big firms themselves are often oblivious.

One is World Innovation Lab, or WiL, a $400 million venture capital fund with offices in Tokyo and Palo Alto, California. The founder, Gen Isayama, is a former banker who left corporate Japan to learn the ways of Silicon Valley. His fund, whose main investors are big Japanese firms and the government-linked Innovation Network Corporation of Japan, looks for would-be entrepreneurs within large Japanese firms, whom it helps to start their own Silicon Valley–style startups. It does this with the full knowledge of the original employer, who is invited to join with WiL in order to share in the benefits from successful startups. For those that fail, the employees are allowed to return to their jobs, reducing some of the risks of entrepreneurship.

"Everyone says Japan's big companies are all terrible, terrible, terrible, but if you take a different view, they are treasure houses filled with gems," Isayama said. "By figuring out how to utilize the underutilized talent and wealth, we should be able to bring out innovations that are globally competitive."

"The current trouble with Japanese large companies is that they are not fully taking advantage of it," Isayama added. "My hypothesis is that if outsiders like us can activate this potential, then Japan can regain its venture spirit."[20]

Unleashing this venture spirit could allow Japan to find better ways to tackle its still-formidable problems, like its shrinking workforce and rapidly aging population. For instance, Japanese startups could pioneer new ways to use artificial intelligence and automation to compensate for the declining number of working-age Japanese. In fact, Japan may be a natural testbed for these technologies, as a society that has refused to embrace mass immigration but has been remarkably accepting of robots and humanlike machines. Similarly, in an era when high-quality data are critical to developing products and services, Japan offers a wealth of information as an advanced society whose population increasingly visits hospitals and elderly care facilities or uses new innovations such as care robots. The data collected from large numbers of people—their health, spending habits, and biometrics—could spur new ideas and innovations in everything from new medical devices and financial products to artificial intelligence and the Internet of Things.

Tapping this potential requires the government to play a role by setting policies that encourage the use of data while also maintaining privacy protections. At the same time, the government must be willing to allow Japan's entrepreneurial ecosystem to move beyond the nation's tired old paternalistic, government-guided model. Government-led approaches, such as direct subsidies or industry promotion, seem less likely to work in the current era of rapid change. This is evident in the pharmaceutical industry, which has become a major success story in Japan largely due to deregulation.

In 2014, a revision of the Pharmaceutical Law shrank the time needed to bring new products to market during clinical testing from a decade down to just two years—the shortest among advanced industrialized countries. Such deregulation has fostered the creation of new startups by Japanese entrepreneurs as well as attracted top biopharmaceutical companies from around the world to conduct trials in Japan. These include Japanese biotech startup SanBio, which was founded in Silicon Valley but relocated to Japan when the regulatory changes made it easier to bring new drugs to market in Japan than in the United States.

It is significant that Japan was able to transform an area long criticized for overregulation—clinical trials and pharmaceuticals—into one of its most dynamic sectors. Similar deregulation could energize the market for individual data or other industries as well.

The bottom line is that Japan is once again a country that can make such leaps, largely due to the hybrid forms of innovation that link big firms with the burgeoning startup ecosystem. This chapter has shown that there are areas in which the nation is once again a leader. Its successes have built upon both the underutilized strengths of its large firms and the underappreciated potential of its new startup ecosystem. While this new Japan is still very much a work in progress, it has ample ability to play an even larger role in the global economy.

Notes

1. Stephen K. Vogel, *Japan Remodeled: How Government and Industry Are Reforming Japanese Capitalism* (Ithaca, NY: Cornell University Press, 2006).

2. Kenji E. Kushida, "Inside the Castle Gates: How Foreign Firms Navigate Japan's Policymaking Processes," PhD diss., University of California, Berkeley, CA, 2010.

3. Vogel, 2006.

4. Kenji E. Kushida, Kay Shimizu, and Jean C. Oi, eds., *Syncretism: Corporate Restructuring and Political Reform in Japan* (Stanford, CA: Walter H. Shorenstein Asia-Pacific Research Center, 2014).

5. "Research and Development Expenditure (% of GDP)," The World Bank, accessed July 10, 2017, http://data.worldbank.org/indicator/GB.XPD.RSDV.GD.Z S?contextual=max&locations=JP.

6. "Protein Materials: A Revolution in Manufacturing," Spiber, accessed July 10, 2017, https://www.spiber.jp/en/endeavor.

7. "Ten People Who Mattered This Year," *Nature*, December 17, 2014.

8. Richard Solomon, "Japan's Biotech Entrepreneur Offers Hope to Those Suffering from Incurable Illness," *Beacon Reports*, October 26, 2015.

9. J. T. Quigley, "She Created Japan's Xiaomi, Launching 21 Gadgets in 2 Months," *Tech in Asia*, August 13, 2015.

10. Soichi Kariyazono, "Japan as a Startup Nation," paper presented at the U.S.-Japan Venture Capital Conference, Stanford University, Stanford, CA, October 30–31, 2015.

11. Erico Guizzo and Evan Ackerman, "Who Is Schaft, the Robot Company Bought by Google and Winner of the DRC?" *IEEE Spectrum*, February 6, 2014.

12. Kenji E. Kushida, "Innovation and Entrepreneurship in Japan: Why Japan (Still) Matters for Global Competition," working paper for the Silicon Valley New Japan project, Stanford University, Stanford, CA, March 15, 2017.

13. James Riney, "7 Things Investors & Founders Need to Know about the Japan Startup Ecosystem," *500 Startups*, May 19, 2016.

14. "About UTEC," University of Tokyo Edge Capital–UTEC, accessed July 10, 2017, https://www.ut-ec.co.jp/english/about_utec/firm_profile.

15. See the Stanford Silicon Valley–New Japan Project, which is compiling a database of Japanese startups in Silicon Valley, accessed November 20, 2017, http://www.stanford-svnj.org.

16. Clayton M. Christensen, *The Innovator's Dilemma* (New York: Harper Business, 2000).

17. "Skycatch Partners with Komatsu to Automate Construction Job Sites World Wide," Skycatch, posted January 20, 2015, http://blog.skycatch.com /2015/01/20/skycatch-partners-with-one-of-the-largest-and-most-innovative -heavy-machinery-makers-komatsu-to-automate-constructor-job-sites-world -wide/.

18. Jordan Crucchiola, "Yamaha's Motobot Will Make Human Motorcyclists Look Pathetic," *Wired*, January 15, 2016.

19. Silicon Valley–New Japan Summit 2016, Stanford University, Stanford, CA, October 4, 2016.

20. Gen Isayama, speaking at Asia Pacific Initiative, February 18, 2016.

CHAPTER FIVE

A Nation of Centenarians: Japan's Revolution in Health and Wellness

Yoshiki Ishikawa

We are entering an era when living 100 years could become common-place. Japan is at the forefront of this revolution in longevity.

Half of all children born in Japan in 2007 will live for at least a century, according to estimates by demographers at the University of California, Berkeley, and Germany's Max Planck Institute for Demographic Research.[1] That would be significantly more than Japan's current average life expectancy, which is already the world's highest. According to the most recent statistics from the World Health Organization, a person born in Japan today can expect to live an average of 83.7 years, long enough to rank Japan first out of 183 nations.[2]

This represents an extraordinary advance compared with the end of World War II, when a Japanese woman could expect to live about 54 years. For a man, the average was just 50 years. Since then, Japan has made steady progress in stretching its citizens' life spans, becoming the world's longest-lived nation for the first time in 1986. It continues to make gains every year, which probably explains the Berkeley–Max Planck forecast of more life spans reaching a century in length.

Various explanations are given for Japan's longevity. Some factors are universal, like improvements in nutrition, immunization against deadly diseases, and medical breakthroughs including antibiotics. Others are more specific to Japan. These include educational campaigns to reduce salt intake and lower Japan's high rate of stomach cancer. Credit is also given to the Japanese diet itself, which traditionally has been low in fat and cholesterol (though fast food has been making recent inroads).

From the standpoint of what Japan has to offer the world, it is important to point out that Japan started making its remarkable gains in longevity in the decade or so after 1945, when it was still a poor nation struggling to rebuild from defeat in war. Some of Japan's most life-extending medical advances, such as containing the deadly contagions cholera and typhus, were accomplished during this period. One of Japan's biggest postwar accomplishments was providing universal care, which it did by creating a national medical insurance program.[3] Japan reached the milestone of full coverage of its population in 1961, years ahead of the United Kingdom's similar national health system, despite having a gross domestic product, or GDP, that was just half the size of the UK's at the time.[4]

More recently, Japan has grappled with the same challenge of skyrocketing health care costs faced by other nations. In fact, the problem may be even more acute in Japan due to its rapidly aging demographics. The cost of medical care as a percentage of GDP has soared in the last decade. In 2005, health-related costs consumed 8.1 percent of GDP, on par with the average for members of the Organisation for Economic Co-operation and Development (OECD) group of advanced industrial democracies. By 2013, however, those costs had jumped to 10.2 percent of GDP, surpassing the OECD average of 8.9 percent.[5] During those same years, the number of retirees age 65 and older rose from about one in every five Japanese to one in four.

As Japan grays, the costs of providing health care have far outstripped the payments into the national insurance program by those still of working age, whose numbers have been shrinking. In 2014, the national treasury made up for the shortfall by shouldering a full 20 percent of the annual bill for health costs.[6] And there is no relief in sight. Current projections show Japan's working-age population continuing to dwindle due to low birth rates. Meanwhile, the number of elderly will only increase as more people not only reach retirement age but also live longer after doing so. These older residents are the heaviest users of health care, placing an ever-larger financial burden on national medical insurance. The system that has given Japan such long lives is becoming increasingly unaffordable.

Japan has thus become a frontrunner in facing one of the most dire health policy challenges of our era: providing quality care for a growing population of seniors. Japan has eschewed the obvious policy response of opening its doors to permanent immigration. This refusal has turned Japan into a stark test case of a nation seeking solutions without increasing the size of its working population. (The nation has made a few lukewarm efforts to raise its domestic birth rate, but with negligible effect.) Japan is also fiscally constrained by one of the world's largest national debts. This means it must find ways to meet the needs of a growing elderly population without big increases in spending.

Poised to become the world's first nation of centenarians, Japan must also lead the world in finding affordable—and creative—ways to care for its elderly and to allow them to enjoy their ever-longer lives.

A U.S. General Launches a Health Revolution

Japan's transformation into a long-lived society began after the war, with the introduction of better sanitation, childhood nutrition, and access to health care. These factors may not be as flashy as the latest medical advances, but they are among the most important steps in increasing life expectancy. In the United States, for instance, the average life span grew by 30 years over the course of the 20th century, reaching 76.8 years in 2000. According to the U.S. Center for Disease Control and Prevention, 25 of those additional years were the result of improved access to public health and sanitation.[7]

The same can be said of Japan, where dramatic postwar gains in life expectancy were largely due to the tireless efforts of a single person, Brigadier General Crawford F. Sams. A medical officer in the U.S. Army, Sams was assigned in 1945 to head the Public Health and Welfare Section of the Allied Occupation of Japan. There, he became a confidante of the U.S. supreme commander, General Douglas MacArthur, who gave Sams wide authority to improve the health of occupied Japan's citizens. In tackling this task, Sams's goals were not simply humanitarian. He believed that controlling the contagious diseases then rampant in Japan was the best way to demonstrate the worth of its individuals and thus advance the Allied occupation's political agenda of promoting democratic values.

These motivations led Sams to launch what he called a health revolution. To combat malnutrition among children, he introduced school lunches, supplemented with bread and powdered milk imported from the United States. He brought deadly illnesses under control with programs such as mass spraying of the pesticide DDT to kill lice and other disease-carrying insects. (The program was stopped after DDT's adverse health effects were discovered.) Sams even had a hand in drafting Japan's new postwar constitution, adding a guarantee that the state will promote public health.[8]

However, Sams's biggest accomplishment may have been creating a national network of 800 public health centers staffed by professional nurses. At the time, Japan had a population of about 80 million people. That meant one of Sams's clinics served an average of 100,000 people. Sams began to build this system on March 15, 1948, when he opened a model public health center in Suginami Ward, a residential district in western Tokyo.

"Today, from this corner of Suginami, we must establish in Japan a system of public health that within two years will be unsurpassed anywhere in the world," Sams told clinic staff. "This is akin to transforming the scene of wreckage into a green garden—it is nothing less than a revolution in Japan's health and hygiene."[9]

Takeko Suzuki became the first nurse at the Suginami Health Care Center. She decided to leave her job at an established hospital after a female physician told her that the clinic represented a major innovation because it offered citizens preventative health care. "From now on, what matters is the period *before* someone falls ill," Suzuki recalled the doctor telling her. "People's daily habits are the foundation of good health, and you can advise them on how to improve those. This is called 'public health,' and it's a new chance that is available to you now."[10]

The nationwide system of public health care centers became the basis for Japan's current health care system. Not only did they provide low-cost care but the nurses also educated the public in hygiene and disease prevention. Sams worked in Japan for just six years, until the Korean War in 1951. Yet during that time, the average Japanese life expectancy jumped by 10 years. By contrast, it took the United States twice as long to achieve the same gains.[11]

Looking over the postwar period, Japan's advances in longevity can be divided into three stages.

The first stage extended from 1945 to the mid-1960s, when Japan rebuilt from the devastation of war. During this phase, efforts to lengthen life spans were focused on reducing infant mortality and deaths from contagious diseases. Japan made huge strides in lowering these rates, thanks largely to Sams's public health initiatives and the subsequent introduction of national health insurance.

During the following period of rapid economic growth, which lasted until the end of the 1980s, Japan's health needs shifted along with its rising living standards. Health policy focused on lowering the number of deaths from heart disease and stroke, which are leading causes of mortality in advanced nations. Japan's increases in longevity outstripped those of other developed countries, allowing Japan to become the world's longest-lived nation.

In the current era of the Lost Decades, which began in the 1990s, these gains were threatened by social changes like the explosive growth of fast foods and a more sedentary lifestyle brought on by the advent of computers. Japan's aging demographics also began to have a significant impact on the finances of the national health insurance system, pushing it into what has been a slowly developing crisis.

Despite these challenges, Japanese life expectancy has continued to increase. One explanation has come from Ichiro Kawachi of the Harvard T.H. Chan School of Public Health. Kawachi believes that social factors not normally associated with health, like cohesive communities and smaller gaps between rich and poor, may actually lead to healthier, longer lives. He argues that something as simple as greater trust among neighbors, or contentment in the workplace, can reduce stress and encourage healthier habits.

Kawachi believes that Japan's success in preserving social ties and avoiding glaring inequalities in income has helped maintain health and extend life expectancy.

"What are the real factors affecting longevity? Since 1996, Harvard's social epidemiologists have conducted large-scale surveys in such countries as the US and Japan," Kawachi was quoted as saying in a recent article. "Our findings suggest that the strong 'social capital' within Japanese culture is strongly correlated with the longevity and health of the Japanese."[12]

The Benefits of Japanese Food

Growing attention has also gone to the health benefits of the traditional Japanese diet. In 2013, Japanese cuisine, or *washoku*, was registered with UNESCO as part of Japan's intangible cultural heritage. But the health benefits of Japan's diet have been studied for decades.

University of Minnesota physiologist Ancel Keys was the first to hypothesize the benefits of Japan's traditional cuisine. Keys is best known for linking consumption of saturated fat with heart disease, a discovery he made in 1947 when studying a sudden increase in heart disease–related deaths in the postwar United States. Keys concluded that the culprit was increased cholesterol from rising consumption of fatty foods like meat, eggs, and cheese. His analysis went against the received wisdom of the time, that the American diet had achieved an ideal nutritional balance. Keys was harshly criticized when he presented his theory in 1955 at an international conference organized by the World Health Organization.

Undaunted, Keys set out to test his ideas with a vast and complex research project, known as the Seven Countries Study. This study established his reputation while also provoking debates over health that continue to this day. The study was unprecedented in its scope, tracking eating habits in seven countries—the United States, Finland, the Netherlands, Italy, the former Yugoslavia, Greece, and Japan—over the course of two decades. All told, Keys studied the diets of 12,763 participants, who were between the ages of 40 and 59 when the study was launched.

The study employed something called the extra tray method. Hisashi Adachi, a medical professor at Japan's Kurume University who helped Keys conduct the study in Japan, describes it as follows: "We would have each household make an additional portion, or tray, of the meals that its members were eating on a particular day. We would compensate them for this tray and then analyze its contents. The tray's contents would be placed into a large mixer, and then the nutritional content would be subjected to raw biochemical analysis—we would measure the amounts of protein, fat, and so on."[13]

When the data from the seven different countries were compared, a startling pattern emerged. Subjects from Finland, which was known for its high rate of heart disease, were also found to have the highest intake of cholesterol. By contrast, the Japanese subjects had far lower intakes of cholesterol—and lower rates of heart disease. The same trends were apparent in other countries, allowing Keys to establish a connection between diet and heart ailments.

Keys used the study to promote what he called the Mediterranean Diet, low in animal fats and high in olive oil and fish, as a defense against heart disease. However, his findings also stoked research into the health benefits of the Japanese diet, which is similarly rich in seafood (think sushi) as well as other low-fat, low-cholesterol ingredients, such as tofu, gelatinous *konnyaku*, and wheat bran. The Japanese diet has been subsequently linked to Japan's low rates of not only heart disease but also rectal and breast cancer.[14]

Most Generous in the World

Japan took a big step toward becoming a centenarian nation more than 50 years ago, when its national health insurance system reached its goal of universal coverage in 1961.

The origins of the system actually go back to 1922 and the era of so-called Taisho democracy, when lawmakers created a national health insurance program for newly industrializing Japan's factory workers. This insurance was voluntary at first, though the government eventually made it compulsory in some industries. The next step came in 1938, when insurance coverage was extended to farmers in an effort to ease rural poverty.

After the war, national health insurance became a high political priority as a defeated Japan sought to rebuild itself into a more prosperous, egalitarian society. A mandatory national health insurance system was created in 1958, achieving universal participation within just three years. According to Yasuki Kobayashi of the University of Tokyo, Japan was able to do this while still relatively poor because of a convergence of favorable factors: a young population, an economy that was starting to take off, and citizens who shared "a sense of solidarity during this difficult post-war period."[15] During Japan's decades of high economic growth, this medical insurance system facilitated the redistribution of wealth and helped create a society of "100 million middle class"—in other words, only modest economic disparities.

With universal health coverage in place, Japan next turned its attention to providing better care for its elderly. In 1963, the Diet, Japan's Parliament, passed the Act on Social Welfare for the Elderly, which created nursing homes and other publicly funded services for older citizens. Ten years later, Japan made health care free of charge for those aged 70 and older. However, it was in the 1970s that the size of Japan's elderly population first started to creep upward, placing a growing burden on both household and national finances. The challenges of caring for the elderly first erupted into public consciousness in 1972, with the publication of novelist Sawako Ariyoshi's *Kokotsu no Hito*, translated into English as *The Twilight Years*, about the challenges of looking after older relatives with dementia. The book, which helped raise national awareness about caring for bedridden elderly, became an instant best seller.

The health system scrambled to keep up with the growing numbers of elderly. New nursing homes were built, with the number of beds increasing from 1,912 in 1965 to 119,858 just 20 years later. However, this was far from enough. In 1992, there were an estimated 1.3 million bedridden people in Japan, mostly elderly, of whom 800,000 were cared for at home. Many others used hospitals as surrogate nursing homes, a phenomenon that came to be called "social hospitalization." Because national insurance coverage had been expanded to cover all medical costs for the elderly, the system had to pay for these extended hospital stays.[16]

As the cost of caring for all these elderly spiraled upward, the government increasingly had to foot the bill, putting pressure on public finances. Yet, rolling back coverage for the elderly faced political resistance. In 1983, the Health Ministry came under intense criticism when it made a public warning about the threat of rising medical costs to national finances.[17] Fiscal concerns finally drove Japan to make a limited retreat from its guarantee of free care to the elderly. Elderly were once again forced to make copayments, though the levels remained quite modest by international standards: in 1994, a patient was expected to contribute just ¥21,000, or about $200, for a month's hospitalization. The bulk of costs were still borne by the government.[18]

Japan's economic slowdown forced more changes. In 2000, the government tried to alleviate the strains on the health insurance system by creating a separate national insurance program that would take over the costs of long-term care of the elderly. The new system, which all workers are required to join at age 40, subsidizes services such as adult day care and home help.[19]

In 2011, *The Lancet*, a British medical journal, proclaimed Japan's long-term care system to be "one of the most generous in the world." It said Japan had fewer restrictions on eligibility and services than Germany's similar system and a higher rate of use by its elderly population.[20] This means that Japan has been able to maintain its goal of providing affordable health care to all parts of its population. But this success is coming at a cost, as medical expenses have spiraled out of control. In 1970, total expenditure on health care in Japan totaled about ¥2.5 trillion, according to the Health Ministry. In 2014, that sum had soared to more than ¥40 trillion.[21]

Indeed, the growing financial burden of caring for Japan's aging population has become a source of increasingly acute national concern as Japan's economy faces uncertain growth prospects. According to Kobayashi of the University of Tokyo, this has contributed to an erosion in Japan's postwar support for guarantees of affordable, universal health care. "People are becoming diversified, income disparities are increasing, and their sense of solidarity may be deteriorating," Kobayashi warned.[22]

Tapping Big Data

As Japan struggles to pay for its growing legions of the aged, it has begun increasingly to experiment. New ideas are being put forth on how to do more with less, or create new revenue streams that can supplement overstrained budgets. Some of these efforts may provide models, or at least inspirations, to other nations facing a similar funding crisis.

One promising avenue is big data. With a population of 127 million, and records of every citizen's use of national health insurance extending back more than five decades, Japan has built up one of the world's largest databases of medical-related information in the world. It is also a very high-quality database: Japan's records are detailed and highly standardized, with 99 percent having already been computerized. There is also a trove of information about healthy individuals, as most of the population receives free annual medical checkups.

Efforts are now under way to compile and make better use of all these data. The biggest initiative began in 2010, when several doctors' associations, including the 23,000-strong Japan Surgical Society, joined forces to create the National Clinical Database. As of early 2017, more than 4,000 hospitals and clinics have enrolled in the database, gathering information on more than 7 million surgical procedures—95 percent of the total number conducted in Japan over the last five years.[23]

This database is available online to researchers and is used to look for waste and redundancy in health care services in order to cut costs and improve distribution of resources. It is also used to identify the most effective treatments for various ailments, both in terms of costs and improvements to health. To help researchers, the database includes subgroupings, called registries, of data on specific types of cancer, such as pancreatic, breast, and liver, to compare the results of treatment methods. Similarly, registries have also been created to assess various procedures in cardiovascular, thoracic, and other types of surgery.[24]

The government has also stepped in to help advance medical research in order to improve care for the aging population and make Japan's health industry more competitive globally. As part of its Japan Revitalization Strategy, the administration of Prime Minister Shinzo Abe has tried to leverage Japan's position as one of the world's most rapidly aging societies into a chance to create a world-leading health care industry. One of the administration's stated goals has been to help Japan "increase its productivity in the healthcare sector and reduce its current ¥2.5 trillion ($21 billion) trade deficit for medical products." It intends to do this by steps "such as doubling the country's medical device exports" by 2020.[25]

To accomplish this, in 2015 the government created the Japan Agency for Medical Research and Development, whose mission is to push more research to market in the form of actual products and services. Often compared to the U.S. National Institutes of Health, the new agency describes itself as a "control tower" for linking scientists and private companies and streamlining the approval process for drugs and medical devices. The agency also took over the government's $1.2 billion medical research budget, which had been divided between three separate ministries. According to the new agency's president, Makoto Suematsu, its mission is to end this "Balkanization" of funding in order to fast-track research projects that promise to yield new medicines and procedures.[26]

Suematsu identified the quality of its databases as a strong point that Japan can use to become a leader in medical innovation. He said his agency is providing financial and technical support to the National Clinical Database, which he called "the ultimate means of data coordination" between doctors, the government, and the private sector. By making the results of treatment available to researchers, he said the database can not only help create new products but also reduce the often onerous costs involved in commercializing them.

"After a new medical device reaches the market, a number of similar medical associations can share studies, thereby reducing the cost of trials," Suematsu said. "So far, Japan is the only country in the world to have developed ways to use this kind of comprehensive surgical database to lower costs and optimize quality of care."[27]

New Wave in Home Care

Another innovation that has sprung from Japan's efforts to care for its growing number of elderly has been an increasing emphasis on home care.

In home care, doctors and nurses no longer wait for the sick to come to the hospitals and clinics but instead proactively go out to visit patients at their homes. Of course, this model is not suited for every type of condition. However, when it does work, treating patients at home can drastically reduce costs, such as by eliminating extended hospital stays. It also has the benefit of allowing patients to take a more active role in managing their own care, either alone or with the assistance of family members. This altering of the traditional relationship between health care providers and patients can yield substantial psychological benefits, as patients feel more relaxed in the familiar surroundings of home rather than in an impersonal hospital room. Reducing anxiety can help the patient recover more quickly, or for those at the end of life, to pass away in the more comforting environment of their own bedroom, surrounded by family.

Doctors say these new approaches to home care differ from traditional house calls. One pioneer of this new wave is Kazuhiro Nagao, founder and director of the Nagao Clinic in Amagasaki, a city near Kobe.

Not long after starting his clinic in 1995, Nagao said one of his first patients, a local merchant suffering from liver cancer, grew so weak that he was no longer able to visit the clinic. Nagao started dropping by the man's home on the way to work to check on him and administer an intravenous drip when needed. While the patient finally succumbed to his disease, Nagao was moved by the fact that he was able to die at home, without a single tube attached to his body. Nagao recalls this as his first experience of at-home nursing and facilitating the peaceful death of a patient at home. Since then, Nagao has provided similar care for more than 800 patients, mostly elderly who desired to spend their final days at home.

As part of his home care, Nagao has tried to give the patient and family as big a voice as possible in preparing for end of life. He does this by means of what he calls "advance care directing," in which he holds repeated discussions with both the patient and the patient's family. The aim, he said, is for them to reach an agreement on how to care for the patient as aging progresses, including the desired stopping point for treatment.

Some of the most expensive treatments involve efforts to keep an elderly patient alive long past the point when the patient might feel a desire to live or even remain conscious and coherent. Nagao said such life-prolonging treatments can bring pain and discomfort to patients facing the inevitable end. Given a choice, he said, many patients preemptively decide to decline such intensive medical treatment in the final phases of life. These patients choose instead to naturally "fade away" without undue medical interference beyond steps to reduce pain and discomfort, Nagao said.[28]

End of life is just one type of care that Nagao offers to home patients. He said that his visits are now part of a package of services that are offered to patients who elect to receive care at home. He said his clinic works with private companies, known as "care managers," that offer a menu of care plans to patients. These can also include regular visits by nurses, who monitor their health, and other caregivers to help with daily tasks such as feeding or bathing.

One way in which these new home care models are reducing costs is by using mobile phones and wireless devices to allow caregivers to maximize the number of patients whom they can visit on a given day. This marriage of new technology and care methods can be seen at You Home Clinic, one of the more innovative care managers.

You Home Clinic was the brainchild of Shinsuke Muto, a cardiologist trained at Japan's elite University of Tokyo who once served as a court physician to the emperor and empress of Japan. In 2010, Muto established the You Home Clinic to provide affordable home care services in Tokyo.

The key to Muto's business model is the rapid sharing of information about patients among doctors and nurses via cell phones. Caregivers give instant updates after completing a home visit, allowing them and the company to make snap decisions about what kind of additional care a patient might need. This method permits fast, personalized care by allowing the company to recognize a patient's changing needs and quickly respond by sending, say, a physical therapist or a specialist like a cardiologist.[29]

You Home Clinic focuses its services on the very old and very sick, including the terminally ill, those suffering from dementia, and those too feeble to leave their homes. At the end of 2015, a staff of approximately 100 caregivers, based at three clinics spread across Tokyo, were responsible for the care of 800 patients in their homes. Muto says home care can be superior to hospitalization because it not only reduces costs but also allows families and even communities to join in giving succor to patients in their final stages of life.

"Death has always been an extremely personal matter, because it is the conclusion of an individual's life," Muto said. "The people who will be left behind must 'produce' this experience for the individual. This isn't something that can be accomplished by physicians alone. I want to create the social infrastructure that can help achieve this type of palliative nursing care."[30]

Home care's utility is not limited to the end of life. After the devastating 2011 earthquake and tsunami in northeastern Japan, Muto found a new opportunity to use his home care methods to help survivors, many of whom were displaced and isolated. Two months after the disaster, he visited the heavily damaged port city of Ishinomaki, where he found thousands of elderly residents in evacuation shelters. He said many were suffering from a visible deterioration in physical and mental health. Worse, many of the city's doctors' offices had been damaged or destroyed, forcing medical professionals to evacuate or relocate to more distant locations. As a result, many of the elderly had lost contact with their primary physicians and had difficulty getting access to care or even filling prescriptions.

Muto realized that his home care strategies could be used to dispatch doctors, nurses, and other caregivers to shelters to help these elderly evacuees. In September 2011, six months after the disaster, Muto established the You Home Clinic Ishinomaki. However, he did not have enough medical professionals to examine everyone on short notice. He innovated by setting up a group called the Health and Life Revival Council of Ishinomaki, which enlisted 20,000 local volunteers to visit elderly evacuees and screen them to find those in the most need of immediate help. Based on their reports, some 3,000 were identified as requiring medical care, which was provided by professionals.

Muto's efforts are seen in Japan as a possible model for responding to a different though not entirely dissimilar crisis: the depopulation of rural areas. As Japan ages and its birth rate declines, its countryside has experienced a hollowing out, leaving many rural communities with dwindling numbers of graying residents. Care for these populations has become a challenge, especially as the number of doctors and caregivers in rural areas has also declined. Home care services like You Home Clinic may provide an answer for allowing a limited number of medical professionals to tend for patients dispersed over a broad area.

Muto's home care model has also begun to get attention overseas. In 2015, he launched a service in Singapore called Tetsuyu Homecare, to which Ee Sian Neo, a Japan-trained Malaysian engineer, later joined as chief innovation officer. Neo says there is growing interest in Japanese health care methods in Singapore, which faces similar demographic challenges.

"Singapore is a rapidly aging society," Neo said. "Even the newest hospitals don't have enough beds to keep up with the need. While many average Singapore households employ a maid, wage increases and cultural differences will make this harder to do in the future. There is a growing awareness of the urgent need for home health care as a support system for community-based care."[31]

Health and Human Security

Japan has recently embraced the relatively new concept of "healthy life years," which is the average number of years that a citizen can expect to live free of disability—before being bedridden or afflicted by a debilitating age-related ailment like dementia. This concept, which originated in Europe and was adopted by the World Health Organization in 2000, differs from traditional measures of life span by emphasizing the quality of life.

The Japanese government has made extending the number of healthy life years a policy goal. It has done so for two main reasons. One is the fact that shrinking the gap between healthy life years and absolute life expectancy is an effective way to reduce overall health care spending. This is because the longer seniors can live healthily, the shorter the time they will spend bedridden or under supervised care, both of which are very expensive. Thus, extending the healthy life years becomes a way of easing the burden on the health care system.

The second reason is that by prioritizing healthy life years, the government hopes to spur innovation and turn preventative care into a new growth industry to lift Japan's overall economy. By encouraging researchers and companies to find new ways to avoid debilitating illnesses before they strike, the government hopes to nurture the creation of more new services like those offered by You Home Clinic or futuristic therapies using stem cells and other scientific breakthroughs. The aim is to place Japan at the leading edge of new developments in elderly care. This will benefit not only Japan's own aging population but also position the nation as a leader at a time when the concept of healthy life years is winning growing acceptance across the rest of Asia, offering new growth opportunities beyond Japan's own borders.

Japan is already the world's leader in healthy life expectancy, but other Asian nations are right behind. According to the World Health Organization, a Japanese born in 2015 can expect 74.9 years of healthy life, longer than any of the other 183 nations surveyed. Singapore comes next, with 73.9 years, followed by South Korea's 73.2 years. By contrast, the United States ranked 36th, with 69.1 healthy years.[32]

The gap is bigger with less-developed Asian countries. While their populations are expected to age at a similar or even faster rate than Japan's, these countries lag behind in the measure of healthy life expectancy. In Thailand, for instance, citizens can expect 66.8 healthy years; in Indonesia, the figure drops to 62.1 years. In India, it is 59.6 years. One reason for these lower expectancies is that many of these countries lack adequate health insurance systems, access to hospitals and clinics, and educational opportunities for professional health care providers.[33]

This is one area in which Japan has a lot to offer its Asian neighbors. Some initiatives are already under way, such as You Home Clinic's move into Singapore, an aging society that is also one of Asia's wealthiest markets. But government officials say much more is possible. For instance, Suematsu, the head of the Japan Agency for Medical Research and Development, says he sees a growth opportunity in "expanding our big data-based medical care initiatives to the rest of Asia."[34]

Keizo Takemi, a governing Liberal Democratic Party lawmaker who chairs the party's Special Mission Committee on Global Health Strategy, has also said that Japan should seize the chance to become a global health leader.

"Japan should provide its system design know-how to other countries," Takemi told the Asia Pacific Initiative. "We should also support the education and training of policy makers to strengthen governance and leadership in the realm of health care."[35]

To become a global health leader, Japan is already on the right trajectory but must continue to innovate. Hospitals and clinics must eschew a one-size-fits-all approach and learn to meet the diverse needs of individual patients. Private companies must be given a larger role as pioneers of new products and treatments. Governments and universities must find ethical ways to use patient data to further improve health and medical care. The Japanese government can enhance its control tower function by sharing Japan's experiences with the world and guiding efforts to turn these into effective growth strategies.

Japan's biggest potential may lie in leading the world toward a paradigm shift in health care. Japan's own recent experiences point toward the need for its aging citizens to take more control of their own health by improving habits to preemptively avoid costly hospitalizations and extend their healthy life expectancy. At the same time, new research shows the value of community and diet in leading a healthful life. Thus, health care may be shifting away from the traditional model of life-extending medical care administered by experts toward an approach with more emphasis on community and individual. This shift in values can be harnessed as a force for both economic growth and social progress.

In this new age of low birthrates, demographic aging, and shrinking populations, personal health has increasingly come to be seen as a basic right, like free speech or protection of property. This is something that Japan already enjoys, thanks to Article 25 of its constitution written by Sams, the American general. Now the rest of the world may be catching up. The world has begun to embrace the concept of human security, which the United Nations defines as "the right of people to live in freedom and dignity, free from poverty and despair . . . with an equal opportunity to enjoy all their rights and fully develop their human potential."[36] Surely, access to quality health care, and the opportunity to extend one's healthy life years, can easily fit into this definition of human security. National governments are already feeling increasing pressure to guarantee access to quality health care, Takemi said.

"When someone loses their health, the opportunity to expand their range of options in life is also inevitably lost," Takemi said. "That is why health lies at the very core of the concept of human security."[37]

As the world's first nation of centenarians, Japan is a frontrunner in the world's longevity revolution. This gives it a unique opportunity to lead in creating not only new technologies and care techniques but also a new value system that enshrines health as a basic right and guarantee.

Notes

1. "The Human Mortality Database," accessed July 12, 2017, www.mortality.org.

2. "World Health Statistics 2016," World Health Organization, posted June 2016, http://www.who.int/gho/publications/world_health_statistics/2016/en/.

3. Nayu Ikeda et al., "What Has Made the Population of Japan Healthy?" *The Lancet*, 378 (2011): 1094–1105.

4. Kenji Shibuya et al., "Future of Japan's System of Good Health at Low Cost with Equity: Beyond Universal Coverage," *The Lancet*, 378 (2011): 1265–1273.

5. "Health at a Glance 2015: How Does Japan Compare?" Organisation for Economic Co-operation and Development, posted November 4, 2015, https://www.oecd.org/japan/Health-at-a-Glance-2015-Key-Findings-JAPAN.pdf.

6. Japanese Ministry of Finance, "Heisei 26 Nendo Sozei Oyobi Inshi Shunyu Kessan Gakushirabe," accessed July 12, 2017, http://www.mof.go.jp/tax_policy/reference/account/h2014.htm.

7. United States Center for Disease Control and Prevention, "Life Expectancy at Birth, at Age 65, and at Age 75, by Sex, Race, and Hispanic Origin: United States, Selected Years 1900–2010," accessed July 12, 2017, www.cdc.gov/nchs/data/hus/2011/022.pdf.

8. Sams was ordered by MacArthur to draft Article 25 of Japan's constitution. This article, which specifies the state's responsibility to protect the health of its citizens, reads as follows: "All people shall have the right to maintain the minimum standards of wholesome and cultured living. In all spheres of life, the State shall use its endeavors for the promotion and extension of social welfare and security, and of public health."

9. Crawford F. Sams, *Medic: The Mission of an American Military Doctor in Occupied Japan and Wartime Korea* (Armonk, NY: Sharpe, 1998).

10. Sei Nishimura, *Nihonjin no Seimei o Mamotta Otoko* (Tokyo: Kodansha, 2002).

11. Sams, 1998.

12. "Habado Daigaku Ichiro Kawachi Kyoju no Chosa Kekka o Tokubetsu Kokai: Nihonjin wa Naze Nagaiki nana no ka—San Man Nin no Chosa de Wakatta Koto," *Shukan Gendai*, September 13, 2012.

13. "Intabyu: 50 nen mae ni Hajimatta Seven Countries Study, Kurume Daigaku Shinzo/Kekkan Naika Junkyoju Adachi Hisashi," epi-c.jp, posted November 5, 2007, www.epi-c.jp/entry/e110_0_interview_01.html.

14. Suketami Tominaga and Tetsuko Kuroishi, "An Ecological Study on Diet/Nutrition and Cancer in Japan," *International Journal of Cancer*, Suppl. 10 (1997): 2–6, February 1997, accessed November 20, 2017, www.ncbi.nlm.nih.gov/pubmed/9209011.

15. Yasuki Kobayashi, "Five Decades of Universal Health Insurance Coverage in Japan: Lessons and Future Challenges," *Japan Medical Association Journal*, 52 (2009): 263–268, July/August 2009, accessed November 20, 2017, www.med.or.jp/english/journal/pdf/2009_04/263_268.pdf.

16. Scott Bass et al., *Public Policy and the Old Age Revolution in Japan* (London: Routledge, 2016).

17. Jin Yoshimura, *"Iryohi o meguru josei to shakai ni kan suru watashi no kangaekata," Shakai Hoken Junpo* (Tokyo: Shakai Hoken Kenkyujo, 1983).

18. Bass et al., 2016.

19. Nanako Tamiya et al., "Population Aging and Wellbeing: Lessons from Japan's Long-Term Care Insurance Policy," *The Lancet*, 378 (2011): 1183–1192.

20. Ibid., p. 1185.

21. Japanese Ministry of Health, Labor, and Welfare, "Estimates of National Medical Care Expenditure, FY 2014," accessed July 12, 2017, www.mhlw.go.jp/english/database/db-hss/enmce_2014.html.

22. Kobayashi, 2009.

23. Tadashi Iwanaka, "Past, Present, and Future of the National Clinical Database," *Kyobu Geka*, 70 (2017): 35–40.

24. Arata Murakami et al., "The National Clinical Database as an Initiative for Quality Improvement in Japan," *Korean Journal of Thoracic and Cardiovascular Surgery*, 47 (2014): 437–443.

25. Michael Mezher, "Japan Launches NIH Analogue," Regulatory Affairs Professional Society, April 1, 2015.

26. "Makoto Suematsu: Fast Tracking Medical Research in Japan," *Eurotechnology Japan*, March 23, 2016.

27. Makoto Suematsu, speaking at Asia Pacific Initiative, June 6, 2016.

28. Kazuhiro Nagao, *Hannin ha Watashi Datta!—Iryou Shoku Hitsudoku 'Heion shi' no Kanaekata* (Tokyo: Nihon Iji Shimpousha, 2015).

29. Shinsuke Muto, speaking at Asia Pacific Initiative, January 26, 2016.

30. Shinsuke Muto, interviewed by author, September 26, 2016.

31. Ee Sian Neo, interviewed by author, October 31, 2016.

32. See World Health Organization, "Healthy Life Expectancy at Birth (Years) 2000-2015," accessed July 12, 2017, http://gamapserver.who.int/gho/interactive_charts/mbd/hale_1/atlas.html.

33. Daiwa Institute of Research, "ASEAN Insaito: ASEAN Shokoku ni Okeru Koreika no Shinten," December 7, 2015.

34. Suematsu, at Asia Pacific Initiative, 2016.

35. Keizo Takemi, speaking at Asia Pacific Initiative, April 11, 2016.

36. United Nations Trust Fund for Human Security, "Human Security at the United Nations," accessed July 12, 2017, www.un.org/humansecurity/sites/www.un.org.humansecurity/files/Human%20Security%20Brochure%20-%20English.pdf.

37. Takemi, at Asia Pacific Initiative, 2016.

CHAPTER SIX

Pursuing Nobels: Japan's Emergence as a Global Leader in Science

David Cyranoski

In 2001, Koji Omi, then Japan's minister of science and technology, reflected on what he called the poor showing that Japanese science had made since World War II: its researchers had won a mere six Nobel Prizes compared to 180 by American scientists and 44 by those in the United Kingdom. "If you just look at these figures, you would probably think Japan's science and technology level is low. It should be higher," he said.[1]

Omi spoke as he announced an ambitious goal for raising his nation's scientific stature: Japan would aim to win 30 Nobel Prizes over the next 50 years. The target was met with heckles both at home and abroad: Nobels are awarded by committees of scientific peers, making the winning of one very different from, say, achieving the output targets of industrial policy. Yet, over the next 15 years, Japanese scientists seemed to heed the call, picking up on average one Nobel per year, outpacing every country except the United States and putting Japan on track to sail past Omi's goal.[2]

The winning streak brought pride and respect to a nation that just a generation earlier had been dismissed as a country of imitators. As Japanese scientists racked up Nobel after Nobel, they overturned the old stereotype that theirs was a nation of engineers adept at improving on the discoveries of others but lacking the creativity to pioneer on their own. Today, Japanese researchers are respected for their novel ideas and willingness to think outside the box as well as for their technical skill, obsessive attention to detail, and relentless work ethic.

These strengths have helped Japanese science make important contributions to a vast array of fields: from particle physics and robotics to photonics and seismology, and from stem cells and immunology to mathematics and space exploration. The country has also gotten a boost from its willingness to invest in large, cutting-edge research facilities, like the Super Kamiokande neutrino detector and SPring-8 synchrotron radiation facility, which have contributed to major discoveries, attracting collaboration from top foreign scientists. Japan's research practices have also added to its success. The tightly bound social relationships of Japan's laboratories have been criticized for impeding free thought, but they have also provided the level of training needed to produce rigorous work and the peer support that allows scientists to take risks in research. Due to often poor communication skills, a dislike of the limelight, and their nation's geographical distance from the United States and Europe, Japanese scientists often work in relative isolation. But even this has at times proven to be an advantage, giving researchers the space to do original research.

Ironically, most of Japan's recent Nobel Prizes were actually recognition of research that was done in the 1970s and 1980s, demonstrating that Japanese scientists have been blazing trails for decades. Even as Omi was bewailing the poor performance of Japanese research, the nation had already matured into a world-class science power. But Omi was right about one thing. Winning a few Nobels did help public perception catch up to that reality.

Japan's successes have also helped establish itself in a different way: as a model to other late-developing nations. Scientifically ambitious countries like China and South Korea have looked with envy on Japan's parade of Nobel laureates. Their scientists and policy makers now study Japan's successes for hints for how to make their own transitions from follower to pioneer. However, if there is one lesson to be learned from Japan's accomplishments, it is that they were not achieved overnight. The roots of Japan's scientific rise extend back to the mid-19th century, when its leaders set out to turn a medieval nation of samurai into a modern industrial empire. In doing so, they laid the groundwork for Japan to become the first non-Western nation in modern times to lead in research as well as technology.

At the same time, Japan also provides a cautionary tale. Even as its scientists win global accolades, many warn that Japan's basic science may already be losing its competitiveness. These observers point to such danger signs as a recent decline in output of published research papers, a key indicator of a country's prowess in basic science. The number of articles written or cowritten by Japanese researchers soared through the 1990s and by 2000 accounted for more than 10 percent of the world's publications. But that proved to be the peak. Even as Japan has upped its take of Nobel Prizes, its publication rate has declined dramatically relative to other countries. According to the National Institute of Science and Technology Policy (NISTEP), Japan dropped from being the fourth most prolific publisher of high-impact scientific papers in 2005 to ninth a decade later. During that same period, China climbed from No. 8 to No. 2, behind only the United States.[3]

There are many reasons for the downturn. One is financial. After the 1990s, scientific research budgets stagnated along with the Japanese economy. After increasing by some 60 percent during the 1990s, spending on basic science plateaued. According to figures collected by NISTEP and the OECD, Japanese government spending on science and technology increased only 10 percent between 2000 and 2015. By contrast, spending over the same period increased by 90 percent in the United States, by 280 percent in South Korea, and by 1,480 percent in China. Japan has also fallen behind in absolute amount of spending: Japanese government expenditures on science and technology reached ¥18.9 trillion in 2015, compared with the equivalent of ¥51.2 trillion in the United States and ¥41.9 trillion in China during the same year.[4]

Demographics may also play a role, as the number of young Japanese going into science has declined along with the size of the nation's overall population.[5] Efforts to rejuvenate its aging, predominantly male scientific community by increasing intake of women and foreigners have met with limited success. Only 15.3 percent of researchers in Japan's public and private laboratories are female, putting Japan at the bottom of all major scientific powers, according to a comparison of data from Japan's Ministry of Internal Affairs and Communications and figures from the OECD.[6] Such glass ceilings have contributed to an overall decline in the prestige of Japan's universities, which have fallen in global rankings as top students from India and China bypass Japan in favor of Berkeley and Oxford.

Despite such challenges, Japanese science is here to stay. While funding is no longer increasing, it has not declined either. Modes of education and training remain in place that are capable of producing top-notch scientists, even if their overall numbers may be shrinking. Japan also benefits from having built a critical mass of research talent, world-class institutions, and perhaps most importantly, widespread support for investment in science among bureaucrats, politicians, and the general public. With such backing, Japanese scientists remain well positioned to find new avenues of research, pursue them with a perfectionist rigor and the most advanced techniques, and offer results that can still dazzle the global scientific community.

"There is a disquieting feeling among young researchers" about the future of Japanese science, says Tadatsugu Taniguchi, an award-winning immunologist at the University of Tokyo who has served on government advisory committees. But, he says, "science is a culture, and these cultures don't disappear so quickly."[7]

Creating a Culture of Science

In Japan, this culture of science took more than a century to develop. Its roots go back to two key decisions in the late 1860s, when a group of young samurai took control of a nation that they saw as too backward to resist the advanced imperialist powers of Europe. The first was the conclusion that learning the West's technological know-how was the only way for Japan to avoid the same fate as Qing China, which Britain had humiliated in the Opium War. The other was less obvious: that such technology could not be effectively adopted without also absorbing the scientific mind-set that made those new inventions possible. With this realization, Japan embarked on a national project that eventually saw it become the first non-Western country to join the ranks of leading scientific nations.

As Japan entered an era of social experimentation and crash industrialization known as the Meiji period, its leaders set out to learn the culture of science by visiting the West itself. The first step was the Iwakura mission, a remarkable two-year tour of Europe and the United States by more than 100 of Japan's top political and intellectual leaders as well as students. After departing Japan in 1871, they visited the West's leading centers of science, where they spared no expense in hiring top researchers and educators to bring back to Japan.

These foreign teachers established many of Japan's top universities and laboratories and are still revered today. They laid the groundwork for the impressive research infrastructure that Japan built before World War II. By 1939, this included seven Imperial universities based on the hierarchical German university chair system; after the war, these became the national universities that still lead academic research today. Many

Japanese scientists also went abroad to work at top laboratories and then used the knowledge that they acquired there to set up research centers back in Japan. One is the Institute for Materials Research (IMR) at Tohoku University, which Kotaro Honda established in 1916 after a stay in Germany's University of Gottingen. Today, IMR is a world leader in advanced materials from metallic glasses to nano-crystalline magnets.

In the prewar period, a few Japanese researchers rose to the forefront of their fields, winning international recognition. Two were nominated for Nobel Prizes: Shibasaburo Kitasato, a codiscoverer of an antitoxin to treat diphtheria, and Katsusaburo Yamagiwa, who in 1915 proved the existence of carcinogens, chemicals that cause cancer.

The establishment in 1917 of the Institute of Physical and Chemical Research—better known by its shortened Japanese form, RIKEN—signaled the beginning of significant, targeted government financial support for science. It also set the stage for the mobilization of science to serve the nation's empire-building. While Japan's wartime achievements lagged behind those of the United States and Germany, its scientists did research in radar, engines, and even short-lived efforts to build atomic bombs.

Defeat in 1945 brought a backlash that split the scientific community. Having allowed themselves to serve the failed war effort, many scientists vowed never again, creating a strongly pacifist streak that is still evident in Japanese science. In 1950, the Science Council of Japan, an advisory group to the government, issued a statement declaring that scientists "will absolutely not engage in research whose purpose is use in war." For many, this took the form of not just rejecting military research but any work that might appear to have national or even industrial benefits. Doing pure research, for the good of all humankind, became a point of pride, leading many university-based scientists to look down on research with commercial applications. One result was a division of the nation's researchers into two distinct tracks, one based at universities and the other in big companies like NEC and Sony.

The government also stepped in to support industrial research, sometimes on a vast scale. In the 1970s, the Ministry of International Trade and Industry established the Tsukuba Science City, an entire community of industrial research and development laboratories. As Japan's postwar economy took off, companies also expanded their in-house research, yielding such transformative technological breakthroughs as the compact disc and the lithium-ion battery. Reinforcing the academic-industrial divide was the Japanese corporate practice of hiring newly minted university graduates and training them internally to be scientists and engineers rather than relying on university graduate programs. As the Japanese economy entered the so-called bubble years in the 1980s, companies flush with cash started pouring money into "blue sky" research, taking chances on visionary projects with no clear commercial applications.

The 1980s were also a boom period for academic science, in part thanks to *gaiatsu*, or pressure from outside Japan. Having emerged as the world's second-richest nation, Japan faced accusations that it had simply copied and commercialized technology that had been developed elsewhere, without giving back. As we have seen, this was not actually the case: much of the research behind Japan's current spate of Nobel Prizes was done in the 1970s and 1980s. Yet, while the label of technological freeloader was at least partially a product of foreign ignorance and economic envy, the criticisms stung Japan. The government responded with a rapid expansion of research budgets. By 1988, Japan spent a larger proportion of its gross domestic product on research than the United States did.[8]

One way Japan cemented its status as a world scientific power and knowledge contributor was by building a series of world-class research facilities. One was the massive SPring-8, run by RIKEN, which came on line in 1999. It quickly established itself as one of the top centers of high-energy beam research in the world, rivaling the Argonne National Laboratory in the United States and drawing scientists from around the world to do experiments in particle physics as well as biochemistry and materials research. Another high-profile project was the Subaru Telescope with its record-setting 8.2-meter mirror, built in 2005 atop Mauna Kea in Hawaii, and the half-billion-dollar *Chikyu* drilling ship, which set a record by bringing up boring samples taken from a seabed under ocean more than seven kilometers deep.

While many of these were clearly intended to be prestige projects, Japanese scientists and the bureaucrats who funded them did their homework, carefully choosing fields in which they could make the biggest impact. The scientists not only successfully convinced the government to set the nation's sights on ambitious targets but took advantage of the new facilities to help establish Japan as a major player in basic science. But their success was the result of more than just building the biggest and newest research facilities. It also reflected the unique culture of science that emerged in Japan after the war and that has contributed to Japan's spectacular breakthroughs, as well as some of its less illustrious moments.

Taking the Lead in Neutrinos

One field in which Japanese researchers gained global attention in recent decades was the search for the neutrino, a subatomic particle that had been postulated to exist but that had eluded detection for decades. Their success in tracking down these ghostlike particles, and particularly neutrinos from cosmic sources, forced a rewriting of the Standard Model, the current conceptual edifice of theoretical physics, a feat that won them two separate Nobel Prizes. While Japan now faces growing competition from overseas researchers, its ongoing experiments in this field continue to address the most pressing riddles of our universe.

Neutrinos were first predicted to exist in 1930 to explain the loss of energy from the decay of neutrons, one of the building blocks of an atomic nucleus. Neutrinos were believed to have neither electric charge nor mass, making them difficult to detect. Some of the best minds in experimental physics sought ways to prove their existence. Of particular interest was detecting neutrinos that emanated from the sun. The discovery of such solar neutrinos would lay to rest the question of what powered the sun by offering definitive proof of the fusion of hydrogen atoms into helium, a high-energy reaction that releases neutrinos as a by-product. An experiment in South Dakota in the 1960s had turned up the first tantalizing traces of solar neutrinos, but many scientists remained skeptical.

Japan's involvement in the hunt for solar neutrinos came by chance. In 1982, a group of scientists decided to turn an old zinc mine in central Japan into a detector to look for decaying protons, another building block of the atomic nucleus. That quest failed, but an astrophysicist named Masatoshi Koshiba, who held a PhD from the University of Rochester, realized that the detector's location one kilometer deep under solid mountain rock would block out most types of radiation—except neutrinos, which pass effortlessly through the mass of the earth.

Koshiba refitted the proton detector to create the Kamiokande II, a tank holding 3,000 tons of water that was lined by thousands of what look like giant lightbulbs. These photo multiplier tubes detect the faint flashes of light created when a neutrino collides with an atomic nucleus in one of the molecules of water, releasing an electron. Kamiokande II was a success, finding not only the telltale flickers of passing neutrinos but also evidence that the direction of some of them could be traced back to the sun. Koshiba's work was heralded as the dawn of what was quickly dubbed neutrino astronomy. In 2002, Koshiba shared a Nobel Prize for his work.

Koshiba's breakthrough whetted the appetite of other Japanese physicists, who sought to build on their nation's lead. They turned their attention to the questions that Koshiba's work had left unanswered. One was the fact that Kamiokande II had detected only a fraction of the number of neutrinos that physicists had predicted should be coming from the sun. Where were the missing neutrinos? One possible answer lay in an earlier theory laid out by three Japanese physicists in 1962 that neutrinos come in three different types, or "flavors," of which Kamiokande II had detected only one. Perhaps the missing neutrinos had converted to another flavor? Finding these other types of neutrinos would be even harder, requiring a much larger and more sensitive detector.

Motivated by a desire to combat the freeloader criticisms, Japan's Ministry of Education, Science, Sports, and Culture decided in 1991 to put up the $100 million needed to construct the new detector. The result was the Super Kamiokande, or Super-K, built in the same location as the original Kamiokande II. The new detector was a massively expanded version of its predecessor, with a tank holding 50,000 tons of water lined by more than 11,000 photo multiplier tubes. It proved sensitive enough to catch a glimpse of neutrinos changing flavors, a phenomenon known as neutrino oscillation. It also produced evidence that neutrinos had a tiny mass, overturning the Standard Model's assumption that they were massless, like photons.

The decision to build the Super-K proved to be a turning point for Japanese astrophysics, putting the nation on the global research map as never before. Building the detector was a huge gamble: if the Standard Model had proved correct, and the theory of oscillating neutrinos wrong, Japan would have come up empty-handed. Even the United States had balked at the price, forcing its scientists to seek spots on the Japan-led program. Success almost eluded the Japanese, with the Super-K's project leader, Takaaki Kajita of the University of Tokyo, admitting that he "almost accidentally" stumbled upon the telltale traces of converting neutrinos in 1998.[9] For his discovery, Kajita shared the 2015 Nobel Prize. On returning to Japan from the award ceremony, Kajita told reporters, "I want to thank the neutrinos, of course."[10] One of his first calls after winning the prize was to his mentor, Koshiba.[11]

Japan was now blazing the trail forward, producing innovative research that was rewriting the laws of physics. The Super-K results forced scientists to reconcile the Standard Model with the finding that neutrinos, trillions of which stream from space through our bodies each second, actually had mass. However, exactly how much mass remained unclear, one of many secrets that the neutrino had yet to yield.

To solve the riddle of neutrino mass, Japanese scientists put the Super-K to novel use, measuring the mass of neutrinos that came not from space but via beams created by the scientists themselves using an accelerator. This success at quickly repurposing the Super-K and generating a neutrino beam moved them ahead of rival researchers overseas, demonstrating the ability to put theoretical knowledge into practice and skill at handling sensitive equipment that had already placed Japan on the leading edge of neutrino science. "The nimbleness allowed the Japanese to establish precedence," said Richard Tesarek, a senior scientist at the Fermi National Accelerator Laboratory near Chicago, which competes with Super-K in neutrino research.[12]

Japan now hopes to build on that lead to crack some of the most fundamental mysteries in physics, such as the nature of the mysterious dark matter that scientists now believe fills the universe. Japanese scientists have drawn up plans to build an even larger Hyper Kamiokande, a next-generation detector 10 times larger than the Super-K. While construction keeps getting pushed back, in February 2017 the Science Council of Japan selected the proposed detector, already dubbed Hyper-K, as a high-priority large-scale science project.[13]

"The Japanese have decided to go with what they know works, and if and when it gets approved, I have no doubt it can be built faster and produce more physics" than competitors, says Henry Sobel, a physicist at the University of California, Irvine, who started working on the Super-K project in 1992.[14]

Weaknesses Can Be Strengths

Japan's breakthroughs in neutrino research cemented the nation's position as a leader in particle physics. It also brought world attention to the ways of doing science that emerged in postwar Japan.

One was a close cooperation between the scientific community and industry, which both Japanese and foreign particle physicists credit with making the Super-K's breakthroughs possible. This new cooperation represents a change for Japanese science, as tighter budgets have made academic researchers shed some of their postwar reluctance to work with government and industry, especially if they can join a prestige project like the Hyper-K. At the same time, it is important to point out that those walls have not fallen entirely. Japanese university scientists are still loathe to work with industry on money-making endeavors or get their hands dirty by doing research for profit. However, they now appear more willing to form relationships with government and industry in order to build the increasingly expensive facilities needed to do cutting-edge basic science.

Similarly, Japanese companies have also shown themselves willing to join in risky, high-profile experiments that allow them to showcase their technological prowess, whether it be creating the world's most powerful atomic-resolution holography electron microscope, the first space probe to bring back pieces of an asteroid, or the super-sensitive detectors used by the Super-K.

To build the Super-K, physicists worked closely with engineers from a small, highly specialized manufacturer called Hamamatsu Photonics. The collaboration produced photo multiplier tubes sensitive enough to capture the faint footprints of passing neutrinos, allowing Kajita to make his discovery. To give the proposed Hyper-K the power to make new discoveries, physicists and engineers are working together to develop a new generation of even more sensitive tubes. This science-industry cooperation has also benefitted Hamamatsu, allowing it to establish itself as the leading producer of highly sensitive photo detectors.

"This technological development resulting from the collaboration with Hamamatsu was absolutely central to this success," says Alain Blondel, a neutrino researcher at the University of Geneva. "It was one of many examples of Japanese researchers working closely with industry to produce the tools they need."[15]

Another, very different strength of postwar Japanese science was put on display during a less-celebrated episode of the Super-K project, an accident in 2001 that almost brought its demise. The detector's water tank was being refilled after routine maintenance when one of the photo multiplier tubes, which contain a vacuum, suddenly exploded, perhaps due to pressure from the incoming water. The resulting shock wave set off a chain reaction, causing some 7,000 of the 11,000 tubes to burst in less than 10 seconds.[16] Faced with a $20 million price tag to repair the damage, the relevant ministry could have opted to close the facility, which had already achieved its original goal of detecting neutrino oscillation.

Instead, the government chose to repair the Super-K, slowly bringing it fully back on line five years later. For many foreign scientists, this decision was a display of another feature of Japan's culture of science: a dogged determination not to give up. Of course, such tenacity is not always a virtue. Japan's electronics giants continued to bet on mainframe computing long after nimbler rivals in Silicon Valley and Taiwan had pivoted to PCs and the Internet. But in the case of neutrino research, often criticized features of the Japanese system—hierarchical organization, complicated internal structures, and consensus thinking—produced positive results. The United States might have been faster out of the gate in beginning neutrino research, but it dropped out once the costs started to mount. By contrast, Japan's more plodding approach allowed it to maintain support for its neutrino detectors, which are now in their third decade and on the cusp of yet another upgrade.

"Like big Japanese companies, the scientific institution in Japan moves slowly but steadily," said Iulia Georgescu, a senior editor at *Nature Reviews Physics* who used to work as a physicist in Japan. "It is not as dynamic as the U.S., but it is thorough and proceeds at its own pace. In slow-moving fields, where planning, building, and doing the experiment takes decades, they have a clear advantage precisely because of this inertia."[17]

The Creative Outliers

Not all of Japan's successes depend on big government-funded projects or the slow, thoughtful style of the neutrino researchers. The nation's scientific community has also given space for the intellectual mavericks willing to strike out on their own to follow risky, often freshly original avenues of research.

One was Shinya Yamanaka, who won the Nobel Prize in 2012 for a breakthrough in stem cells that many expect to revolutionize medicine. In 2006, he used a specially designed virus to coax the skin cells of adult mice into behaving just like stem cells, the all-purpose cells in unformed embryos that later develop into the myriad types of tissues found in the body: nerves, muscles, bones, blood. Yamanaka's so-called induced pluripotent stem cells, or iPS cells, promise to make possible the futuristic field of regenerative medicine, in which doctors may one day be able to take a sample of a patient's own cells and grow them into different types of tissue—such as new pancreatic tissue to help diabetic patients—in order to treat disease or injury. Since such a graft would be made from the victim's own cells, there would be a far lower chance of it getting rejected by the immune system. Yamanaka's discovery has made him perhaps Japan's most prominent celebrity scientist and a much-needed role model for younger generations of would-be Nobel laureates.

Yamanaka followed an unlikely career path. Trained as an orthopedic surgeon, Yamanaka said a lack of confidence in his surgical skills made him decide against practicing medicine. Instead, he ended up in biomedical research, eventually landing an enviable position at the Gladstone Institutes in San Francisco, where he studied the role of proteins in cancer. Returning to Japan in 1996, he suffered what he called post-America depression—the disappointment felt by many Japanese academic researchers who return home to find underfunded, poorly equipped laboratories. Yamanaka said he got little support from the government for his research, which required the use of hundreds of mice. He often felt like he spent more time taking care of them than doing actual research, and he faced the mockery of colleagues who saw working with mice as beneath them. Yamanaka said he reconsidered his decision to eschew medical practice.[18]

Two developments put him back on course. His personal career had received a boost in 1999, when Yamanaka was hired as an associate professor at Nara Institute of Science and Technology, a national university. The new position put him in charge of his own independent research group and gave him a staff to help with laboratory work. Yamanaka had begun researching the embryonic stem cells of mice, looking for possible medical uses. This research suddenly began to look more promising in 1998, when a group in the United States announced that they had successfully removed stem cells from a human embryo and grown them in a petri dish. According to the group, these cells had retained their pluripotent ability to turn into other tissues, raising the first early hopes for regenerative medicine. Yamanaka saw the American breakthrough as a route to vindication for his own research.

While the embryonic stem cells promised a new era of medical treatments, their use still faced substantial obstacles. One of the biggest was moral. Many doctors were unwilling to enter into the new field, and many politicians unwilling to publicly fund research, because the cells could only be obtained by the destruction of human embryos, typically leftovers from in vitro fertilization clinics. The use of human embryos also posed technical challenges: since the cells came from a different individual, they still faced a high probability of rejection by the patient's own immune system.

Yamanaka recognized that a possible solution lay in somehow reprogramming the patient's own cells to act like embryonic stem cells. Scientists already knew that such reprogramming was at least theoretically possible from research into another morally fraught new field, cloning. In 1996, a cell from a sheep's mammary glands had been placed inside an unfertilized egg, where it had reverted to the state of an embryonic stem cell. It was this process that produced Dolly, the first cloned mammal. But cloning had its own ethical and technical issues, including the need for unfertilized eggs. Anything that smacked of human cloning would face enormous resistance from scientists and the public.

Scientists wanted to figure out how cells could be reprogrammed without using embryos or eggs. However, many feared that cracking the mystery of reprogramming would be hopelessly complex given the cascading sequence of changes that a cell undergoes as it matures into adult tissue.

Yamanaka was undeterred. He started with a search for the genes in DNA that could hold the key to reprogramming adult cells. This was a huge gamble because it was unclear how many genes were involved. Yamanaka later recounted how he did not even know if the number was less than 10 or more than several hundred. Either way, the number of possible genetic combinations could quickly grow to astronomical figures. "I thought it could take decades, that it might never be achieved while I was doing research," Yamanaka said.[19]

Other researchers were pursuing a similar avenue, systematically testing candidate genes one or two at a time. Scientists learned a lot about the function of these genes, but none could get to the point of reprogramming actual cells. Yamanaka, who had moved to Kyoto University in 2004, was also trying this strategy. His laboratory had zeroed in on 24 genes and was testing, without success, the ability of each to reprogram mouse skin cells. On a whim, Kazutoshi Takahashi, a postdoctoral researcher in the laboratory, tried a different strategy. He took the skin cells from adult mice and inserted all 24 genes, using viruses to add the genes to the skin cells' DNA. After a few weeks, Takahashi could not believe his eyes. The modified cells had formed into small cobblestone-patterned colonies—behavior exhibited by embryonic stem cells but not fully formed skin cells. Excited, he called over Yamanaka. The two tested and retested the procedure until they were sure that they had indeed found a way to make adult cells revert to acting like stem cells. With additional experiments, they eventually whittled the number of genes needed to create stem cells down to four.

Scientists credit Yamanaka and Takahashi's breakthrough to out-of-the-box thinking. Other stem cell researchers were moving in the opposite direction, trying to catalog the contribution to reprogramming of an ever-larger number of individual genes. No one had thought to narrow down the number by trial and error. Even if they had, few researchers would have seen inserting a small number of genes as a gamble with enough chance of success to justify the use of time and precious laboratory resources.

"The idea to screen small libraries of candidates was a masterful and essential epiphany that none of the rest of us had," says George Q. Daley, a prominent stem cell expert and dean of Harvard's Faculty of Medicine.[20] "In retrospect, this is the type of experiment that the NIH [the National Institutes of Health in the United States] would dismiss as harebrained and impossible, but it's so brilliant that it has spawned countless efforts to apply the same strategy in lots of other settings, leading to an explosion of new insights."[21]

In Japan's recent string of Nobels, perhaps none has been as instantly transformative as Yamanaka's. The prize came a mere six years after publishing his first research paper on the breakthrough, a sign that the scientific community immediately recognized the value of his work. It also led quickly to real-world applications: researchers have already begun taking cells from patients with Huntington's disease and other genetic disorders to turn into stem cells, which can be more easily studied in a laboratory. Pharmaceutical companies now use such "diseases-in-a-dish" methods to test new treatments.

The Japanese government also recognized the possibilities opened by Yamanaka's research, moving with uncharacteristic speed to pour billions of yen into development of the reprogrammed cells, which Yamanaka dubbed iPS cells. In its excitement over Yamanaka's breakthroughs, the government may also have overextended itself, passing a new law to fast-track the commercialization of laboratory advances that many criticize for putting ineffective and possibly dangerous treatments on the market.

Still, the government's swift moves were aimed at putting Japan at the forefront of one of the most promising new fields in medicine. And in this goal, it seems to be succeeding. In 2017, RIKEN researcher Masayo Takahashi led a team that conducted the world's first transplant using retina cells created from iPS cells.[22] Her husband, Jun Takahashi, a professor at Kyoto University, is planning the first clinical trials to treat Parkinson's disease, in which brain cells deteriorate, by growing healthy new neurons from a patient's own blood using iPS cell technology.[23] Nor is Yamanaka simply sitting on his laurels. A tireless worker, he is now trying to create what he calls an iPS cell bank that could speed up regenerative treatments by storing stem cells for quick use by patients.

Freedom to Take Risks

The fast pace of change in fields like stem cells have challenged one of the dominant features of Japan's research landscape: its formation into highly organized and hierarchical laboratories. These labs tend to be the creation of large companies or to be located at universities and government institutes where they are led by senior researchers with established channels to funding sources. Young scientists join with the promise of lifetime jobs; once inside, they receive training from senior members including the leader, who also sets the direction of research.

The closed nature of these labs has made them the target of frequent criticism. They are faulted for grouping researchers into isolated silos, which can hinder communication with other labs and the fruitful cross-pollination of research and ideas. The lab system has also been blamed for playing a role in recent scientific fraud cases that have tarnished Japan's image, such as the retractions of dozens of papers by University of Tokyo molecular biologist Shigeaki Kato found to contain what the university called fabricated data.[24] Critics say Japan's lab system can be vulnerable to abuse because of its opacity and reliance on trust instead of careful oversight.

However, Japan's scientific community is not so rigid as these criticisms might make it appear. The guarantees of lifetime employment give researchers a level of job stability, and a resulting freedom from pressures to publish or perish, that can be enviable compared to the dog-eat-dog world of American universities, with their fierce battles over tenure and research grants. What is more, not all Japan's academic researchers belong to a large lab. Those who do not still enjoy job security in which salaries and grants, though maybe not as generous as those in the United States, are reliable once obtained.

This can lead to clear benefits in research, as Yamanaka's success shows. Even though his first academic position in Japan was at the lesser-known Osaka City University, where he was not a member of a large, established lab, he enjoyed job security as a "lifetime faculty member," he said. He said this gave him the freedom to take risks without worrying about losing his position due to failure or the disapproval of colleagues who said he was spending too much time taking care of his mice.[25]

While Yamanaka was able to get his own independent laboratory, even researchers who join one of the big traditional labs can find that to be similarly liberating. Under the command of a capable lead professor, Japanese laboratories can foster a culture of creative experimentation in which younger researchers feel they belong to a tightly knit group that allows them to take risks. One such leader is Makoto Fujita, a professor at the University of Tokyo who has won numerous international awards for his work in supramolecular chemistry. At his laboratory, Fujita "consciously steers his group away from the traditional 'boss' model, devolving responsibility, and credit, to his team members," according to one editor at *Nature* familiar with the group.[26]

The hierarchical structure can also nurture Japan's high levels of technical skill and perfectionist attention to detail. The labs use an apprentice system in which younger researchers learn by working alongside their seniors and the lab boss. This allows the lab leader to provide guidance and mentor the younger researchers by example. Taniguchi of the University of Tokyo emphasized the importance of passing down to the next generation what he called tacit knowledge—using hands-on experience to teach the subtle techniques and nuances in research methodology that can be difficult to articulate verbally, much less in a written manual.[27] This approach allows younger lab members to absorb the necessary research skills and approaches over time, says Taniguchi, who has also worked in the United States and Europe.[28]

Indeed, Japanese researchers are well known for their technical skill, something that can be in high demand overseas. Teruhiko Wakayama of the University of Yamanashi in Kofu, Japan, is perhaps the world's leading master of cloning animals in a laboratory, a distinction he has held since

1998, when he became the first person to successfully clone a mouse. He did this using the standard method of replacing a cell's nucleus with a nucleus taken from the animal to be cloned. However, his technique is so demanding that he is frequently invited to laboratories, including some of the most prestigious in the United States, to teach scientists who failed to replicate his method by following his published descriptions.

Cloning can be a hit-or-miss proposition, often requiring the replacement of nuclei in hundreds of eggs just to get a single successful birth. Wakayama has worked to turn cloning into a more predictable and routine process. He has also used his skills to take cloning in new directions. In 2008, he cloned a mouse that had been frozen for 16 years, raising the possibility of one day reproducing extinct animals like mammoths found frozen in ice. In an extended experiment, he cloned 25 generations of mice, producing 580 healthy pups, a feat that proved DNA does not deteriorate.[29]

His research has also pushed the envelope on ethical issues. In one experiment, he cloned a mouse from urine. While this technique could offer new ways to rescue species on the brink of extinction, the ability to clone someone from their waste products also raises disturbing, potentially dystopian possibilities.

Japanese scientists often present such potentially controversial breakthroughs with a startling disregard for moral ambiguities. Many ignore the potential ethical questions raised by their work, demonstrating a form of tunnel vision that allows them to view their job solely as conducting science for science's sake. (In Wakayama's case, this refusal to look beyond his own work landed him in trouble when he was one of several researchers who played a supporting role in the discredited stem cell research of Haruko Obokata. While Wakayama was not involved in the questioned laboratory work that sparked the scandal, he later admitted that his narrow focus on his own portion of the project prevented him from seeing the flaws in other parts of the experiments.[30])

However, problems such as Obokata's are hardly the norm in Japanese science. Far from it: the hierarchical lab system can actually nurture a high level of research rigor. Conscious of the watchful eyes of their seniors, Japanese researchers can set their own standards quite high when interpreting data—to the point of seeming overly cautious to sometimes frustrated overseas collaborators. "The most striking thing is the extraordinary care our Japanese colleagues take to avoid mistakes, and their focus on constant incremental improvements," neutrino scientist Jeffrey Wilkes, who has collaborated off and on with Japanese scientists for four decades, said in an e-mail. "This involves careful checking of methods and results, constant review of work, and frequent group meetings where juniors report to senior members and are critiqued (sometimes, to American eyes, in a bullying manner!)."[31]

While Japan has had its scandals, this careful approach is likely to pay off in the long run. This is especially true when science globally is facing what might be called a crisis of reproducibility. There has been growing attention on the fact that, for a disturbingly large number of published research papers, other laboratories have failed to replicate the experimental results. This has raised serious doubts about their findings, a problem that some now fear may apply to more published papers than previously thought.[32] Sloppy laboratory techniques and methods for recording data may be the culprit more often than outright fraud, but in either case, the cautious rigor demonstrated by many Japanese researchers may win increasing admiration.

Crisis in Science?

But the practice of science is changing in Japan, and many fear for the worse. Over the last decade, the government has taken a larger role, funding science projects that have industrial or even military applications, raising the hackles of researchers who remember the post-1945 vows of never again. But one of the biggest causes of concern has been an erosion of the freedom to pursue the risky, original research that many credit for making Japan a powerhouse in basic science in the first place.

Many scientists blame policy changes by the government that they say are borrowing less savory aspects of the American model. They warn that these changes are eroding the ability of young scientists to take risks and gamble on innovative research. The biggest is a 2004 legal change in which national universities like the University of Tokyo, which had been under direct control of the central government, were reincorporated as independent public corporations. The reform was intended to free up the universities to innovate on their own, a goal that the government reinforced by forcing them to compete for funding. The once-steady flow of research budgets from the Ministry of Education has been replaced by an annual scramble for research grants, many of them short-term. As funding has grown less predictable, universities have responded by hiring fewer professors to secure, tenure-track jobs, opting instead to take on lower-paid researchers in temporary positions. Many Japanese scientists say that this has created an environment in which young researchers no longer feel secure enough to follow hunches into risky projects that may turn up unexpected results. Instead, career-conscious scientists now feel compelled to do work that offers the prospect of quicker, more predictable results so they can churn out papers in order to win the next grant and the next job.

The changes have brought expressions of concern from top scientists, including Yamanaka. Asked if he would have been able to do the research today that led to his breakthrough in stem cells, Yamanaka said the drop in funding for permanent posts has created greater uncertainty. "I think this environment drives young researchers to focus on something immediately achievable to establish their career," he warned.[33] At his center for iPS cell research, Yamanaka said he is trying to compensate by giving young researchers permanent posts.

Despite such individual efforts, the new uncertainty has made science a much less attractive career for the nation's youth. This is reflected in sharp declines in the numbers of young Japanese pursuing doctoral degrees, a necessary step toward a career in scientific research. The percentage of master's degree students in the sciences who have continued into PhD programs has fallen to just 8.9 percent in 2015 from 14 percent in 2004. Over the same period, the number of students enrolling in PhD programs in the sciences has dropped by a third, to slightly more than 4,000.[34]

The perception that a scientific career may not be the ticket to a stable, rewarding career that it once was has also been exacerbated by another government policy misstep. A program in the 1990s aimed at bolstering Japan's scientific prowess by adding 10,000 postdoctoral researchers backfired. Universities did not have enough spots to absorb them all, and the companies did not step in to hire the rest despite offers of government subsidies to do so. This left Japan with a glut of scientists of the same age who have struggled ever since to find work.[35]

"After watching postdocs unable to relax and do research, PhD students decided not to become researchers," says atomic physicist Akito Arima, a former president of the University of Tokyo who also served as the head of RIKEN. Arima says the impact of the university overhaul has been so destructive that new incentives are needed to get young people back into scientific careers.[36]

Of course, declines in funding are an inevitable outcome of slower economic growth and tighter government budgets. Japan is hardly the only country to face such realities, and its researchers have no choice but to accept the changes. But this is also an important transition period and one that requires reforms every bit as momentous as those Japan implemented in the 1990s to catapult itself into a leadership role in basic science. Once again, Japan's policy makers must rethink how the nation pursues science, this time to fit a new set of financial and demographic realities. As they do so, Japan's leaders must be careful not to overreach by expending precious resources on unrealistic efforts to stay ahead of rising neighbors with deeper pockets. Japan must find a way to protect its successes, even as it finds a new path forward. It must be careful not to undo the very system that has given it pioneers like Yamanaka and Koshiba. It is important to recognize the strengths that lie within Japan's current system, many of which are not fully recognized or appreciated. For this reason, it may be critical for those who know the system best—Japan's own scientists—to step forward and take a more aggressive stand to protect the culture of science in Japan, even while accepting the reality of financial cutbacks. In that struggle, they will find that Japan has significant advantages, including a long history and a system that has shown surprising success in producing new discoveries, as seen by the bevy of Nobel prizes.

Notes

1. "Competing with the World in Brain Power," *Koizumi Cabinet Mail*, posted August 2, 2001, http://www.kantei.go.jp/jp/m-magazine/backnumber/2001/0802 .html.

2. Ministry of Education, Culture, Sports, Science, and Technology, "White Paper on Science and Technology 2016," p. 15, accessed August 10, 2017, http:// www.mext.go.jp/en/publication/whitepaper/title03/detail03/1384513.htm.

3. National Institute of Science and Technology Policy, "Japanese Science and Technology Indicators 2017," p. 8, accessed August 23, 2017, http://www.nistep .go.jp/research/science-and-technology-indicators-and-scientometrics/indicators.

4. Ibid., pp. 17–19.

5. Ministry of Education, "2017 White Paper," http://www.mext.go.jp/b _menu/hakusho/html/hpaa201701/detail/1388434.htm. See figure 9.

6. National Institute of Science and Technology Policy, Japanese Science and Technology Indicators 2017, p. 78.

7. Tadatsugu Taniguchi, interviewed by author, April 18, 2017.

8. OECD, "Gross Domestic Spending on R&D," accessed August 10, 2017, https://data.oecd.org/rd/gross-domestic-spending-on-r-d.htm.

9. "Interview with Takaaki Kajita," Nobelprize.org, accessed August 10, 2017, https://www.nobelprize.org/mediaplayer/index.php?id=2625.

10. Dennis Overbye, "Takaaki Kajita and Arthur McDonald Share Nobel in Physics for Work on Neutrinos," *The New York Times*, October 6, 2015.

11. "Japan's Takaaki Kajita Shares Nobel in Physics," *The Japan Times*, October 6, 2015.

12. Richard Tesarek, e-mail to author, May 9, 2017.

13. Science Council of Japan, "Japan Master Plan of Large Research Projects," posted February 8, 2017, www.scj.go.jp/ja/info/kohyo/kohyo-23-t241-1.html.

14. Henry Sobel, e-mail to author, May 10, 2017.

15. Alain Blondel, e-mail to author, May 11, 2017.

16. David Cyranoski and Geoff Brumfiel, "Neutrino Physics: Picking Up the Pieces," *Nature*, February 14, 2002, accessed November 27, 2017, http://www.nature.com/nature/journal/v416/n6877/full/416118a.html.

17. Iulia Georgescu, e-mail to author, April 11, 2017.

18. Shinya Yamanaka, "Every Cloud Has a Silver Lining," speech to high school students December 2010, accessed August 10, 2017, http://logmi.jp/37600.

19. Ibid.

20. George Daley, e-mail to author, April 30, 2017.

21. Ibid.

22. "Japanese Team Conducts World's First Eye Transplant Using Donor iPS Cells," *The Japan Times*, March 28, 2017.

23. "Kyoto University's Potential iPS Cell Therapy for Parkinson's May Be Delayed," *The Japan Times*, November 11, 2015.

24. "Four Tokyo University Researchers Involved in Cover-up of Dubious Papers," *The Japan Times*, August 1, 2014.

25. Yamanaka, 2010.

26. Editor in e-mail to author, May 2, 2017.

27. See Kengo Kuma and Dana Buntrock's description of similar hands-on training of Japanese architects in chapter 2.

28. Taniguchi, 2017.

29. Elle Hunt, "Space Sperm Produces Healthy Mice, Raising Prospect of Future Human Settlement," *The Guardian*, May 22, 2017, https://www.theguardian.com/science/2017/may/22/space-sperm-produces-healthy-mice-raising-prospect-of-future-human-settlement.

30. Teruhiko Wakayama, e-mail to author, December 30, 2014.

31. R. Jeffrey Wilkes, e-mail to author, May 11, 2017.

32. Thomas Gall et al., "The Credibility Crisis in Research: Can Economics Tools Help?" *PLoS Biology* 15 (4, 2017): e2001846, April 26, 2017, https://doi.org/10.1371/journal.pbio.2001846.

33. Shinya Yamanaka, e-mail to author, May 11, 2017.

34. Ministry of Education, 2016 White Paper, p. 22.

35. David Cyranoski et al., "Education: The PhD Factory," *Nature*, 474 (2011): 276–279.

36. "A New Law for Human Resources," Nihon Keizai Shimbun, April 17, 2017.

CHAPTER SEVEN

Deciphering Japan: China's Fascination with Its Neighbor

Mao Danqing

In the spring of 2016, the Shanghai Translation Publishing House reissued the Chinese-language edition of Harvard University professor Ezra Vogel's classic, *Japan as Number One*. Appearing 36 years after Vogel's book was first published in Chinese, this newly released edition immediately became a best seller, selling 40,000 copies in just four months.

Against the cover's white background, the sun is depicted rising behind Mount Fuji. In a review in China's *Economic Observer* entitled "Can We Still Learn from Japan Today?" Yan Jiefu observes, "Japan's growth has stalled following the burst of the bubble economy. Yet Japan's low levels of income disparity and relatively clean politics, robust systems of social security and health insurance, low crime rate and good public manners, and sanitary living environment still contain important lessons for China. This book can teach the Chinese a great deal."[1]

When the original English edition of *Japan as Number One* was published in 1979, Japan was in a very different position than it is today. Having emerged from the ruins of wartime defeat to become the world's second-largest economy, Japan by the 1970s was a global force in trade and finance. As made-in-Japan products flooded global markets, and the Japanese yen became an international currency, the entire world wanted to know the secret to Japan's success. Vogel's book was an attempt to respond to this intense interest, though the book did best in Japan itself, where it sold 700,000 copies.

Why would a four-decade-old book about Japan stir so much interest in China today? After all, the political and diplomatic relationship between Japan and China is at its most difficult juncture since the normalization of ties between the two countries in 1972. Strategically, China and Japan have clashed over their competing territorial claims to the Senkaku/Diaoyu Islands and over maritime security in the East and South China Seas.

However, lost in all the noise over islands and history is the fact that Chinese interest in Japan has never been higher. This is most evident in Chinese tourism to Japan, which is in the midst of an unprecedented boom. Every year, a new record is set in the number of Chinese visiting Japan, testimony to the fact that Chinese interest in Japan is only growing and deepening. Much of this attention is focused on Japan's society and culture, particularly its arts, lifestyle, and popular trends.

Moreover, this rise in interest by China comes as Japan itself seems to have lost confidence in its own appeal. Almost 20 years of deflation, a plummeting birthrate, and fiscal deterioration have prompted intense discussion within Japan of its so-called Lost Decades. Japan's myriad problems have even led many Japanese and foreign observers to write the country off. However, when it comes to the attraction of Japanese culture overseas, and particularly in China, it is clear that Japan has not "lost" anything at all. On the contrary, Japan has gained an enormous amount of social and cultural prestige during the past two decades, so much so that this period may be better described as a period of gain rather than loss.

The renewed appeal of Vogel's book reflects a feature of this growing fascination with Japan: the inclination of many Chinese to view Japan as a model of emulation, or at least a guidepost as their nation tries to repeat Japan's successful emergence as a non-Western economic powerhouse.

According to Wang Taiping, a former Chinese consul in Osaka who made the first translation into Chinese of Vogel's book in 1980—

> The practical significance of the book's re-publication in China is that it offers the Chinese a form of "counseling" regarding the various anxieties we have developed over the course of China's growth. This is an opportunity to consider the social challenges that have arisen during the push for economic reform and development. Forty years ago, Japan experienced the various problems confronting China today. Moreover, in many cases Japan solved these problems admirably—environmental pollution was one such example.[2]

When the book first appeared in Chinese four decades ago, China was just embarking on a path of economic liberalization and reform. The turmoil of the Cultural Revolution had only ended a few years earlier, and China had just begun opening to the world. The enormous disparity at the time between a prosperous Japan and an impoverished China was readily apparent, and many Chinese harbored images of Japan as a land of wealth and luxury. While geographically close, Japan seemed a distant, unattainable presence to many in China.

These days, many Chinese have come to see their nation as following in the footsteps of Japan, as a fellow latecomer trying to break into what had been a Western-dominated club of leading nations. Many in China try to locate their own nation's place in history by comparing the China of today with the Japan of 40 years ago. As income levels rise in China, the Japan that Vogel describes seems less remote.

In fact, the two countries appeared for a time to be trading places, as China began a period of remarkable growth and globalization in the 1990s, while Japan entered its long, dark tunnel of deflation and debt.

However, the days of China's double-digit growth are now over, and the country has entered a long period of lower growth and perhaps even stagnation that many are calling the "new normal." Once again, China is finding itself following in Japan's footsteps, this time in dealing with the social problems of a slowing economy, aging population, low birthrate, and debt-laden banks.

For this reason, the nature of China's interest in Japan has changed. Gone is the old image of Japan as a rich but distant neighbor. In its place has appeared a more life-sized version of Japan, as a complex and yet accessible place that still has much to teach China. In this sense, Japan has become a mirror into which many Chinese gaze in search of China's own image. They view Japan with more empathy, as a place with superlatives and faults, charms and blemishes, and its own answers to the common challenges faced by China and all humankind.

Moreover, while Japan remains different in many ways, it is now a country that China is capable of deciphering. New developments in Japanese arts, culture, and lifestyle are immediately gathered, interpreted, dissected, enjoyed, and analyzed in China. This is occurring because Chinese society has developed the kind of intellectual space in which such a process can unfold.

Norwegian Wood and Honest Poverty

Let us look at the Chinese-language editions of the novels of Haruki Murakami, who enjoys enormous popularity in China. Tokyo University Professor Shozo Fujii studies the work of Murakami and observes—

The Murakami craze in the Chinese-speaking world began with the publication of *Norwegian Wood* in Taiwan in 1989. In Taiwan, the Murakami craze gave birth to the Taiwanese buzzword *Feichang Cunshang,* or "Very Murakami." Two years later, the book was published in Hong Kong. Ten years later, the enormous success of the novel in the Chinese-speaking world continued with the appearance of Chinese editions of *Norwegian Wood* in Shanghai and Beijing. From Taiwan to Hong Kong, Hong Kong to Shanghai, Shanghai to Beijing. Like the hands of a clock, the Murakami phenomenon wound its way through the Chinese-speaking world. In Taiwan and Hong Kong, the Murakami craze broke out as economic growth halved after two decades of economic growth. In China, the Murakami boom began in the late 1990s, just as high economic growth, spurred on by the re-acceleration of economic reforms, began to show signs of slowing down. Readers' enthusiastic reception of Murakami became an indication of a maturing urban society.[3]

Norwegian Wood was the Chinese-speaking world's first introduction to the works of Murakami. Originally published in 1987 in Japan, Murakami's novel quickly became a best seller in its home country. In mainland China, translations of *Norwegian Wood* were published in 1989 by both Lijiang Publishing House and the Northern China Literature and Art Publishing House. However, the latter edition featured a suggestive cover picture of a woman sitting alone at a bar and the subtitle "a young girl's farewell to the world." Murakami's novels were thus originally treated much like pornographic novels. The early Chinese translations of the novel also left much to be desired: for example, a reference in the text to "Hey Jude" was simply rendered phonetically in Chinese, not in a form that Chinese readers would recognize as the title of the Beatles song

In the 1980s, Japanese movies made their way to China, where Japanese actors like Ken Takakura became superstars. Japanese singers such as Masashi Sada, Hideki Saijo, and the folk group Alice began performing in Beijing. Popular television shows like the NHK series *Oshin* debuted in China, and Japanese anime, including *Ikkyu-san* and *Astro Boy*, also proved popular. This was the first period in which ordinary Chinese could experience Japanese arts and culture. Japanese novels, however, were slower to appear in China. The primary reason for this delay was the dearth of skilled Chinese translators and lack of copyright protection.

The latter problem was addressed with the June 1991 implementation of China's first copyright act, a move that allowed the Chinese translations of foreign novels to finally take off. In 1992, the pace of reform accelerated following Deng Xiaoping's Southern Tour, in which the aging leader launched China on a course of rapid economic development. Shortly thereafter, Murakami's novels began to be widely read in China.

By the end of the 1990s, China had become an avid consumer of Japanese novels. When books won Japan's prestigious Akutagawa and Naoki prizes for fiction, the Chinese translations would appear within a year, faster than they appeared in English in most cases. At the same time, the Chinese government began restricting the import of Japanese anime and movies, including those that had proved most popular in the 1980s; the number of Japanese movies shown at Chinese movie theaters decreased.

The Murakami boom is perhaps the best example of the enormous appeal that many Chinese saw in Japanese fiction. Murakami has gained an avid following in China, winning countless Chinese readers. His work is also admired in literary circles, where *Norwegian Wood* was evaluated not as a mere story of youth but as a more complicated tale that instilled a sense of justice and morality in an absurd, irrational world. The empathy-inspiring loneliness, sense of helplessness, and urban sensibilities of Murakami's characters resonated strongly with Chinese readers and critics.

In 2015, the Shanghai Translation Publishing House issued revised editions of many Murakami novels. Most of these new editions, such as *The Wind-up Bird Chronicle*, *Kafka on the Shore*, and *After Dark*, were post-1990 Murakami novels that exceeded 4 million characters in length.

Chinese translator Lin Shaohua, a professor at the Ocean University of China in Qingdao, says that when he first began translating Murakami, he would summarize numerous portions of the text. This was because a direct translation of the original text would have failed to make sense to Chinese readers at the time. Twenty years later, however, Chinese readers are capable of engaging and understanding Murakami's novels in their original form. Today, translators cannot omit a single word of the original text. *Norwegian Wood* is no longer associated with pornographic novels; it is regarded as a literary masterpiece. Lin believes that *Norwegian Wood* will continue to be widely read in China.[4]

Another book that became a best seller in China was Koji Nakano's *Seihin no Shisho*, often rendered in English as *The Philosophy of Honest Poverty*. This book was originally published by Soshisha Publishing Company in 1992, immediately after the collapse of Japan's bubble economy. In the book, Nakano discusses such figures of classical Japanese literature as Heian-era poet Saigyo Hoshi, 14th-century essayist Yoshida Kenko, and haiku master Matsuo Basho, and urges readers to follow in their footsteps by relinquishing material desires in favor of enriching the spirit. Nakano's book became a best seller in Japan, with the term "honest poverty" suddenly catching on in a nation that faced collapsing stock and real estate markets.

In 1997, a Chinese translation of *The Philosophy of Honest Poverty* was published by Beijing's Joint Publishing Company. While the initial response from Chinese readers was not unfavorable, the book suddenly began to receive frequent coverage in Chinese magazines and newspapers starting in about 2013, as China's own economy slowed. Seemingly overnight, honest poverty, pronounced *qingpin* in Chinese, became a frequently used term on social networking services. In January 2015, China Youth Press released a revised translation. As one Chinese commentator noted, "This book is a Japanese self-portrait. It contains many lessons that we [Chinese] must now learn."[5]

The Chinese began reading *The Philosophy of Honest Poverty* two decades after it was originally published in Japan. In fact, interest in the book surged just as the so-called binge shopping tours, in which rich Chinese tourists flocked to Japan to buy everything from luxury European watches to Japanese-made rice cookers, were beginning to wane. This was no coincidence. As China's once red-hot economy slowed, many Chinese began to show more interest in Japan as a place to enrich their souls rather than just fill their shopping bags.

Interestingly, even as China's economy has slowed, the number of tourists visiting Japan continues to grow. Many of these Chinese tourists are now coming in search of rich experiences. I once joined a tour of Kyoto that catered to wealthy Chinese tourists. Most of my fellow tour participants had read *The Philosophy of Honest Poverty*; the goal of the tour was to help them put the book's teachings into practice. Many had come on a Buddhist-inspired "Meditative Contemplation Tour of Japan," in which they spent a full day practicing Zen and meditating over tea at Kyoto's Daitokuji Temple. They told me they were enormously satisfied with the experience, notwithstanding the ¥900,000, or almost $9,000, price tag for the four-night, five-day tour.

Once again, Japan seems to be pointing the way for Chinese in search of understanding the changes within their own country. More than 20 years after the burst of the Japanese economic bubble, China may be reaching a similar juncture after their own years of double-digit growth. Two decades after Japanese readers began to question the meaning of growth, consumption, and material wealth, Chinese readers are turning to *The Philosophy of Honest Poverty* to make their own, similar self-examination.

Private Initiatives in Cultural Exchange

The current, new phase in the Chinese discovery of Japan has also been marked by a shift away from previous top-down, state-led initiatives.

Until recently, Chinese attempts at understanding Japan had been fundamentally state-led endeavors. This was true even of academic research and cultural exchanges. An example was the visit in 1984 of some 3,000 young Japanese, who came to China at the invitation of the general secretary of the Communist Party at the time, Hu Yaobang. This was a classic example of top-down cultural exchange, and one component of the Chinese government's policy toward Japan. This state-orchestrated exchange was very different from the current surge in Chinese tourism, which reflects a bottom-up, grassroots curiosity about Japan.

The same is true of academic research. The Chinese Academy of Social Sciences, a research organization under the State Council, the highest organ of China's central government, established an Institute of Japanese Studies in 1981. This official think tank has set the agenda in Chinese academic work on Japan from the early days of China's economic reform period and still conducts research projects commissioned by the Chinese government. In this sense, the institute continues to manage the efforts to interpret Japan by major universities and policy research institutes.

At the same time, there have also been more organic efforts to understand Japan, which take place not in the official spheres of academia and think tanks but in the domain of popular culture and mass consumption.

This popular interest in Japan took shape as part of a broader growth in interest in foreign cultures that spread in Chinese society in the lead-up to the 2008 Beijing Olympics. As it prepared to enter the global spotlight as host to international athletes and spectators, China experienced a surge of interest in the outside world, including Japan. This rising popular fascination with Japan built upon the already growing embrace of Japanese literature among Chinese intellectuals. The result was a boom in production of Japan-related books by the Chinese publishing world that began in the late 2000s and shows no signs of abating; in 2013 alone, more than 2,000 Japan-related titles appeared in bookstores or online. The majority of readers are young Chinese.

I have experienced this boom firsthand. In January 2011, I launched *Zhiri (Know Japan)*, a monthly magazine in Chinese that aims to introduce personalities and trends in Japanese popular culture and arts to mainly young Chinese readers. Since then, I have served as editor in chief of the magazine, whose circulation by the end of 2015 had reached 3 million.[6]

China's enormous population size can give publications on a popular theme sales figures that can seem large in comparison with Japan or even the United States. But that is not the only factor to explain the boom in publications about Japan. Oddly enough, the structure of censorship in China's publishing world also favors the promotion of books and magazines about the society and culture of foreign countries.

Unlike movies or music, books and other publications from abroad are legally permitted to be imported and published in China free of direct government control. The reality, of course, is that they remain subject to state examination and censorship. China's state-managed publishing houses include an internal department widely referred to as "the Dharma's eye." The staff of this department read through an enormous volume of potential publications in search of any content that might conflict with the official government stance on such potentially sensitive subjects as religion, politics, the military, finance, economics, and foreign relations. When any questionable content is discovered, "the Dharma's eye" sends a report to the relevant officials to seek their guidance. For instance, potentially sensitive references to religious matters are referred to the State Administration for Religious Affairs, while questions about foreign policy matters go to the Ministry of Foreign Affairs, and so on. If authorities deem the subject matter to be problematic, these portions of the imported text cannot be published.

To avoid such heavy-handed interference, publishers dislike taking on publications with delicate themes. This helps to explain the popularity of publications like my own, which introduce popular culture in other countries and have little to do with sensitive themes directly related to China's domestic politics.

Popular efforts to understand Japan also help explain the rapid growth in the number of ordinary Chinese citizens traveling to Japan as tourists. Of course, the depreciation of the yen since 2012 played a role, making once-expensive Japan far more affordable to regular Chinese citizens. But this is only part of the story. There has also been a discovery of a Japan that is very different from what they were taught in school and that resonates with China's own spiritual and cultural aspirations.

When Chinese come to Japan, they often experience it as a storehouse of an older spiritual culture that has its roots in China but that China has since lost. For instance, many Chinese have started visiting Mount Koya, a Buddhist holy mountain near the ancient Japanese capital of Nara. They stay in priests' lodgings and rise early to read scripture, copy sutras by hand, and experience the meditation methods of the Shingon sect of Buddhism. They have also been permitted to attend the rites performed in the inner sanctum of the temple, where food is offered to a statue of Shingon's founder, a Japanese monk named Kukai who died in 835.

Part of Kukai's appeal lies in the fact that he traveled to China in the early ninth century to bring back the latest Buddhist teachings from the Imperial Chinese court. China was then in the Tang dynasty, now regarded as a high-water mark of Imperial Chinese influence, when the nation was a global center of not just wealth and material power but philosophy and religious thought.

China has lost much of its history to the more recent upheavals of the Cultural Revolution and the headlong rush toward economic development. What is left in China is only what the officials want preserved. But as China has grown wealthier, ordinary Chinese have felt a growing urge to recover some of that vanished past. They have found some vestiges of old China abroad, preserved in neighboring countries that were influenced by China in the past. What is more, these surviving traces of old China seem more authentic, since they were not preserved by official decree but as living parts of those societies. There is now a saying in China: "If you want to see the Tang and Song dynasties, go to Japan. To see the Ming and Qing dynasties, go to South Korea. To see the pre-1949 Republic of China, go to Taiwan."

To find vestiges of their own past, the Chinese must travel. So much of what China once had—and lost—can still be discovered in nations like Japan and South Korea. This is part of the appeal of Japan. Chinese visitors can encounter remnants of their own nation's Tang and Song dynasties that have been preserved, absorbed, and developed by generations of Japanese. This rediscovery inspires feelings of nostalgia in Chinese visitors, experienced as pangs of both pride and loss. These emotional reactions may be the stirrings of desire for a new and more authentic Chinese identity.

There has always been a complex interplay of cultural borrowings between China and Japan. At roughly the same time when Kukai was seeking Chinese Buddhism, Japan was also importing China's written characters into its own language. As a result, both countries can be said to belong to a wider region sharing the cultural legacy of Chinese characters. However, the flow of linguistic change and innovation has not been just one way.

There have been times when Japan has "reexported" Chinese characters back to China. The first such wave occurred after Japan's Meiji Restoration in the mid-19th century, when the nation opened to the West and successfully transformed itself into Asia's leader in science and industrialization. As it rushed to absorb new concepts in science, governance, and society from the West, Japan invented novel combinations of Chinese characters to express such terms as "human rights," "duty," "philosophy," "economy," "separation of powers," "parliament," and "consumption." These new combinations of Chinese characters then made their way to China, which was also struggling, less successfully, to respond to the West's supremacy.[7] Chinese also began to use these newly coined words: approximately 70 percent of the specialized terms now used in the social sciences and humanities in China originally came from Japan.

Today, there is a second wave of Japanese language exports to China. However, this wave is very different from its 19th-century predecessor. The Japanese words being exported to China today do not come from the West but from Japan's own popular culture. Young Chinese now use words like "*kala OK*," a phonetic rendering of karaoke created by adding two Chinese characters to the Roman letters O and K, and "*yuzhaizu*," a literal translation of the Japanese slang term "*otaku*," or "geek."

The Appeal of Decluttering

The word *danshari*, or "decluttering," is the title of a 2009 book by Hideko Yamashita, published by Magazine House. Yamashita's book was widely discussed in the media and went on to become a social phenomenon in Japan. The term *danshari*, a neologism composed of three Chinese characters meaning refusal, disposal, and separation, is a call for a simpler, unencumbered way of life. As the name suggests, *danshari* is a rejection of modern materialism rooted in a refusal to buy extraneous things, a willingness to dispose of unnecessary items, and an embrace of a deeper spiritual separation from both material possessions and the culture of consumption that they represent.

Danshari is about far more than simply ridding oneself of unneeded possessions. It involves opening one's eyes to one's surroundings in order to gain a clearer view of oneself and a heightened sense of self-affirmation. A number of Chinese students living in Japan were influenced by this new thinking, which extends into the smallest nooks and crannies of one's personal lifestyle. Their interest may be explained by the crowded, cluttered dormitories in which Chinese students typically reside. Reading Yamashita's book gave these students the resolve to clean up their personal space and in the process find a new sense of self-worth.

Their embrace of *danshari* can only be explained by the fact that decluttering seemed relevant to their own lifestyles and aspirations. This was not a concept from a remote and more advanced society but something that resonated with their own experiences in a direct and compelling manner. These Chinese students found the book to be describing their lives as they lived them, and it equipped them with a new and emotionally meaningful view of life. These students then introduced the concept of decluttering to other Chinese, who also found the message appealing.[8]

This is not an unusual pattern. Chinese residents of Japan often act as cultural intermediaries, conveying resonant aspects of Japanese culture to a broader audience back in China. On social media, they can be seen relaying the thrills and joys of discovering even the small details of life in Japan. They serve not only as conduits of the latest social trends but also as interpreters of how Japanese culture can improve and enrich the lives of themselves and by extension other Chinese.

"The Chinese Binge Shop. The Japanese Declutter." This was the title of an essay published in a Chinese newspaper by a Chinese writer living in Japan who goes by the pen name "Hot Pepper." The essay helped launch China's own decluttering boom. Yamashita became so popular in China that she visited the country and held book-signing events at major bookstores.[9]

Several books on decluttering have been published to a warm reception by Chinese readers. Another is Marie Kondo's *The Life-Changing Magic of Tidying Up: The Japanese Art of Decluttering and Organizing*, which sold more than 5 million copies worldwide and has been translated into 31 languages.[10] Her book also proved enormously popular among Chinese readers, who embraced her advice to gather all objects of a certain kind in a single place and to ask themselves whether these objects "spark joy."

In China as in other countries, the appeal of Yamashita and Kondo lies in the fact that both were able to elevate the act of cleaning into an expression of philosophical or even spiritual purpose, in which tidying one's personal space reflected an unfettering of the soul. Both women showed their readers how even daily tasks could be filled with a deeper meaning. This was a message that resonated with Chinese readers, who were finding their own society too obsessed with consumption and accumulation of material wealth. Yamashita and Kondo gave their Chinese readers a model lifestyle, a philosophy of life, a source of joy, and a mode of self-discipline and self-improvement that made as much sense in China as it did back in Japan.

The search for something philosophical or spiritual has become an increasingly common goal of Chinese visitors to Japan. According to Peach Aviation's chief executive officer, Shinichi Inoue, "Hong Kong tourists fly to Japan on Peach Airlines to visit peach orchards in Wakayama Prefecture in search of 'the Land of the Peach Blossom Spring' [an East Asian version of Arcadia or Eden]. They message their friends and family back in Hong Kong on social media, who in turn come to Japan in search of the same. Tourists from both Hong Kong and mainland China arrive in Japan looking for this type of healing-travel experience."[11]

Inoue said he was surprised to learn that Chinese tourists are content to visit simple peach orchards, not Japan's more heavily promoted tourist attractions.

"I think there is often a mismatch between the needs of foreign visitors and Japanese expectations of what tourists want," Inoue said. "By deftly matching these needs and expectations we can rapidly expand the frontier for inbound tourism."

A Japanese Feline Wins Over Chinese Hearts

On January 5, 2007, a cat named Tama became the official station master of a small railway station in Wakayama Prefecture, not far from Osaka. This was a lifelong position; the primary purpose of Tama's job was to attract tourists, for which she was compensated with a lifetime supply of cat food. Tama proved a huge success, winning widespread attention in Japan's national news media. Her story warmed the hearts of many in China as well.

Tama was much reported upon in the Chinese press, in books, and in the magazine *Zhiri*. Following Tama's death in the summer of 2015, many books and magazine articles on the furry station master were reissued. While Tama was a phenomenon in her native Japan, her reception in China was arguably even more significant. That an entirely ordinary Japanese feline could inspire such attention and empathy in China represented an unprecedented development in cultural exchanges between the two countries.

Why was Tama so popular in China? Her story reflects the growing desire of many in China to scour Japan's popular culture for deeper meanings and for clues to filling the spiritual and cultural shortcomings they feel in their own growth-obsessed society. When confronted with the spectacle of Tama's popularity in Japan, many in China embraced the story of the feline station chief as well, hoping to find more clues for deciphering what they find so appealing in Japan.

In particular, Tama became a vehicle for discovering the Japanese popular-culture concept of *moe*, a word that originally referred to the sprouting of new plants. Within Japanese popular culture, however, the word is used to express the infatuation inspired by the cute characters in anime, manga, game software, and in this case, a station cat. The interest in *moe* comes as related popular culture concepts such as *iyashi*, the feeling of emotional comfort or "healing" that a cute character can produce, have also taken hold among China's youth.

Asia's Rediscovery of Japan

The appeal of Japanese popular culture among so many of China's youth may lie in the fact that it feels to them closer and more familiar, and thus more accessible, than does the popular culture of the West. Japan seems to point the way to a more meaningful present for many people in China and other Asian countries who are starting to catch up with or even surpass Japan's levels of material wealth. For this reason, this discovery—or rediscovery—of the common cultural ground that Japan shares with its neighbors, particularly China and South Korea, will have a significant impact on Japan's relations with the region.

In March 2016, a South Korean master of the game Go, Lee Se-dol, made history by facing off in Seoul against a computer program called AlphaGo. Go is an ancient game of strategy, originating in China, that is played with slightly different rules in South Korea and Japan. In this case, Chinese rules were applied in the five-match showdown, in which AlphaGo ultimately defeated Lee, four matches to one. On one level, the victory of AlphaGo, a form of artificial intelligence capable of "deep learning," marked the triumph of machine over man, an outcome that was as thrilling as it was unsettling.

But the match had another, unanticipated consequence. It became an opportunity for Japan, China, and South Korea to rediscover something in common.

Following AlphaGo's victory, Joichi "Joi" Ito, the director of the Media Lab at the Massachusetts Institute of Technology, said, "Go has never been so exciting. Membership in the MIT Go club doubled overnight."[12] There are reportedly more than 340 million Go players worldwide, mostly in East Asia. Until now, they have shown little interest in creating organizations that stretch outside their national borders or transcend the national differences in game rules. But AlphaGo's defeat of a human competitor has sparked a sudden sense of shared community among Go players, raising awareness of the common cultural heritage of Japan, China, and South Korea.

A Fascination Gap

Looking toward the future, what is the trajectory of this Asian rediscovery of Japan, and what does this mean for Japan?

From a Chinese perspective, one trend that I foresee is a growing imbalance in what might be called the fascination gap. In particular, while China will show continuing or even rising levels of fascination in Japan, Japan has not shown the same positive interest in China.

The Japanese columnist Kei Nakajima reports being both surprised and delighted by the number of books on Japan that she discovered during a recent visit to a bookstore in China.[13] As discussed above, there is a proliferation of books about Japan, many from a very positive standpoint. Regrettably, there are very few Japanese bookstores that feature similar books on China. The books on China that are prominently displayed in Japanese bookstores tend to be alarmist or negative in tone. Many dwell on China's growing assertiveness and nationalism and present China as a threat. This characterization is not baseless. Viewed from Japan, or elsewhere in the outside world, the youth of China may appear nationalistic, self-centered, and materialistic.

Yet it is equally true that young Chinese are intensely interested in foreign cultures and starving for opportunities to experience them firsthand. Today, they are greedily taking every opportunity to do so. And they are just as interested in Japan as in the West.

My fear is that young Japanese do not seem to share this intense interest in Chinese culture—or in any other foreign culture, for that matter.

During its 19th-century opening to the world, and again after World War II, Japan's development was fueled by a deep intellectual interest in the outside world and active efforts to absorb foreign cultures. By contrast, today's Japan is turning inward in an attempt to rediscover its own culture and values. This is not in itself a bad thing—far from it. The rediscovery of what is worthwhile in the past, and the creation of values and lifestyles based on that, can be a constructive process. And Japan's new cultural trends are indeed eliciting increasing interest from China and the rest of the world, as I have discussed.

If I were to offer one suggestion, it would be for Japan not to make this inward turn come at the expense of its curiosity about the outside world. Just as China is looking to Japan for hints and ideas for forging a new, more prosperous, and more spiritually balanced modern, middle-class society, so should Japan continue to look abroad for its own inspiration and stimulus. Japan's own history shows us that development and improvement come through the dynamic, complex interplay of internal and external perspectives. Shutting itself off from the world would result in a true stagnation of Japan.

Notes

1. Yan Jiefu, "Can We Still Learn from Japan Today?" *The Economic Observer* (in Chinese), May 27, 2016.

2. Wang Taiping, "Thirty-Six Years On, Why Is *Japan as Number One* So Popular?" *China Reading Weekly* (in Chinese), May 22, 2016.

3. Shozo Fujii, *Higashi Ajia ga Yomu Murakami Haruki* (Tokyo: Wakakusa Shobō, 2009), p. 3.

4. Lin Shaohua, "China and the Literature of Murakami Haruki," *Shenzhen Shangbao* (in Chinese), June 1, 2015.

5. Li Zhangsheng, "Honest Poverty Is the Start of a New Ideology," *Caijing* (in Chinese), posted May 4, 2016, http://magazine.caijing.com.cn/20160504/4114899 .shtml.

6. Launching *Zhiri* was not smooth sailing. The general lack of interest in a magazine about Japan by China's national publishing houses was the primary reason for the magazine's rocky start, but the dearth of veteran editors who believed they could profit from a Japan-related publication was another reason. *Zhiri* changed publishers three times in just one year. Strictly speaking, China does not have private publishing houses but rather private "publication planning" companies. These planning companies can only publish if they first contract with a state-managed publishing house and receive a permitted publication number certifying the legality of their publication. In order to obtain this permitted publication number, they pay administrative costs to the state-managed publisher. State-managed publishing houses are supported by government funds, but such payments have increased their revenue in recent years.

7. Sun Jianjun, *Kindai Nihongo no Kigen—Bakumatsu Meiji shoki ni Tsukurareta Shinkango* (Tokyo: Waseda University Press, 2015), pp. 287–295.

8. *Zhiri* dedicated its July 2013 edition to the subject of *danshari*. The magazine's cover featured the characters for *danshari* in a metallic type. In order to convey the subject's relationship to lifestyle, the words for *danshari* were depicted as if written with a lead pencil, creating an almost three-dimensional effect.

9. Tang Xinzi, "The Chinese Binge Shop. The Japanese Declutter," *Tengxun Dajia* (in Chinese), posted March 3, 2016, http://dajia.qq.com/original/japan/txz 20160303.html?pgv_ref=aio2015&ptlang=2052.

10. "The 100 Most Influential People," *Time*, April 16, 2015.

11. Shinichi Inoue, speaking at Asia Pacific Initiative, April 22, 2016.

12. Joichi Ito, speaking at Asia Pacific Initiative, May 16, 2016.

13. Kei Nakajima, "Chugoku no Shoten ga 'Shinnichi' De Aru no ni wa Wake ga Aru," *Toyo Keizai Online*, posted June 15, 2016, http://toyokeizai.net/articles/- /72968.

PART 3

Global Contributor

CHAPTER EIGHT

Lessons of Tohoku: The Sources of Japan's Resilience to Disaster

Daniel P. Aldrich

When a magnitude 9.0 earthquake struck off northeastern Japan on March 11, 2011, it unleashed a towering tsunami that left more than 18,400 people dead or missing and destroyed communities along 500 kilometers of coastline. Hundreds of thousands of homes, businesses, and factories were destroyed or literally swept away. Half a million survivors relocated to temporary shelters, a mass evacuation made even larger by the meltdowns at the Fukushima Daiichi Nuclear Power Plant.

Despite such devastation, a handful of communities were able to bounce back and rebuild within as little as two years. One was Rifu, a small town near the city of Sendai in Miyagi Prefecture that lost nearly half of its structures, including most of its downtown, to the tsunami. By March 2013, the town had cleaned up some 15,000 tons of debris, restored essential public services including police and fire, and repaired or replaced most of its destroyed homes.[1] Rifu was even able to grow, adding an additional 2,000 residents to its predisaster population of 34,000, an accomplishment even in the best of circumstances for one of Japan's demographically challenged rural areas. Rifu was one of only three communities out of the 42 towns and cities damaged by the tsunami that have seen their population increase since the disaster.[2]

This swift rebound stands in contrast to most other towns and cities in Japan's disaster-struck northeastern Tohoku region, where populations have on average declined by 15 percent since the triple disaster of earthquake, tsunami, and nuclear accident. The worst-hit towns around the Fukushima nuclear plant remain uninhabited years after the accident. But even in towns near the plant where evacuation orders have been lifted, such as Naraha, only 10 percent of the population has returned.

In sociological terms, we would describe Rifu as being resilient, that is, able to rebound from crisis and quickly resume the rhythms of daily life. To some degree, all of northeastern Japan demonstrated a remarkable resilience to the devastation of the 2011 tsunami, as Tohoku's residents bore their losses with a quiet fortitude that won sympathy and admiration around the world. However, cases such as Rifu's show that the ability to overcome disaster was not uniformly shared across the region. Rather, the speed of revival appears to spring from not just a broadly shared national culture but specific attitudes and practices within particular communities and the nature of their interactions with the broader national polity. Identifying the sources of their swift recovery will point to some of the most important lessons that disaster-resilient Japan has to offer the rest of the world.

Resilient Japan

Like other nations sitting on the Pacific's Ring of Fire, Japan is no stranger to calamity. The 1923 Great Kanto earthquake destroyed nearly half of Tokyo, killing an estimated 140,000 people. Seventy years later, more than 6,000 people died in the port city of Kobe as a result of the 1995 Hanshin Awaji earthquake. Nor are all of Japan's recent catastrophes natural in origin. During World War II, Allied bombers leveled most major Japanese cities, including Tokyo, and incinerated Hiroshima and Nagasaki with a terrifying new weapon. All told, natural and manmade disasters have cost Japan more than a million lives over the past century and inflicted destruction costing the equivalent of hundreds of billions if not trillions of today's dollars.

Yet, time and time again, Japan has recovered to continue its remarkable development into one of the world's most advanced and prosperous industrialized nations. Cities like Tokyo, Hiroshima, and Nagasaki have risen from the ashes to become thriving urban centers. How Japan has achieved this remains open to debate. Many have argued that a national culture—some constellation of shared beliefs, language, experience, and education—make Japan uniquely more resilient. This was evident in commentary after the 2011 disaster, when journalists and scholars frequently cited culture to explain the stoic self-restraint of Tohoku residents, seen in the patience of victims waiting hours for food and water or the lack of crime in disrupted communities. Reporters regularly pointed out differences with postdisaster behavior in other parts of the world, such as New Orleans, where reports of looting were widespread. Perhaps the most common version of this cultural argument holds that Japan's location on a number of active seismic faults has made its population more resigned to the possibility of losing everything in a moment's notice once the ground starts to shake.

However, such broad-brush explanations miss important details of Tohoku's response to the 2011 catastrophe. While outside observers have praised the forbearance of Tohoku's survivors, the region has actually seen a flourishing of political protest, often in the form of music and art expressing anger with the central government and the Fukushima plant's operator, Tokyo Electric Power Company, or Tepco. By the same token, there has also been wide variation in the abilities of individuals and communities to bounce back from the devastation.

These differences are most evident in the large and growing discrepancies in recovery rates seen among the villages, towns, and cities across Tohoku struck by the tsunami. Visit some communities today, more than six years after the disaster, and life has returned to something close to normal. Students attend schools, residents live in their own homes, convenience stores are open, and city halls bustle with citizens engaged in the mundane tasks of filing taxes or claiming pensions. However, step across the border into a neighboring town and it is not uncommon to enter a very different world: residents still in emergency housing, empty fields where neighborhoods and downtowns once stood, and city halls set up in temporary locations that remain eerily empty. These disparities are also evident in data on 40 disaster-hit communities in Tohoku gathered by the National Institute for Research Advancement, a government-established think tank in Tokyo. Comparing statistics on debris removal, business restarts, infrastructure repairs, and restoration of bus and train lines two years after the disaster, I found that while some communities like Rifu had fully recovered to predisaster levels, others had succeeded in restoring only 40 percent of their businesses, schools, and transportation.[3]

Such inconsistent rates of recovery were also evident following Japan's other past crises. After Japan's wartime defeat in 1945, some prefectures proved themselves better able than others to regain a peacetime normalcy by resuming regular mail service, reopening schools and shops, and restoring health and other services.[4] Similarly, different recovery paths also appeared after the 1995 Kobe earthquake. This was seen not only in reconstruction of dwellings and other physical infrastructure but also in rates of emotional recovery. Some residents were able to overcome the stress by creating new narratives in which the disaster was a challenge to overcome and learn from. Others, however, struggled to overcome the trauma, reliving the disaster in their minds while failing to focus on the present.[5]

No one-size-fits-all answer, like national culture, can account for these variations. What, then, can explain the speedy recoveries demonstrated by Japan's most resilient communities?

The answers appear to lie in two important social factors that are separate but often intimately connected. The first is the cohesiveness of local communities. By this, I am talking about the connections within a society that bind together its residents or that link them to decision makers at local, regional, and national levels. These connections are a form of social capital that are built through regular interaction and the creation of trust. Communities with high levels of such social capital are more likely to collaborate in resolving problems and to come to shared conclusions about challenges and their solutions. Even in relatively homogenous Japan, the levels of trust, communication, and bonding can vary widely between communities.

The second is the quality of governance. No matter how cohesive, a local community can achieve only so much if forced to stand alone, if for no other reason than it often faces extreme constraints on capital and other resources, particularly in the aftermath of a devastating disaster. The speed of its recovery can be determined by the ability of local or national political institutions to allocate resources in a timely and effective manner. Despite sometimes unimaginative policy responses, Japan has often shown itself capable of solid and responsive governance in the aftermath of disasters. When it has failed, as many argue happened after the Kobe earthquake due to extreme stovepiping and petty turf fights between government ministries, Japan's decision makers have shown themselves able to learn from those failures, as we shall see below.

Deemphasizing cultural explanations also allows us to find what is transferrable to other nations in Japan's experiences, and particularly in the ability of some of its disaster-hit communities to rebound quickly. One of the biggest lessons of 2011 was not only the importance of the ties that bind but the fact that communities can actually take steps to strengthen such connections in order to increase their resilience to disaster. Using the experiences of the Tohoku earthquake, groups in Japan such as nongovernmental organizations have created community-building programs aimed at fostering the development of such social capital. These programs are now being used not only within Japan but also in other disaster-struck nations to help them rebuild and become more resilient to future catastrophes.

As we shall see, another takeaway from the 2011 disaster is the importance of not only effective governmental response but also of more bottom-up, decentralized efforts to empower victims and communities. This was seen in energy policy. Local governments in Fukushima and elsewhere in Tohoku have pushed into cleaner solar and wind energy sources despite Tokyo's insistence on restarting unpopular nuclear plants. A similar movement toward democratization is also evident in the so-called citizen's science that has proliferated in Fukushima since the nuclear accident, as new nongovernmental organizations have taught residents how to measure radiation with do-it-yourself Geiger counter kits.

Social Connections Save Lives

If there is a single, compelling lesson to take away from Japan's experiences during March 2011, it is that social ties save lives. Nowhere is this more evident than in the testimony of survivors such as a farmer in the coastal town of Watari, just south of Sendai, whom we shall call Mitsuhide Wakasugi. (He asked that his actual name not be used.) Wakasugi says he is alive only because of the actions of relatives and neighbors long before the arrival of professional rescuers.

Wakasugi, a man in his late seventies, was working in his greenhouse sowing carrot seeds when the earth began shaking at 2:46 p.m. on Friday, March 11. He tried to hold the structure to stay upright but was soon knocked to the ground until the shaking subsided. He, like a number of other evacuees with whom I spoke, was not immediately aware of the impending tsunami and did not hear any sirens, cell-phone warnings, or radio announcements. "I knew the disaster prevention alarm was announcing something, but other noises interfered, and I couldn't catch the announcement at all," he said.[6]

Wakasugi has a disability that prevents him from being able to walk without assistance, and he stood up and slowly used a walker to return to his home. He and his wife went inside, unsure of what to do. He told me:

The first person who came to my house was my sister, and she told me, "Brother, we have to evacuate." And I told her "I'll catch up later so you go on and escape on your own," and let her escape before me. And then, young officials from the neighborhood association (*chonaikai*) came to my house and told us to evacuate. They were standing in front of our entrance telling us to evacuate. And that moment, I saw in front of our house, around 150 meters ahead, a lot of water running through the area carrying cars and many other things.

The tsunami was rushing toward them. The Wakasugis got into their car to flee but were surrounded by water almost as soon as they closed the doors. The waves stalled the car's engine and threatened to carry the vehicle away. To escape, the Wakasugis broke one of the car's windows, only to find themselves marooned by the water swirling around them. It was then that they were rescued by a younger member of the neighborhood association who himself had clambered onto a nearby roof for safety.

"This young man saw us from the roof, and he came down from the roof and carried us both on his back from the car and helped us," Wakasugi said. "We were saved because there was a third person, but if there were only two of us, then we might've not been able to make it, for sure." The man carried the Wakasugis back into their house and up to the second floor to stay above the water. There they spent a cold, miserable night. The next day, a Self-Defense Force helicopter arrived to transport them to a nearby hospital. Only then did Wakasugi learn that some 300 people from Watari had died in the tsunami.

Wakasugi's decision to flee, and he and his wife's survival after escaping from their car, were clearly the result of help from others—in other words, tight social connections. Nor was this an atypical case. I heard similar stories in dozens of interviews conducted across Tohoku following the disaster. I have become convinced that this is a key variable for understanding one of the most intriguing findings to come out of my research into the disaster and its aftermath: the widely varying death rates between communities.

According to data from the National Police Agency, while some Tohoku communities lost as much as one-tenth of their population to the tsunami, other communities suffered few or no deaths at all. These differences in mortality rates appeared even between communities that had been struck by waves of the same size or that had been protected behind sea walls of the same height. To find out why, a colleague and I compared the communities by looking at possible factors such as average age, income levels, population density, coastal exposure, and quality of roads. We also conducted dozens of interviews. In community after community, we came to the same conclusion: it was trust and social ties that had saved lives. Neighborhoods where people made the effort to check in on and help each other had higher rates of survival, regardless of any other factor. Survivors told us time and time again that neighbors had saved their lives by providing crucial warnings and assistance. This was particularly true of the elderly and infirm, who were moved from their beds and wheelchairs to safety by relatives and neighbors.

In the communities with higher mortality rates, we found the opposite: residents did not check in on each other. Death rates were particularly higher among vulnerable groups.

To confirm the importance of social connections, we looked at predisaster crime rates in Tohoku communities, a widely accepted measure of levels of social capital. We found a direct correlation: the higher the predisaster crime rate, the higher the death rate during the disaster. In fact, predisaster crime rates proved a far more accurate predictor of disaster death rates than the height of a community's wave walls or whether it had taken other, more conventional measures to prepare itself for a tsunami.[7]

Social cohesion increases not only chances of survival but also the speed of recovery. This is seen in the case of Masayuki Kimura, a baker whose decision to rebuild his business in his devastated hometown of Rikuzentakata was made possible by social connections.

Rikuzentakata was a bustling fishing port in northern Miyagi Prefecture when the tsunami struck, killing 10 percent of its population of 23,000 and washing away 80 percent of its businesses. By any rational logic, Kimura admits he never should have come back. Not only did he have to rebuild his completely destroyed bakery from scratch, but staying in Rikuzentakata also meant he had to resume payments on the equivalent of $370,000 in business loans from before the disaster, making a profit unlikely, he said. Kimura said he considered starting afresh somewhere else, a decision made by other town residents, more than 1,200 of whom had left by the end of 2011.[8]

Nonetheless, Kimura decided within less than a year to restart his bakery in the town. In an interview with *The Wall Street Journal*, he said this was not a business decision but a show of support for his community. He said he was swayed by what he learned as a volunteer distributing supplies to evacuation shelters, where he overheard survivors longing for a return to their lives before the tsunami, including the flavors of foods from local stores and restaurants: "People are longing for our local taste," he concluded.[9]

He said he realized that reviving his bakery could encourage others to rebuild the community, where his family has deep roots. The bakery was started in 1926 by Kimura's grandfather, who later adopted Kimura's father into the family to inherit the enterprise. He also said he felt an obligation to his mother, who began telling other evacuees that she wanted to bake sweets for the community again.

When he did decide to rebuild, he said he received help from an unexpected quarter. Suppliers with whom he had worked before the disaster offered a secondhand oven and other baking equipment and ingredients free of charge, refusing to take his money when they found out that he was living in a shelter. Without such moral and financial support, he said it was unlikely that he would have been actually able to rebuild.

Over and over again across Tohoku, these kinds of connections determined not only whether residents lived or died but whether survivors could later return to rebuild their lives. While the popular assumption is often that disaster recovery is a function of external factors, such as the amount of aid from the government or severity of damage, the testimonies of Kimura and others like him show that loyalty to and support from communities could be more important.

Tellingly, villages with weak connections and low levels of trust saw their recovery process stalled. This was evident not only in Japan but also in New Orleans neighborhoods following Hurricane Katrina in August 2005. Some neighborhoods in the city, such as the highly cohesive Vietnamese community in Village de L'Est, were able to mobilize and return quickly. Members of the local Mary Queen of Vietnam Church community not only worked together regularly before the storm, they also created an outreach network to communicate with authorities and nongovernmental groups during the evacuation process. Other areas in the city lacked such internal cohesion and ability to connect to outside agencies and as a result were slower to return and rebuild.

The Lessons of Tohoku

The importance of social ties in saving lives and recovering from disaster has gained growing attention in Japan since 2011, leading to the creation of nongovernmental organizations that seek to strengthen such communal bonds. One is the Ibasho project, founded by architect Emi Kiyota. This group promotes an insight that Kiyota said she drew from the disaster: that the elderly should be seen as an asset for strengthening a community's resilience, not a liability. All too often, Kiyota said, the elderly were treated during the 2011 disaster as an extra burden on rescuers or as a target of social services into which they had no input.

Kiyota, who had done graduate research on nursing homes, said she came to view the elderly as an untapped resource that could help heal Tohoku's damaged communities. She said their deep roots in the community meant they could serve as an eager pool of volunteers to join in rebuilding. Just as importantly, their experience and relative calm could offer a rock of emotional stability in a time of disorienting dislocation and destruction. According to its Web site, Ibasho seeks to "create a better place, one where the elderly can be valued as human beings and give back to their communities."[10]

One result was the Ibasho House, which Kiyota helped create in 2012 in the tsunami-struck city of Ofunato. The house is a restored farmhouse with an open floor plan and outdoor area for activities. It provides a free gathering place for survivors of all ages, where they can eat at a volunteer-run café, meet friends, bring children, or do homework. It also provides free exercise classes for adults, cooking classes for seniors, field trips for schoolchildren, and events for mothers with young children, all organized and led by volunteers from the community. Many are elderly, who often have the time and relish the chance to interact with younger residents. In this way, the elderly play a leading role in helping the scarred community by building new communal bonds, says Ibasho.

"How can we reduce the vulnerability of elderly populations affected by disasters and empower them to strengthen resilience?" asks the group's Web site. The Ibasho approach "improves the community's ability to withstand shocks caused by natural hazards by creating a strong informal support system in which elders are the catalyst to strengthen social capital among community members of all ages."[11]

Ibasho also organizes volunteer work in the broader community in order to strengthen social ties. Volunteers help build shared spaces, such as communal rooms in apartment buildings, meeting areas in parks, and sidewalk spaces where people can gather to talk. To entice evacuees and residents to use these spaces, Ibasho has tried to make them more attractive by adding BBQ pits and benches as well as convenient parking. Ibasho also "pays" its volunteers in community currencies, which can be used at local stores and farmers' markets in Ofunato.[12]

To date, Ibasho has held more than 350 events with more than 11,000 participants. Their efforts seem to be paying off. In interviews, individuals who participated regularly in Ibasho events reported that they have built deeper ties with their community as measured through number of friends, involvement in activities, and a subjective sense of belonging. They were also more likely to express a belief that they can improve their environment than individuals who had no contact with the program.[13]

Ibasho's outcomes show that it is possible to deliberately create strong social ties that help rebuild a damaged community. Ibasho has been so successful that it is now seeking to take its methods overseas. In 2014, Ibasho launched a project in the Philippines to help the community of Bagong Buhay, in the city of Ormoc, recover from the devastation of Typhoon Yolanda a year earlier. Ibasho sent a team from Japan, partly funded by donations from the Ibasho House in Ofunato, to organize the community's elderly into such grassroots community-building efforts as recycling drives and the creation of communal vegetable plots. In the latter, local schoolchildren were invited to participate in the harvest. The intention was to help the disaster-struck community learn from the experiences of the Ibasho House in Ofunato and other projects in Japan, where the building of social ties and trust speeded recovery.

The Bagong Buhay project aims to "strengthen the social ties of elders in the community . . . by harnessing the elders' skills and experience to help mend a community traumatized by a natural disaster," according to Ibasho's Web site.[14] The Philippine effort has been so successful that Ibasho launched a similar project in Nepal after the 2015 earthquake there.

Good Governance Makes a Difference

So far, we have focused on social bonds within communities. Tohoku's experience shows that a community's connections with outside people and organizations can also speed recovery. Some of the most important are those between survivors and people in positions of authority, particularly in the government.

In my research of disaster-hit communities in Tohoku, I found one of the most telling indicators of a community's speed of recovery is its relationships with power holders in Tokyo. Specifically, towns and cities represented by established, long-serving members of the Diet, Japan's parliament, were better able to access the budgets and other resources needed to accelerate their recovery.[15] Similarly, towns whose native sons had become members of the cabinet or highly placed officeholders in the elite national bureaucracy also demonstrated greater success in winning central government approvals and funding for reconstruction plans.

The local leaders of Rikuzentakata, for example, immediately moved to connect with national political figures after the tsunami destroyed much of city, including its city hall. This effort was led by a local leader who had extensive domestic and international contacts through his past work at the United Nations and also at an investment bank. Rather than waiting for the government to reach out, he established a routine of weekly contact with the cabinet office by phone. One of his aims was to bypass the prefectural government to speed the flow of funding and other resources from Tokyo into Rikuzentakata. At the cabinet office's suggestion, this leader eventually established a nongovernmental organization to help communities build and maintain channels to the central government.

Such connections allowed Rikuzentakata to pursue an ambitious plan: to rebuild its downtown safely out of reach of future tsunamis by using landfill to elevate the ground level by some 14 meters. No other city in Tohoku has undertaken so monumental an earthmoving project, sheering off the tops of nearby mountains to gather the dirt, which was then transported via a three-kilometer, ¥12 billion conveyor belt. The partially leveled mountains have also become the site of new residential neighborhoods far above the reach of the sea.

This is not to say that Japan unfairly favors communities with the best connections within government. Rather, Rikuzentakata's experience points to the obvious but important fact that national governments must play a leading role in helping local areas rebuild because of their ability to command far greater financial and organizational resources. For this reason, systems of governance are important in aiding—or hindering—the resilience of local communities. In Japan, a democratic political system showed itself able to respond more effectively to large-scale disasters because it was sensitive to public needs. This made it superior to alternatives such as authoritarian or elite-serving systems, which may place a higher priority on protecting elite privilege over the popular welfare.

Another area in which the quality of governance can make a big difference is in survival rates. This linkage can be better seen in a negative example: the high mortality rates in the Indian state of Tamil Nadu during the 2004 Indian Ocean tsunami.

In India alone, that disaster on December 26 claimed more than 10,000 lives, mostly in Tamil Nadu, and forced tens of thousands more to evacuate. While India is a democracy, its governance systems lack financial and administrative transparency, and few of its coastal areas had invested in early warning systems. Further, few of the residents in Tamil Nadu with whom I spoke even knew the names of their government representatives or agents, and fewer yet reported having any kind of contact with them. Perhaps as a result, the government had taken few measures beforehand to protect citizens from such an event. Lacking early warning systems, most residents of the state's poor coastal fishing villages had no idea the tsunami was coming. The few who received advance warnings did so via informal channels, usually phone calls from family in distant urban areas who had access to television or radio.[16]

When the government did act, in the form of providing aid to survivors in the disaster's aftermath, these efforts were often hampered by a lack of the kinds of social bonds that I described earlier in Tohoku. In Tamil Nadu, the existence of strong ethnic and caste divisions excluded many from aid distribution lists, slowing down the region's recovery. Widows, Dalits, Muslims, and other peripheral social groups found it difficult to receive the same level of aid as members of the more dominant fishing caste.

Japan benefited from stronger social bonds and more responsive authorities. The relatively high quality of Japan's governance system is evident in a telling measure, the ability of its government officials to learn from past failures. As mentioned above, the national government was widely criticized after the 1995 Kobe earthquake for a slow, disorganized response that many blame for raising the death toll. In 2011, the government appeared to take the lesson to heart, reacting promptly by using all the resources at its command, including the military. While the government hesitated to use the Self-Defense Forces after the Kobe earthquake because of political sensitivities, the prime minister in 2011, Naoto Kan, quickly ordered 100,000 soldiers into the disaster zone, Japan's largest military mobilization since World War II. To centralize decision making, Kan set up an emergency headquarters at the prime minister's office in central Tokyo.

Another lesson learned was the decision by the government, via a newly created Reconstruction Agency, to set as its goal not *fukkyū*, or "reconstruction," but *fukkō*, or "renewal." This may sound like semantic quibbling, but the word choice in fact reflects a strategic decision by the government to focus not just on reconstructing roads and buildings, as officials did following past disasters, but also on restoring quality of life and mending communities. Such holistic approaches are also evident in decisions by local emergency management agencies across Japan to adopt the language of *gensai*, or "disaster mitigation," in place of the previous *bōsai*, or "disaster prevention."

The question of whether Japan's lessons of governance can be transferable to other countries is a tricky one. With its antiwar constitution and bitter experience during World War II, Japan has long avoided interfering politically in other countries, even in support of its main ally, the United States. While Japan remains one of the world's largest donors to developing countries, its billions of dollars in overseas aid have gone to civilian uses, such as economic assistance and technology transfer. However, the rise of China has pushed Japan to seek new, if still nonmilitary ways to expand its influence abroad and particularly in its own region.

In recent years, Japanese leaders have come to see disaster preparedness and recovery as a major field of international assistance in which their nation can take a leading role. Through its main aid agency, the Japan International Cooperation Agency, or JICA, Japan has provided not only grants and loans but also technical expertise on disaster mitigation. In Thailand, which lost some 8,000 people in the 2004 Indian Ocean tsunami, Japan has helped increase disaster preparedness at the community level by providing early warning systems, educating children, and conducting drills and workshops for residents. In Fiji, a Pacific island nation visited by frequent typhoons, Japan has helped to build early warning systems for floods and educate residents on what to do when they strike. Over the last decade, Japan has spent more than $300 million per year on disaster-related grants and technical assistance.

Disaster relief has also given Japan a chance to claim a larger regional and even global role in areas outside development aid. Following the 2013 typhoon in the Philippines, which killed more than 6,300 people and left half a million homeless, Japan responded with one of its largest overseas military deployments since World War II. Japan's Self-Defense Forces sent 1,000 personnel, 10 aircraft, and some of its largest warships, including the helicopter carrier *Ise*, on a relief mission that won praise in the Philippines. In March 2015, Japan was able to demonstrate leadership of a different sort by hosting more than 6,500 leaders, officials, and experts from around the world at the United Nations World Conference on Disaster Risk Reduction held in the city of Sendai, near the epicenter of the 2011 earthquake and tsunami.

According to Akihiko Tanaka, who served as president of JICA from 2012 to 2015, growing global attention on disaster preparation and response has offered Japan a chance to step forward as a global leader. "In specific fields of international cooperation, Japan has begun to use its own experiences to speak out more clearly in advising other countries on what to do," Mr. Tanaka said.[17]

Decentralization and Nongovernment Actors

However, just as national culture is not the sole creator of social cohesion, national governments are not the only actors with resources to help residents survive and recover. In fact, one of the key lessons from the

Tohoku disaster for both Japan and the world is the importance of non-state actors, including nongovernmental groups and private businesses as well as local governments.

One of the most effective early responses to the Tohoku disaster came from delivery companies like Yamato Transport, better known in Japan as Kuroneko Yamato for its black cat (*kuro neko*) logo. In normal times, companies like Yamato and rival Nippon Express operate some of the most efficient and reliable delivery networks in the world, using sophisticated tracking systems to keep their fleets of compact trucks moving like clockwork. After the 2011 earthquake, the Japanese government asked Yamato to put this formidable network to use in delivering relief supplies to disaster-struck regions.

The delivery companies were able to do what the Self-Defense Forces could not and deliver small packages of food and other goods to individual households isolated by the disaster. This was particularly important during the first weeks and months, when surviving stores were often emptied by panicked shoppers and unable to restock due to disrupted supply lines. According to Makoto Kigawa, the chairman of Yamato's parent company Yamato Holdings, his company used its know-how in delivering packages to track relief supplies that were arriving at government and military-run collection points and avoid the bottlenecks and man-made shortages that can plague logistics in relief efforts:

> The Self-Defense Forces can do the large-scale logistics and carry large volumes of supplies up the main roads. But when they come to the smaller local roads, or to reaching families who were not in the big shelters but who had remained home, the Self-Defense Forces' big trucks just can't deliver the relief supplies as needed. So we found ways to do this, such as using systems to minutely manage what supplies were in stock, determine what was needed, and deliver these supplies.[18]

Kigawa said this trial went so well that delivery companies have come to see themselves as an integral part of Japan's response to any major natural disaster. When a large earthquake struck the southern prefecture of Kumamoto in April 2016, killing 49 people and forcing the evacuation of some 44,000, Yamato and Nippon Express swung into action right away, delivering relief supplies more quickly than government responders, Kigawa said. He said one by-product of these relief efforts has been Project G, for "government," an effort by Yamato to work with local governments even in times of nondisaster to deliver food and other essentials to elderly and disabled residents living in isolated rural areas.

Another lesson of Tohoku has been the need for a more robust role by local governments, which can lead to a valuable decentralizing of disaster responses. This has been evident in Japan's post-2011 energy policy. The triple meltdown in Fukushima punctured the safety myth of Japan's nuclear industry and has left the country divided on the future of atomic energy. While the governing Liberal Democratic Party has tried to push through a restart of the nation's nuclear reactors, opinion polls still show a majority of the public opposing a return to atomic power. Amid these mixed emotions, many local communities in Fukushima and elsewhere in northeastern Japan have taken matters into their own hands by investing in renewable energy sources. Towns and cities are turning to geothermal, solar, and wind power to fill the gap left by the disappearance of nuclear energy. Such actions at the local level make it clear that Japan has already entered into an era of what the Germans would call *Energiewende*, or energy transition.

Moreover, instead of relying on large utilities like Tepco, which many blame for failing to prevent the accident, some towns have created energy cooperatives that sit outside traditional frameworks of top-down, large-scale energy production. Iitate, a village northwest of the destroyed Fukushima plant that was evacuated due to high radiation levels, has built a 50-kilowatt solar farm on former rice paddies that will sell excess power to Tohoku Electric Power Company, the local power company. The village is also finishing up a far larger, 10-megawatt solar farm financed by Toho Bank. Similarly, the village of Izumizaki in Fukushima has constructed a 1.2-megawatt solar plant financed by the national farmers co-op, the Japan Agriculture Group. These projects can also generate revenues for local governments, helping to make up for lost income as radioactive contamination prevents resumption of farming.

Similar moves toward decentralization and democratization have also been evident in efforts to measure the radiation released by the Fukushima nuclear disaster. Loss of trust in the central government and Tepco due to failures to disclose information about radioactive contamination, especially in the first months following the accident, spawned a proliferation of citizen science. Believing that the central government was covering up critical information about radiation exposure, residents in Fukushima and elsewhere began to buy or build their own measuring devices. These grassroots efforts have made a point of providing their findings in a transparent, open-source manner on the Internet. Since the accident, more than 50 citizen or community-based food-monitoring labs have sprung up across Japan, mostly in Fukushima. Of these, more than half post their measurements on a Web site called *Minna no data saito*, or Everyone's Data Site.[19]

This trend quickly jumped national borders, blossoming into a global movement led by nonprofit organizations such as Safecast. Safecast began as a crowd-sourced, do-it-yourself approach to measuring radiation across Japan. According to Azby Brown, an American university professor in Tokyo who has served as a lead researcher for Safecast, the organization responded to the government's failure to provide timely and reliable information by teaching citizens how to collect and analyze radiation data on their own. Safecast helps residents build radiation detectors with affordable kits and offers workshops on how to use them. It has asked citizens around Japan to place the detectors in their cars, bicycles, and backpacks, where they can collect radiation readings as the citizens go about their daily lives. These data are uploaded to a Web site, where the results have been compiled into a color-coded map.

Brown said the group promotes a bottom-up approach to keeping people informed that relies heavily on the democratizing power of the Internet: "Safecast's response was, 'We'll do it ourselves.' Develop devices, make maps that can be online, and then build a community that can do this sort of thing. A citizen science community. And it started off with hackers, basically. Tokyo Hacker Space and other people like that just sort of whipping together quick solutions that would allow people to drive and measure radiation and then make maps available on the Internet."[20]

Though it has encountered indifference and even vague warnings from the government, Safecast has built up trust by avoiding a political agenda and instead just offering an objective database of radiation levels in Fukushima and elsewhere. It has been so successful, with more than 70 million pieces of information uploaded to its site as of mid-2017, that its maps are among the most accurate and detailed available about radiation levels in Japan. Its rich database and lack of a pro- or antinuclear message has helped Safecast win over some of the public agencies that once viewed it with distrust. Safecast has even partnered with the Japanese post office, Japan Post, to place its radiation detectors on the motorcycles and other vehicles used by mail deliverers on their routes in Fukushima.

"I think the disaster and the citizen response, the citizen refusal to just accept the information and accept some of the decisions, has forced the government to be more open with certain kinds of data," Brown said.

Brown says Safecast is just one example of how citizens in Japan have turned to the Internet to free themselves of dependence on the government and to inform themselves about radiation. He said people around the world can learn how Japanese citizens used the disruptions caused by the disaster to start more grassroots initiatives and "free up latent or potential social abilities and social organizations," a process that has been called "emancipatory catastrophism."

"This growth in citizen science in our project is only one case, and there are quite a few in Japan and quite a few overseas," Brown said.

Citizen science was not the only bottom-up movement to appear in the aftermath of 2011. Nongovernmental organizations of all sorts sprang up across Tohoku and Japan, founded by citizens moved to change their lives by their experiences during the disaster. One example is RCF, a nonprofit organization founded by Retsu Fujisawa, a former management consultant, that seeks to use private investment to speed recovery in the disaster-struck northeast. The group serves as a pro bono advisor to companies, making it easier for them to build factories and other facilities by helping them choose sites, hire workers, and clear regulatory hurdles. Fujisawa said the new jobs boost not only the economy but also the spirits of local residents by making them feel more confident about their future.[21]

According to Fujisawa, nonprofits like his have emerged to do things that governments cannot or will not do. Many like RCF are by necessity heavily domestic in their activities. But their very appearance illustrates what might be the most important lesson from Japan's deadly catastrophe in 2011: that resilience to disaster comes less from physical infrastructure, like roads and wave walls, and more from the social infrastructure of community ties and responsive leadership. It will be such bottom-up, community-led initiatives that keep Japan on the leading edge of resilience strategies and allow it to serve as a model of best practices to the rest of the world.

Notes

1. "Status of Recovery and Current Problems in Three Disaster-Hit Prefectures, What the Data Tells Us, Indexes for Recovery and Reconstruction Following the Great East Japan Earthquake," National Institute for Research Advancement, posted August 2013, http://www.nira.or.jp/pdf/1301english_summary.pdf.

2. "Population Shrinks by 92,000 in 39 Disaster-Hit Municipalities," *Asahi Shimbun*, March 9, 2015.

3. Daniel P. Aldrich, "It's Who You Know: Factors Driving Recovery from Japan's 11 March 2011 Disaster," *Public Administration* 94 (2, 2016): 399–413.

4. Rieko Kage, *Civic Engagement in Postwar Japan: The Revival of a Defeated Society* (New York and London: Cambridge University Press, 2011).

5. Shigeo Tatsuki and Haruo Hayashi, "Seven Critical Element Model of Life Recovery: General Linear Model Analyses of the 2001 Kobe Panel Survey Data,"

paper presented at the Kyoto University Disaster Prevention Research Institute, Research Center for Disaster Reduction Systems, 2nd Workshop for Comparative Study on Urban Earthquake Disaster Management, February 14–15, 2002.

6. Mitsuhide Wakasugi, interviewed by author, July 24, 2011.

7. Daniel P. Aldrich and Yasuyuki Sawada, "The Physical and Social Determinants of Mortality in the 3.11 Tsunami," *Social Science and Medicine* 124 (2015): 66–75.

8. Patrick Barta, Daisuke Wakabayashi, and Gordon Fairclough, "After Tsunami, a Mayor Plants Seeds of Renewal," *The Wall Street Journal*, December 10, 2011.

9. Daisuke Wakabayashi, "Making Home Sweet Again," *The Wall Street Journal*, November 12, 2011.

10. "Welcome to Ibasho," accessed August 15, 2016, ibasho.org/web/.

11. "Elders Leading the Way to Resilience," pp. 1–2, accessed November 27, 2017, http://www.ibasho.org/web/wp-content/uploads/2015/03/150318Elders -Leading-the-Way-to-Resilience-Conference-Version.pdf.

12. Daniel P. Aldrich and Michelle Meyer, "Social Capital and Community Resilience," *American Behavioral Scientist*, 59 (2015): 254–269.

13. Daniel P. Aldrich and Emi Kiyota, "Creating Community Resilience through Elder-Led Physical and Social Infrastructure," *Disaster Medicine Public Health Preparedness*, 11 (2017): 1–7.

14. "Philippines," Ibasho.org, accessed July 17, 2017, http://www.ibasho.org /web/projects/ibasho_cafe/philippines.

15. Aldrich, 2016.

16. Daniel P. Aldrich, "The Externalities of Social Capital: Post-Tsunami Recovery in Southeast India," *Journal of Civil Society*, 5 (2011): 81–99.

17. Akihiko Tanaka, speaking at Asia Pacific Initiative, November 5, 2015.

18. Makoto Kigawa, speaking at Asia Pacific Initiative, June 8, 2016.

19. "Mina no Data Site," accessed August 15, 2016, http://en.minnanods.net /MDS/.

20. Azby Brown, speaking at Asia Pacific Initiative, May 13, 2016.

21. Retsu Fujisawa, speaking at Asia Pacific Initiative, April 13, 2016.

CHAPTER NINE

Bridges Make Good Neighbors: Building Soft Power with ODA

Hiromi Inami

Since the end of World War II, the United States has used foreign aid to build Cold War alliances, spread democracy and human rights, and even dismantle Soviet-era nuclear weapons. Japan has used foreign aid to build bridges—lots of bridges.

Since becoming a donor nation in the 1950s, Japan has spent ¥950 billion, or $8.7 billion in today's dollars, to fund the construction of almost 2,000 bridges across the developing world. One of Japan's first big foreign aid projects was the Chroy Changvar Bridge, a 711-meter span completed in 1966 on the outskirts of the Cambodian capital of Phnom Penh. Damaged by the Khmer Rouge in the 1970s, the bridge was rebuilt with Japanese aid in 1994 as the Cambodia-Japan Friendship Bridge. Today, it links central Phnom Penh with the rapidly growing Chroy Changvar district.

This is just one of many bridges that Japan has helped build in Cambodia and other nations in the Mekong River basin. In fact, bridge construction seems to be a specialty of Japanese aid efforts. And these bridges are not only in Southeast Asia. The Fatih Sultan Mehmet Bridge is a towering, 1.5-kilometer-long suspension bridge that links Europe and Asia by spanning the Bosporus strait in Istanbul. It was built in 1988 with Japanese aid, as was the Suez Canal Bridge, also known as the Egyptian-Japanese Friendship Bridge, which was completed in 2001 to connect Africa with Eurasia. Built by Japan's Kajima Corporation, the 3.9-kilometer span has become an important part of a highway linking Morocco to Turkey and Greece and to the Asian Highway system that extends across central Asia to link the Middle East with China.

These bridges, built with Japanese aid, connect not just cities but nations, continents, and even civilizations. They have improved people's lives by shortening travel times and providing vital infrastructure to nurture commerce and economic growth. They have connected people across natural barriers and political borders, strengthening social and cultural ties. For nations torn by war or natural disaster, these bridges have served as monuments of peace and recovery, connecting their citizens to a future of greater stability and prosperity.

Of course, Japan's foreign aid is not limited to building bridges. In the 60 years from 1954 to 2014, the Japanese government provided a total of $334.5 billion in foreign aid—more formally known as official development assistance, or ODA—to 190 countries and regions around the globe. This is second only to the United States, which provided $609.3 billion during that same time.[1] Japan is also the second-largest contributor to the World Bank and the largest donor alongside the United States to the Asian Development Bank, making it a major supporter of the international institutions that finance economic development.

But while spending on bridges represents a drop in the bucket of Japan's overall aid budgets, the bridges are highly symbolic of what Japan has tried to achieve and of what sets its aid efforts apart from those of other developed nations. These bridges are not just showpieces, erected by Japan to enhance its boasting rights. Rather, they are emblematic of how Japan designs its projects to help the economic development of recipient nations. These bridges are intended to do more than just connect geographical locations. Their construction is an opportunity to transfer engineering know-how and to train citizens of the recipient nations in such vital skills as design, construction, and maintenance.[2] Bridge building reflects a strategic focus on infrastructure projects that generate lasting economic benefits, linking people together into larger marketplaces that can foster greater prosperity.

This highlights Japan's overall approach to foreign aid, which has emphasized projects that are intended to help recipients help themselves. Rather than swoop in and try to save developing nations, or condescendingly tell them how to manage themselves and their economy, Japan has striven to give recipients the means to better themselves on their own terms. This is true not just of bridges but of other Japanese aid programs, from providing impoverished farmers with new, more productive strains of rice to giving pregnant women the knowledge to protect the health of both themselves and their infants. Japan's aid has been heavily focused on providing practical knowledge and skills, seen in its emphasis on technical and developmental assistance. The approach behind Japan's aid has been to give poorer countries the tools to improve themselves, and then get out of the way to let them develop as they see fit.

This "customer-focused" approach was a lesson of Japan's own experience after World War II, when it rose from the ruins of defeat with the help of overseas aid, mainly from the United States. As the first non-European aid recipient to make the transition to becoming a major donor, Japan knows that aid projects work only if the poorer nation is given control and allowed to find its own solutions instead of being forced to adhere to the donor's methods or values. Aid projects such as bridges are not just one-off acts of charity but a means of creating self-reliance that empowers the recipient nation. For this reason, they enjoy higher chances of success.

In this sense, Japan's foreign aid offers a different approach, perhaps even a different model, from the aid programs of other developed nations. It is also an approach that is winning growing recognition at a time when the effectiveness of foreign aid has been questioned and when new donors are stepping in to fill the gaps created by shrinking aid budgets in Japan and the West. One such recognition came in 2007, when President Hamid Karzai of Afghanistan awarded Sadako Ogata the Medal of Malalai, his nation's highest award bestowed upon a woman, for her work as head of the Japan International Cooperation Agency, or JICA. The agency has stayed in war-torn Afghanistan to create almost two dozen projects ranging from wheat breeding and tuberculosis control to administering scholarships for young Afghans to attend Japanese universities.

Thailand has also given Japan the highest form of flattery by using JICA as the model for its main aid agency, the Thailand International Cooperation Agency, or TICA. Taking a page from JICA's playbook, TICA has emphasized technical assistance to help the development of poorer neighboring countries like Vietnam and Myanmar.

Japan's aid efforts have also earned new appreciation in the West, including from philanthropic-minded celebrities. In 2006, Bono, the lead singer of the Irish band U2, met with Prime Minister Shinzo Abe during a concert tour in Japan to talk about increasing aid to Africa. Bono, widely known for his campaigns to fight poverty on that continent, told Abe that he admired Japan's accomplishments in helping lift Asia out of poverty. "There would be something to learn from that experience in helping Africa," he said, according to a summary of the meeting provided by the Ministry of Foreign Affairs.[3]

In a revealing response, Abe told the rock star that Japan's aid was based on his nation's own experience of "receiving aid from other countries during its postwar recovery." Abe said Japan's efforts focused on "helping aid recipients establish their own industries."

According to the ministry readout, Bono replied, "Africa needs a new, business-minded approach in assistance."

From Recipient to Donor

As the prime minister suggested, Japan's experiences were formative in creating its current approach to foreign aid. After devastating defeat in 1945, Japan rebuilt by accepting aid from other nations, mainly in the form of loans. This was especially true right after Japan regained its postwar sovereignty with the San Francisco Peace Treaty of 1951. The following year, Japan joined the World Bank, which became one of its biggest lenders.

At the same time, Japan showed a determination to preserve its newly regained autonomy by keeping its industries under domestic control while acquiring the latest technologies from the United States and Europe. In this way, Japan was able to eventually catch up with the West and become the first non-Western member of the group of advanced industrial democracies. The loans gave cash-strapped Japan much-needed capital, which it used to help successfully figure out its own way to organize its economy and society. While relying on the United States for military protection, Japan built a more egalitarian economic system that departed from the liberal Anglo-American model.

Still, aid from abroad was of great assistance to Japan in the first decades after the war, when its top priority was reconstructing its devastated cities and industries. In 1953, Japan took its first loan from the World Bank to build the Osaka Tanagawa thermal power project. This was one of many energy projects at the time, as Japan faced an urgent need for more electricity to power its new steel foundries and shipyards. A decade later, in the 1960s, the main focus of development became improving transportation links. During this era, Japan borrowed heavily to fund construction projects such as the Meishin Expressway, connecting the port of Kobe to the auto-making hub of Nagoya. World Bank loans also helped Japan pay for the Tokaido Shinkansen bullet train, which links Japan's main cities of Tokyo and Osaka. The bullet train was completed just before the 1964 Tokyo Olympic Games, in time to make it a symbol of Japan's recovery and reacceptance by the world community.

Japan's last loan was received in 1966 and was repaid by 1990. All told, the nation received 31 loans from the World Bank, worth some $863 million.[4]

Japan was also quick to begin helping poorer nations in Asia. In part, this was testimony to the success of Japan's own economic recovery. The nation was also driven by a desire to atone for its wartime conduct and support the Cold War–era efforts of its new ally, the United States. In 1954, Japan joined the Colombo Plan, a multinational effort based in Sri Lanka that was originally intended to fight communism by aiding the capitalist development of economies in Southeast Asia. A year later, Japan began providing technical assistance to that region in the form of training programs and the dispatch of engineers and experts to help build factories, roads, and other infrastructure.[5]

Japan made the switch from ODA recipient to donor as its economic miracle took off in the 1960s and 1970s. In 1976, Japan completed its compensation payments to the victims of its wartime imperialism and announced its intention of becoming a full-fledged ODA donor two years later. One of its first steps was to announce a target of doubling its foreign aid spending in just three years. Also in 1974, it created JICA as the main agency to oversee its aid projects and also launch a new program of sending Peace Corps–style volunteers to developing nations.[6]

By 1989, Japan's ODA spending outstripped that of the United States, making it No. 1 in the world. For most of the next decade, Japan remained the world's largest aid donor, until the United States regained the top spot in 2000.[7]

Japan embraced ODA as a means of both showing contrition for its expansionist past and shoring up its newly won status as a leading industrialized democracy. In this regard, ODA was one of Japan's first efforts to build up its "soft power," a measure of national influence that emphasizes the ability to persuade rather than coerce. Creating goodwill through generous economic and technical aid was a natural fit for Japan, which had built itself into a technological and industrial powerhouse, but one whose military was tightly constrained by a pacifist constitution.

The timing was also right: ODA was an idea that was winning adherents in the West just as Japan's economy was taking off. "The idea of wealthier countries giving away aid blossomed in the late 1960s," according to a report by the World Economic Forum, "as the first humanitarian crises reached mass audiences on television. Only a quarter-century after Auschwitz, humanitarian aid seemed to offer the world a new hope for fighting evil without fighting a war."[8]

Cold War rivalries also played a role, as the United States and western Europe used foreign aid to try to keep poorer nations from aligning with the Soviet Union and China. As a result, many of these efforts were aimed at spreading Western models of democracy and market-based economies.[9]

Checkbook Diplomacy

These political motives have also led to some of the biggest criticisms of aid spending. By treating aid recipients as pawns in superpower rivalries, ODA came under fire as a way of continuing Western domination of former colonial subjects. Instead of helping these nations grow wealthier and stronger, critics said the United States and its allies used aid to prop up corrupt, pro-American authoritarian regimes. They also said even well-intended ODA programs created dependencies that perpetuated the recipient nations' second-class status.[10]

Regardless of such criticisms, foreign aid spending surged starting in the 1960s, peaking at the end of the Cold War. After dropping off during the 1990s, it rose again as the United States discovered a need to promote its soft power in the post-Cold War world. In an influential 2000 article, Carol Lancaster, former deputy administrator of the U.S. Agency for International Development, argued that foreign aid can enhance "the credibility and trust that the United States can command."[11]

During the Cold War, some of Japan's ODA was also used to support the strategic goals of its American ally, as seen in its early support of the anticommunist Colombo Plan. At the same time, Japanese aid programs increasingly departed from the goals of the United States. This divergence was evident in the American and European criticisms of Japan's ODA as being used to promote Japanese exports or acquire energy resources. While there was truth in some of these criticisms, Japanese aid is also widely recognized as helping lay the foundations for the Asian region's later economic takeoff.[12]

Japan's aid reached a turning point in the early 1990s, when the nation came under criticism for "checkbook diplomacy" after providing money but not troops to the 1991 Gulf War to drive Saddam Hussein out of Kuwait.[13] Stung, Japan responded by broadening its aid agenda beyond construction and infrastructure to support multilateral efforts in security-related fields such as nation building. It also started using its still tightly constrained military, the Self-Defense Forces, to support these efforts in a noncombat role. Japan's first postwar deployment of troops abroad came in 1991, when it sent Self-Defense Force soldiers to Cambodia as peacekeepers during that nation's transition to democracy following the collapse of the bloody Pol Pot regime.[14]

In 1993, Japan raised its profile in Africa by launching the Tokyo International Conference on African Development, or TICAD, which it billed as an effort "to promote high-level policy dialogue between African leaders and development partners."[15] Japan served as host for the conferences, which brought African leaders to Japan. The conferences continue to be held every five years. In 2016, Japan convened the sixth TICAD meeting in Kenya, the first time the event was held in Africa. Japan has also used TICAD to articulate its approach to foreign aid, saying that assistance to Africa should stand on the three pillars of "consolidating peace," "poverty reduction through economic growth," and "human-centered development." The last pillar was an emphasis on not only infrastructure building but also training locals in fields such as agriculture, education, and health.[16]

In the 21st century, Japan has continued to use its foreign aid to support the United States, as seen in development assistance to Afghanistan and Iraq aimed at backing American efforts to eliminate terrorism. However, Japan has also adhered to its own approach to foreign aid. Despite expectations that Japan's foreign aid policy would eventually "normalize" by converging with the practices of Europe and the United States, this has not happened. While Western aid has long focused on so-called social infrastructure projects, such as building schools and hospitals, Japan's aid has gone in a different direction, funding economic infrastructure projects, such as roads, communications networks—and, yes, bridges.

In fact, recent studies have shown that Japan has continued to be what some aid experts have called an anomaly among major developed nations. According to OECD statistics, most wealthy donor nations spend twice as much on social infrastructure projects as on economic infrastructure. "For Japan, however, the opposite is true," concluded one academic study. "Indeed in 2010, economic infrastructural aid made up almost 50 percent of all Japanese bilateral ODA commitments."[17]

Miracle Rice

"Economic infrastructure" is a broad term that can encompass anything that helps foster or raise incomes, including helping farmers grow more productive crops. In fact, one of Japan's most successful aid efforts has been in Africa, where a Japanese agronomist has fought hunger by promoting a miracle variety of rice. Tatsushi Tsuboi, a technical advisor at JICA, has traveled to Africa more than 100 times during the past three decades, teaching more than 14,000 people how to grow food using the rice, which is called Nerica, or "New Rice for Africa."

One of the appeals of the rice is the fact that it was developed by Africans themselves. Tsuboi first came across Nerica in 1992, when he visited the West Africa Rice Development Association, a research laboratory based in the Côte d'Ivoire. (It has since grown and changed its name to the Africa Rice Center, a "pan-African rice research organization committed to improving livelihoods in Africa through strong science and effective partnerships."[18]) There, he was shown the rice variety, which had been developed by Monty Jones, a scientist from Sierra Leone. Jones had successfully bred together Asian and African varieties to create a hybrid that combined the higher yields of Asian rice with African rice's hardier ability to thrive in dry climates.

Tsuboi said he immediately recognized that Jones had achieved a breakthrough. While scientists had long tried to cross Asian and African rice, Jones was the first to create a variety whose seeds were not sterile. In an interview, Tsuboi said that when he first held three grains of Jones's rice in his hand, he knew immediately that they contained the promise of easing Africa's chronic food shortages.[19]

Tsuboi was well positioned to help spread this new miracle variety. He had spent his career studying rice, living for a decade in the Philippines and Indonesia to teach cultivation techniques.

Still, he said it was an uphill battle at first. He started his effort in Uganda, which was politically stable and known as one of the better-run economies in Africa. However, he soon learned that no one in the country had much actual experience in growing rice. He started from square one, training local agronomists in the cultivation of rice while traveling all over Uganda trying to convince farmers to give the unfamiliar crop a try.

Unsurprisingly, farmers were cautious at first, but they came around as a few risk takers achieved more profitable harvests. Tsuboi said he felt the value of what he was doing when Ugandan farmers started coming up to him and testifying that Nerica had improved their lives.

"See this house, this house was built with Nerica rice," he said the farmers told him. "They told me, 'I was able to buy this bicycle' or 'I was able to buy this motorcycle with Nerica.'"[20]

One advantage of rice is that, because its plants grow more densely together, it yields far more output per acre than grains like wheat. This makes it easier for even farmers with small plots to feed their families and have a surplus left over to sell. By helping them earn cash, Nerica improves the farmers' lives in additional ways, giving them the means to buy homes, bicycles, medicine, and education for their children.

"It's my dream that in, say, 50 or 100 years, African families will gather about the table for a dinner of rice and reminisce about how their grandfathers and grandmothers used to tell them, 'A long time ago, we couldn't eat this much rice. But now we can because a Japanese person taught us how to grow it,'" Tsuboi said in one JICA publication.[21]

Tsuboi is a good example of Japan's approach to foreign aid. His focus on teaching farmers to feed themselves reflects Japan's emphasis on training people in poorer nations to reduce poverty and develop their economies on their own. Over the past more than 60 years, JICA has dispatched 157,500 Japanese experts like Tsuboi to developing countries to work as teachers and instructors. It has also brought 587,400 people from overseas to Japan for training. They stay at places such as JICA's Tokyo International Center, a 441-room dormitory-like facility that hosts some 4,000 participants every year in JICA's Knowledge Co-Creation Program.[22]

Putting Locals in Charge

Indeed, these people-to-people links are perhaps the most effective type of bridge that Japan has built. This was evident in Tsuboi's efforts to teach Uganda's farmers how to raise themselves above subsistence levels. It is also apparent in the battle that one Japanese doctor has waged against Africa's scourge of AIDS.

In 1995, Tomohiko Sugishita was a freshly trained, 30-year-old heart surgeon when he joined the Japan Overseas Cooperation Volunteers, JICA's version of the Peace Corps. He was sent to Malawi, where he was assigned to work as the director of surgery at Zomba Central Hospital, over 200 kilometers southeast of the capital, Lilongwe.

Sugishita said he arrived ready to take charge of what he thought would be the hospital's team of surgeons. Instead, he was shocked to learn that he would be the only surgeon at Zomba Hospital—and in fact, one of only five trained surgeons in the entire country.

Worse, the nation was in the grips of an epic health crisis. In Malawi, the prevalence of HIV, the virus that causes AIDS, was close to 14 percent among the country's adults.[23] Among patients at Zomba Hospital, the rate was an astounding 70 percent. Many did not survive. Of the 1,000 patients crammed into the 450-bed hospital, half eventually died of AIDS, Sugishita said.

Sugishita said he tried to fill the gap by operating on every patient he could, not only those in his specialty of heart surgery. He said he did emergency procedures to save the lives of accident victims while also operating on ailments in almost every major field of medicine, from gynecology and urology to orthopedics and even neurosurgery. As the only surgeon, he said there were days when he spent 24 hours in the operating theater, performing 21 operations. During his two-and-a-half-year stay, he said he performed some 3,100 operations.[24]

On the most demanding days, Sugishita said he had to remind himself why he had volunteered for this. His interest had been sparked back in junior high school, when he saw a television program on famine in Ethiopia. He said he was appalled by the images of passersby refusing to offer a helping hand to dying children his own age. He dreamed of becoming a doctor and going to Africa to help.

However, when he got to Africa, he quickly realized that Malawi's problems would not be solved by a foreign doctor coming to the rescue. The roots of the crisis, he realized, went deeper than a lack of surgeons to the ways in which locals viewed sickness and its causes.

"Many people in Africa think death is caused by a curse," Sugishita said in an interview. "I saw many cases where the cursed person was lynched. They also believe that disease is caused by the family's misdeeds. I encountered a case where it was thought the father has caused his child's measles, so they tried to cure the child by pouring boiling water on the father."[25]

Moreover, in the face of Malawi's AIDS epidemic, many people were relying on local traditions for treatment. To understand these practices, Sugishita said he took time from his hospital work to visit traditional healers. He began to learn the customs of the locals, who were mostly the Chewa people, and their views on sickness.

"There was only a little that a doctor trained in Western methods could do," Sugishita recalled. "Even if you are able to cure an illness with the latest medical technology, a patient will reject that medical care unless his society accepts that such a procedure will help."

After returning from Malawi, Sugishita earned a master's degree at the University of London in medical anthropology, the study of how diseases are understood within different cultures. He said he wanted to convince the Chewa and peoples like them to improve their health practices in ways that they could understand and accept.

Sugishita's chance came in 2002, when JICA asked him to be the chief advisor for a project to strengthen health services in the Tanzanian region of Morogoro. He realized that local residents would improve their health habits and use the new services only if persuaded to do so by local leaders. Sugishita focused his efforts on convincing local government officials of the value of modern medical techniques. He also developed a leadership training program to put control of health services in the hands of local leaders, not foreign doctors or aid donors. He reasoned that they would show leadership only if they knew that they had actual autonomy.

"I felt it was really important that we specialists acted as catalysts for the administrative officers to act on their own accord rather than us telling them what to do," he said.

His technique came to be known as the catalyst approach, and it has been used by JICA ever since. The training program that Sugishita developed in Tanzania inspired similar leadership-building programs in 26 African countries.[26]

"The administrative officers see with their own eyes, think with their own minds, listen with their own ears, and take action," Sugishita said. "Their motivation is raised even further when they get a real sense via feedback of the improvement their action has made in the field."

Passport to Life

Japan has also tried to promote aid programs derived from the experiences of its own postwar development. One has been the Mother and Child Health Handbook, or *Boshi Techo*, a simple but empowering idea from Japan's own health care system that is now widely used across the world.

The handbook is a small paper booklet given to pregnant women to record prenatal checkups as well as all vaccinations and care received by both mother and infant after birth. It was developed in Japan right after World War II to allow mothers to take their health care records with them to doctors and hospitals of their choice, as Japan tried to create a seamless national health care system. When it was first introduced, the handbook was 20 pages, printed in black and white. Today, it is more than twice that length with color photos and illustrations and also charts to keep track of checkups, shots, and changes in the baby's weight and height.

Researchers have cited the handbook as one reason that Japan was able to dramatically reduce its infant mortality rate after the war. In 1950, Japan's rate was about 60 deaths per thousand births, or double that of the United States. Just 13 years later, Japan had managed to cut that rate to less than 25 deaths per thousand, lower than the American rate, despite the fact that Japan was still classified as a poor country. Researchers say the handbook helped reduce infant deaths by putting health information at the fingertips of new mothers while also promoting checkups that increased early detection of health problems.[27]

Some regions have adopted the handbook on their own accord, such as Thailand, South Korea, and the U.S. state of Utah. In the 1990s, Japan began promoting the handbook as part of its foreign aid administered by JICA. The handbook is now widely distributed in close to 30 nations, including Afghanistan, Brazil, Kenya, and Vietnam.[28] About 8 million copies are printed annually, eight times the number used in Japan.[29]

One place the handbook has won quick acceptance is the State of Palestine. In 2005, Japan introduced the handbook to the Palestinian Ministry of Health, paying for the creation and distribution of an Arabic-language version. The idea took off, and within three years, some 120,000 were being handed out annually to women via hospitals and clinics—the same figure as the annual number of births in Palestine.

In Palestine, 66 percent of the population lives on two dollars or less a day. Such grinding poverty has led to high infant mortality rates. In 1960, more than 1 in 10 infants died in Gaza, one of the poorest parts of Palestine. By 2008, that rate had dropped to nearly 1 in 50. While the handbook is just one reason for this improvement, Palestinians have come to call it the "passport to life."[30]

Of course, not all is rosy. Israel's blockade of Gaza, as well as its walls, road blocks, and checkpoints have prevented women from reaching medical facilities, hampering early detection of illnesses and abnormalities. Some women have actually given birth while waiting in the long queues at checkpoints. Akihiro Seita, a Japanese doctor who directs the health program at the United Nations Relief and Works Agency for Palestine Refugees in the Near East, has said these may be one reason why infant mortality has begun to creep upward again in Gaza, from 20.2 deaths per thousand births in 2008 to 22.4 in 2013.[31]

Afghanistan and Iraq

Since the early 2000s, Japan has increased its experience in extending aid to conflict-ridden areas during the American-led war on terror. While the United States' efforts were not always successful or even well conceived, JICA did try to support them in a humanitarian manner by taking a major role in nation-building projects in Afghanistan and Iraq.

In 2002, Japan hosted the first International Conference on Reconstruction Assistance to Afghanistan, which brought then Afghan President Karzai as well as American, European, and Saudi Arabian officials to Tokyo. The conference was cochaired by Ogata, the first Japanese to serve as United Nations high commissioner for refugees. Believing that national reconstruction and humanitarian aid should go hand in hand, Ogata created model development areas in Kandahar, Mazar-e-Sharif, and Jalalabad.

Ogata continued her focus on Afghanistan after being named president of JICA in 2003. She prioritized development of the area around the capital of Kabul, supporting agricultural and rural development programs as well as education and health care. She became known for her emphasis on long-term goals rather than quick, flashy accomplishments. She also pushed her staff to go out into the field and meet as many local people as possible, to get better information about what was actually happening on the ground. While she did withdraw JICA personnel when she judged the danger to be too high, she kept them in place when possible, to maintain contact with locals.[32] These efforts were appreciated by Afghan leaders. After his inauguration in 2014, President Ashraf Ghani called Ogata to tell her how "deeply indebted" the people of Afghanistan felt to her.[33]

During the United States–led war in Iraq, Japan took an even larger role, announcing in 2003 aid grants of $1.5 billion for "immediate support" in building water and sewage-treatment systems, power generation, and schools. The same year, Japan also offered $3.5 billion in longer-term loans to rebuild infrastructure. This $5 billion aid package was second in size only to that of the United States, which offered $20 billion in aid.

More significantly, Japan departed from its checkbook diplomacy of the 1990s by sending troops, who served in a noncombat role of helping reconstruct power lines, ports, bridges, roads, and other infrastructure in the southern cities of Samawah and Basra. Some Japanese also paid the ultimate price in Iraq. In November 2003, two Japanese diplomats, Katsuhiko Oku and Masamori Inoue, were killed when their car was ambushed on a road near the city of Tikrit, north of Baghdad. Oku, who was 45, was a popular former rugby player who had overseen projects to restore electrical power and dredge a port for commercial use.

JICA officials say Japan's efforts in Iraq stood out for two reasons. One was Japan's persistence to stick with a project until it was finished, even when other aid agencies pulled out because of security risks. In many cases, Japanese aid officials and contractors had to move about Iraq in guarded convoys or helicopters. The other was a focus on creating infrastructure that allowed local people to better their own lives. This latter goal was greatly appreciated by the Iraqis, who often singled Japan out for praise. When one Japanese company built a gas power plant with grant aid, it trained Iraqi engineers to do much of the work by setting up a training facility in Jordan and sending them to similar construction sites in other countries. The purpose was to teach them skills that they could take back to Iraq.

All told, Japan completed 19 aid projects despite the risks of working in an environment in which suicide bombers could strike at any time.[34]

Takema Sakamoto, who served as head of JICA's bureau in Iraq for two years until 2013, said he and other Japanese aid officials stayed in the country despite the risks in order to build rapport with the Iraqi people.

He said he saw many international aid groups deal with the mental and physical stress of working in Iraq by creating generous R&R breaks, in which foreign staff would spend four weeks in country followed by four weeks of vacation. Sakamoto said JICA did not do this because it feared that this would prevent them from winning the trust of the Iraqis, who enjoyed no such breaks. JICA employees followed a cycle of 12 weeks in Iraq followed by just 2 weeks outside.

Japan also maintained its presence in Iraq even as world interest died down. A decade after the war, JICA's office still had eight Japanese employees and four local staff who oversaw the distribution of ¥35.2 billion (about $320 million) in aid in fiscal 2015.[35] In an interview, Sakamoto said much of this came in the form of low-interest or other concessional loans instead of outright grants, a practice that Japan follows in most developing countries. He said even in war-torn Iraq, this emphasis on loans was successful because recipients were made to feel not that they were living off the charity of others, but rather that they had received a vote of trust in the form of a loan that they would repay. He said the recipients felt motivated to live up to that trust by putting the money to good use, building projects that yielded results and created financial return to help pay the loan back: "The basis of Japan's aid philosophy is support of self-help. There is a risk that hand-outs and charity may actually undermine the recipients' will to help themselves. In order to help developing countries ride their bikes alone, JICA doesn't hold on to their bikes forever but works continually to help them remove the training wheels. Our ultimate goal is for developing countries to reach the point when they no longer need JICA."[36]

South China Sea

In the last decade, Japan has begun a major rethink of some aspects of its aid policies, spurred by two developments: Japan's own economic decline and the rise of neighboring China.

Japan can no longer afford to be as generous as it once was. From the world's top aid donor in the 1990s, Japan has slowly fallen behind other leading nations: in 2012, it was ranked fifth in ODA spending behind the United States, the United Kingdom, Germany, and France. Similarly, Japan's ODA budget peaked in 1997 at ¥1.16 trillion. Since then, its aid budget has shrunk by roughly half, to ¥550 billion in 2014. These declines mirror cuts in most other types of Japanese government spending, as the nation has tried to control its ballooning debt.[37]

At the same time, China has grown more assertive in pushing its claims to the South China Sea and also over islands controlled by Japan in the East China Sea. Japan has been forced to respond by reorienting its defense forces toward its southern flank, away from Cold War–era threat Russia. To offset China, Japan has tried to build stronger alliances with other Asian nations that face similar pressure from China, mostly in the South China Sea.

This has led Japan to make more strategic use of ODA to back up these efforts, though still within the constraints of its constitutional rejection of war. One step has been to use foreign aid to strengthen the nonmilitary capabilities of friendly nations, such as their coast guards. One of the first such efforts came in 2006, when Japan provided three patrol ships to Indonesia. While nominally donated to augment Indonesia's ability to combat piracy, these ships also give it new means to patrol its claims to the South China Sea against encroachment by Chinese fishers.

More recently, Japanese coast guard personnel have been dispatched to Malaysia under the ODA budget to teach search-and-rescue techniques. Japan has also provided patrol vessels to the Philippines and Vietnam, two nations that face rising tensions with China over sovereignty of islands in the South China Sea. In 2013, Japan formalized these new, more strategic uses of ODA in its official National Security Strategy, adopted by the cabinet, which called foreign aid a resource for shoring up regional stability.[38]

One result has been new types of ODA, such as the Maritime Security Policy Program, begun in 2015 by JICA and the Japanese coast guard. The goal of the yearlong program is "capacity building," or strengthening the capabilities of coast guards in Southeast Asia to police their own waters. The program pays for junior officers at Asian maritime safety agencies to learn from Japan's coast guard, widely regarded as the most capable in the region.

Following their admission each year in October, the students spend six months studying at the National Graduate Institute for Policy Studies, one of Japan's top graduate schools. After that, they attend the coast guard's officers' training college in the port of Kure, near Hiroshima, where they learn Japan's approach to rescue and also maritime law enforcement. In the first year, two students each from the Philippines, Vietnam, Malaysia, and Indonesia participated in the program. At the end, they wrote policy papers with titles such as "Combatting Illegal Seaborne Migration" and "Enhancing the Capacity of Vietnam's Coast Guard to Respond to Oil Drilling" by China.[39]

Takashi Shiraishi, president of the National Graduate Institute for Policy Studies, said that the program has been deemed a success and is being expanded.

"In the future, I see attending the program as becoming increasingly prestigious," Shiraishi said in an interview. "The inaugural graduating class was given the opportunity to meet Prime Minister Abe on finishing. In the future, I would like to see midcareer officers from coast guards in other coastal states such as Thailand, India, and Myanmar. We would like to expand to 14 to 15 students, two from each country."[40]

These changes are coming at a time when foreign aid programs around the world are in flux. As growing advanced nations cut back on aid spending, a growing portion of financial assistance to the developing world now comes from the private sector: companies, nongovernmental organizations, and foundations.[41] A larger amount of aid also comes from newly emerging nations like China, South Korea, and Thailand, which seek to expand their soft power by demonstrating their transition from recipient to donor. As noted earlier, Thailand's TICA has borrowed many ideas from JICA, including its emphasis on training locals in technical skills.[42]

Nonetheless, foreign aid remains one of the pillars of Japan's influence in the region and its efforts to be a "global civilian power"—a leading nation whose strength is rooted in nonmilitary capabilities. (See chapter 10.) JICA appears in public opinion polls as one of the most trusted public institutions in Japan, alongside the coast guard and the Self-Defense Forces. Foreign aid also remains highly popular among the Japanese people; a 2015 survey by the Gates Foundation found that more than 80 percent of Japanese supported ODA.[43]

This popularity underscores the fact that foreign aid has been one of Japan's must successful means of raising its profile abroad and also contributing to the world. Japan has won wide for aid efforts that help poorer countries learn how to help themselves. Now, at a time when the balance of global power—both hard and soft—is shifting away from the West, perhaps Japan's approach to foreign aid can find new relevance. Perhaps it can serve as a model for both newly emerging nations making the transition to aid donor as well as an inspiration for advanced countries in search of fresh ideas.

Notes

1. Calculation provided by Development Cooperation Planning Office, International Cooperation Bureau, Japanese Ministry of Foreign Affairs.

2. International Development Journal, *Bridges Connecting the World* (Tokyo: Maruzen Publishing, 2015).

3. "Bono of U2 Pays a Courtesy Call on Mr. Shinzo Abe, Prime Minister of Japan," Ministry of Foreign Affairs, posted November 29, 2006, http://www.mofa.go.jp/announce/announce/2006/11/1129.html.

4. For a list of the 31 projects for which Japan received World Bank loans see http://worldbank.or.jp/31project/introduction/#.V5TMSriLSM8.

5. "Basic Facts about ODA," JICA, accessed July 19, 2017, http://www.jica .go.jp/aboutoda/basic/01.html.

6. "Annual Report, 2016," JICA, accessed July 19, 2017, https://www.jica .go.jp/english/publications/reports/annual/2016/index.html. Prior to JICA, ODA was overseen by the Overseas Economic Cooperation Fund, established in 1961. In 1991, this fund was integrated with the Export-Import Bank of Japan to become the Japan Bank for International Cooperation. In October 2008, the bank's ODA department was integrated into JICA.

7. "Japan's International Cooperation, 2015 Development Cooperation White Paper," Ministry of Foreign Affairs, accessed July 19, 2017, http://www.mofa.go .jp/mofaj/gaiko/oda/files/000137901.pdf.

8. "Does Foreign Aid Always Help the Poor?" World Economic Forum, posted October 23, 2015, https://www.weforum.org/agenda/2015/10/does-foreign -aid-always-help-the-poor/.

9. Ibid.

10. "Foreign Aid—Foreign Aid's Critics," in *Encyclopedia of the New American Nation*, Paul Finkelman, ed., accessed July 19, 2017, http://www.americanforeign relations.com/E-N/Foreign-Aid-Foreign-aid-s-critics.html.

11. Carol Lancaster, "Redesigning Foreign Aid," *Foreign Affairs*, September/ October 2000.

12. Bruce M. Koppel and Robert Orr Jr., eds., *Japan's Foreign Aid Power and Policy in a New Era* (Boulder, CO: Westview Press, 1993), p. 364.

13. "U.S. Used Japan's Gulf War Isolation to Push It onto World Stage," *Kyodo News*, in *The Japan Times*, December 18, 2005.

14. "ODA Policy for the Kingdom of Cambodia," Ministry of Foreign Affairs, accessed July 19, 2017, http://www.mofa.go.jp/mofaj/gaiko/oda/files/000072231.pdf.

15. "Toward Sustainable Development for All in Africa," United Nations Development Program, July 29, 2016, accessed November 27, 2017, http://www.africa .undp.org/content/rba/en/home/library/outreach-material/sustainable-develop ment-for-all/.

16. "TICAD 20th Anniversary Review: Main Report," JICA and Mitsubishi UFJ Research and Consulting, February 2013, accessed November 22, 2017, http://open_jicareport.jica.go.jp/pdf/12149092.pdf.

17. Evan Takuya Kratzer, "Japanese Foreign Aid: Convergence, Divergence, and the Formulation of ODA Policy," research paper, accessed July 19, 2017, http://www.eastasiareview.org/issues/2015/articles/Japanese%20Foreign%20 Aid.pdf.

18. Africa Rice Center, http://www.africarice.org.

19. Tatsushi Tsuboi, interviewed by author, June 25, 2016.

20. Ibid.

21. "Rice Will Save Africa!" JICA, accessed July 19, 2017, http://www.jica.go .jp/aboutoda/ikegami/04/index.html.

22. "Tokyo International Center," JICA, accessed July 19, 2017, https://www.jica.go.jp/tokyo/english/office/index.html.

23. "Prevalence of HIV," The World Bank, accessed November 22, 2017, https://data.worldbank.org/indicator/SH.DYN.AIDS.ZS?locations=MW.

24. Tomohiko Sugishita, interviewed by author, June 2, 2016.

25. Ibid.

26. "The Person Behind JICA's Health System Strengthening Project—Tomohiko Sugishita, JICA International Cooperation Specialist," JICA, accessed July 19, 2017, http://www.jica.go.jp/topics/person/20150219_01.html.

27. Yasuhide Nakamura, "Maternal and Child Health Handbook in Japan," *Japan Medical Association Journal*, 53 (4, 2010): 259–265, accessed July 19, 2017, https://www.med.or.jp/english/journal/pdf/2010_04/259_265.pdf.

28. Ibid.

29. "International Cooperation Protecting Lives and Health: The Untold Story of the Mother & Child Health Handbook," JICA, accessed July 19, 2017, http://www.jica.go.jp/topics/2016/20160520_01.html.

30. "Mother & Child Health—Protecting Precious Lives," *Monthly JICA*, July 2008, accessed July 19, 2017, http://www.jica.go.jp/publication/monthly/0807/01.html.

31. "Infant Mortality Rate Rises in Gaza for First Time in 50 Years," United Nations Relief and Works Agency, posted August 8, 2015, https://www.unrwa.org/newsroom/press-releases/infant-mortality-rate-rises-gaza-first-time-fifty-years.

32. Sadako Ogata, "Afghanistan: Accelerate the Shift from Reconstruction to Development," JICA, posted January 15, 2008, http://www.jica.go.jp/about/president/archives_ogata/message/20080115.html.

33. Interview by author with Masataka Nakahara, former head of the Afghanistan bureau at the Ministry of Foreign Affairs, who worked closely with Ogata, August 30, 2016.

34. Hideki Masunaga, "A Decade after the Iraq War: Japan Carved in Iraqi People's Heart," JICA, posted March 19, 2013, https://www.jica.go.jp/english/news/opinion/2012/130319.html.

35. "Annual Report 2016," JICA.

36. Takema Sakamoto, interviewed by author, June 10, 2016.

37. "National ODA Performance in 2015," Organisation for Economic Co-operation and Development, Ministry of Foreign Affairs, April 13, 2016, http://www.mofa.go.jp/mofaj/press/release/press4_003209.html.

38. "Abe Looks to Put His Stamp on Foreign Aid," *The Japan Times*, June 23, 2014.

39. "Maritime Safety and Security Policy Program," National Graduate Institute for Policy Studies, accessed July 19, 2017, http://www.grips.ac.jp/jp/education/inter_programs/maritime/.

40. Takashi Shiraishi, interviewed by author, September 15, 2016.

41. "'Beyond Aid' and the Future of Development Cooperation," briefing paper by the German Development Institute, June 2014.

42. Yasutami Shimomura, John Page, and Hiroshi Kato, eds., *Japan's Development Assistance—Foreign Aid and the Post-2015 Agenda* (New York: Palgrave Macmillan, 2015).

43. "Report on Public Attitudes about ODA," Japan Institute for Global Health, posted December 15, 2015, http://jigh.org/news/jigh/2953.

CHAPTER TEN

Japan's Strategic Position: Global Civilian Power 2.0

Yuichi Hosoya

The rise of China, the relative decline of American military supremacy, and the inward turn by a more populist West are forcing Japan to rethink its security strategy. A growing number of Japanese, including the current prime minister, are calling for Japan to take a more active diplomatic and military role, both in the region and in the world. This has prompted a national soul searching: What does Japan have to offer as an actor in diplomatic and security issues? To what extent should Japan shed what some call the "passive pacifism" that the country has embraced since World War II? What should a more assertive Japan look like?

To consider these questions, it is first necessary to understand Japan's strategic position in the world, and that requires looking at two separate but closely linked issues: the changes in Japan's geopolitical environment and its identity as a nation within the international community.

It is important to remember that such questions are not new. They first began to appear after the fall of the Berlin Wall, when Japan found itself no longer able to follow its postwar strategy of keeping a low profile while relying on the United States for security. The Iraqi invasion of neighboring Kuwait in 1990, and the massive United Nations–sanctioned military response that resulted in the Gulf War, created the first crisis of the post–Cold War world.

This war proved to be a turning point for Japan as well, forcing the nation to face existential questions of a sort that it had not had to answer since 1945. What should Japan, with its postwar constitutional commitment to eschewing war, do? Should it adhere to those constitutional principles underwritten by the United States? Or should it join the international community in dispatching its military, the Self-Defense Forces, to the Middle East? Opinions were divided, and not just in the public. There was no consensus inside government, where calls for expanded military action were opposed by the Cabinet Legislation Bureau—the bureaucratic organ charged with interpreting the constitution.

Other pressures were also changing Japanese views of their own place in the world. This was an era of intense trade friction between Japan and the United States, when the so-called revisionists were arguing that Japan played by different rules and that its political economy was unique and impenetrable. Such theories of "Japanese heterogeneity" were being voiced amid mounting concern about Japan's growing economic power vis-à-vis the United States, a shift in the power balance that was shaking the very foundations of the United States–Japan alliance.

In the face of such changes in the international environment, the debate over Japan's international role, and over its identity rooted in its postwar pacifism, became more animated. Two contending strategic visions emerged.

One was the "normal country" theory. Its adherents argued that, as a member of the United Nations and of the global community, Japan needed to shoulder its responsibility for international security, not only economically but also in political and military terms. This would mean acquiring sufficient military capabilities to join other nations as an equal in collective action on security issues.

According to a 1992 report by a special committee of the governing Liberal Democratic Party, or LDP, this would require Japan to adopt a "spirit of proactive pacifism that differed completely from passive pacifism or one-country pacifism" to which it had adhered since its 1945 defeat. This new, proactive pacifism would permit the use of force in the name of maintaining international peace and in cooperation with the international community. Such a normalizing of Japan would also require drastic reforms at home, not just to the constitution but to the organization of the military and the civilian decision-making apparatus that would oversee its use.[1]

These arguments were most forcefully made in the 1993 book *Blueprint for a New Japan* by the former LDP secretary general, Ichiro Ozawa, whose name has long been associated with the normal nation position. The book, which sold more than 600,000 copies in Japanese, called on the nation to take a more active role in global affairs, including joining UN military operations.[2]

The opposing position was the "civilian power" theory. In this view, Japan's differences, at least in security policy, could actually be a source of strength. This theory called on Japan to adhere to its nonmilitary approach, which should continue to serve as the basis of Japan's strategic position within the international community. The key elements of postwar Japan's so-called Yoshida Doctrine—the security alliance with the United States, contrition over its wartime history, and constitutional constraints on its military—should be kept, though adapted to fit the changed, post–Cold War world. In a 1991 article in *Foreign Affairs* entitled "Japan and the New World Order," Yoichi Funabashi argued that Japan should eschew the traditional superpower model, based on military strength, in favor of becoming what he called a "global civilian power." In this approach, Japan would improve its global image, and thus increase its international influence, by emphasizing its own nonmilitary strengths in areas such as economics, technology, and culture.[3]

These two perspectives formed two poles between which Japan debated its post–Cold War security strategy and its international identity.

Today, a quarter century later, Japan is standing at an equally critical inflection point. The regional and global power balances have changed dramatically for Japan, which has had to face the reality of its own relative decline and the rise of regional rivals. Once again, Japan faces profound questions about its place in the world. In the 21st century, what direction should Japan take? Is it time to finally become a normal nation? If not, what sort of strategic position should Japan seek?

Building on the original theory of "global civilian power," perhaps the answers lie in an updated version of this approach, a new "global civilian power 2.0." The Japan of today can better respond to challenges brought by the changing geopolitical power balance if it does not completely discard its antiwar message as somehow outdated or illegitimate but instead builds on its postwar experiences to forge its own new direction. This approach will also allow Japan to best contribute to sustaining and perhaps revitalizing the postwar liberal international order from which Japan has benefited so much. How this strategy differs from the original "civilian power" and how it can be manifested in specific actions will be discussed below.

Civilian Power or Normal Nation?

As I noted, two competing visions of Japan's security strategy, and of its role within the international community, arose in response to changes in the geopolitical environment at the end of the Cold War. They took shape in the debate over the nation's future that followed Japan's surprisingly bitter experiences during the 1990–1991 Gulf War.

The prime minister at the time, Toshiki Kaifu, rejected calls for dispatching the Self-Defense Forces to the conflict, which drew a coalition of 700,000 troops from 39 nations by some accounts. Kaifu still viewed overseas military action through the lens of Japan's wartime experience and the national disaster that resulted from the nation's failure to control its own military. Kaifu appeared to view a decision to send the Self-Defense Forces abroad as the first step on a slippery slope, saying that calls to dispatch troops to the Middle East "remind me of the Manchurian Incident"—the staged 1931 bombing of a Manchurian railroad that the Japanese military used as a pretext for invading northeastern China.[4]

However, as a result, Japan found itself widely criticized for practicing "checkbook diplomacy," just offering money while other nations sent troops into harm's way. Many Japanese people felt humiliated, an experience that left a searing impression of just how Japan's postwar one-country pacifism had left it powerless, even emasculated.[5]

One response was the normal nation discourse, which gained credence as an effort to recover Japan's ability to command international respect. Normal-country advocates wanted to remove Japan's self-imposed constraints on the military so the nation could join collective security activities, such as fighting alongside other nations during the Gulf War. In particular, they argued in favor of changing the war-renouncing Article 9 of the postwar constitution to permit Japan to maintain a full-fledged military like other nations. If constitutional revision was impossible, they argued, the Japanese government should at least loosen its interpretation of Article 9 to allow so-called collective self-defense—the right to join international military actions that advance Japan's own national security. They argued that such changes would allow Japan to build closer military ties with the United States while also improving its own defense capabilities.

The civilian power advocates pushed back, arguing that Japan's non-military approach to diplomacy after World War II should continue to be the basis for its foreign policy and its international identity. They said Japanese diplomacy should maintain its postwar emphasis on economic and development aid, and particularly official development assistance, or ODA, instead of military action. To increase Japan's global voice, civilian power advocates called for expanding Japan's economic and development aid on a global scale while also offering the lessons of Japan's own dramatic postwar economic recovery as a resource for other nations (see chapter 9).

This advocacy of peaceful diplomacy was at least partly driven by concerns about the reaction overseas, and particularly among former victims of Japan's wartime aggression, to a return by Japan's military to the world stage. But there were also more forward-thinking reasons for eschewing a military-based approach and embracing a more peaceful identity. Civilian power advocates said Japan could win international trust and admiration by acting as an economic and technological power committed to nonviolent resolutions of disputes and to improving global lives by fighting poverty and raising living standards. Such an international image, said civilian power advocates, could be a source of diplomatic capital that would allow Japan to expand its influence.

"Taking the position that Japan's 'success story' rise into a global consumer superpower under its postwar Constitution is not a quirk of history but a replicable concept," writes Funabashi, "Japan is a power that embodies this and is committed to building an international system to share that philosophy with others."[6]

As Japan entered the new century, an attempt to reconcile these visions and create a cohesive national strategy took place at a January 2000 roundtable conference held by the Prime Minister's Commission on Japan's Goals in the 21st Century. Established as a consultative group for then prime minister Keizo Obuchi, the commission's some 50 members included a broad range of leading intellectuals, including normal-country proponents like Shinichi Kitaoka, a politics professor who later became Japan's ambassador to the United Nations, and also civilian-power advocate Funabashi, then a member of the editorial board of the *Asahi Shimbun*, Japan's second-largest newspaper. (In 2011, Funabashi founded the think tank that later became the Asia Pacific Initiative, which compiled this book.)

They produced post–Cold War Japan's first in-depth examination of the nation's goals and identity by a consultative group for the Japanese government and thus merit a deeper look.

The group wrote a lengthy report with recommendations on what course Japan should take in the new century, saying that Japan should seek forms of power and influence that match its vision of itself and also that would be accepted by the international community. It also sought to create a new vision by fusing the concepts of normal nation and civilian power into a new national strategy, which it dubbed a "global civilian power" approach.[7]

This new theory argued that Japan should seek a broader, global scope to its actions and also a more proactive engagement with the world. At the same time, it called on Japan to keep what had made it special during the postwar period, when it became a "non-military economic superpower."[8] The new formulation said Japan should strike a balance by taking a more active role in security issues while drawing a line at becoming a full-fledged military power in its own right:

> Although self-help is essential, a turn in the direction of achieving Japanese security alone would not necessarily increase Japan's safety despite the huge costs it would incur. On the contrary, it would destabilize the global security system, and lead possibly to unnecessary friction and tension with neighboring countries. The prestige and function of the U.S.-Japan alliance should continue to be the economic, political and military cornerstone supporting peace and stability in the Asia Pacific region. To that end, the necessary legislation should be put in place, and a national debate on exercising the right to collective self-defense take place.[9]

The report reflected growing acceptance in Japan of a gradual easing of constraints on its still tightly controlled military that was already under way. In response to its experiences during the Gulf War, Japan made its first dispatch of military forces overseas since 1945, sending the Self-Defense Forces to join UN peacekeeping operations, or PKO, first in Cambodia in 1993 and then in the Golan Heights and East Timor. These actions won praise at home and abroad, giving the Self-Defense Forces new self-confidence. They also played a role in changing the public outlook, building domestic support for Japan playing a more active role in international security. "When the Cambodian PKO (UNTAC) was successful in rebuilding peace and the government of Cambodia," the commission's report noted, "Japanese public opinion shed its postwar pacifist stance."[10]

Citing these steps, the report called on Japan to assume a constructive, peaceful role in the international community by emphasizing "a commitment to security, participation in the global system centered on the international economic order, and cooperation with developing countries (ODA)." In military policy, it said Japan should adopt a more robust but still restrained posture focused on self-defense and increased cooperation with allies and friendly countries. Japan should strengthen defense ties with the United States while passing new laws to remove some of the self-imposed limits on its Self-Defense Forces. At the same time, Japan should dedicate itself to nonmilitary action, strengthening the system of international cooperation and working for peaceful resolution of conflicts.[11]

This new approach shared the civilian power concept's commitment to nonmilitary action. However, as the name suggests, it differs from the earlier approach by calling for Japan to proactively engage with the world beyond its own backyard, as a global player. In that sense, it seeks to unleash more of Japan's latent potential as the world's (then) second-largest economy and only non-Western member of the top industrialized nations. The focus on peaceful action was also intended to allay the concerns of neighboring countries that still remember Japan's more violent foray into global affairs in the 1930s and 1940s.

After the commission's report was published, a prominent Chinese intellectual told members of the group, "I agree with Japan's civilian power argument, but why does it have to be global?"[12] This episode reflects the suspicion with which China still viewed a more proactive Japan. But it also underscores an emerging consensus within Japan itself that the post–Cold War era required a new strategic vision and a more global involvement in the international community.

Updating the Concept of a Global Civilian Power

The international environment has changed since the vision of a global civilian power was first articulated in 2000. Whereas the Atlantic was formerly the focus of world politics, the geopolitical center of gravity has clearly shifted toward the Asia Pacific. The world's dominant bilateral relationship during the Cold War was the global contest between the United States and Soviet Russia; today, it is the more complex relationship between the United States and a rising China.

Japan is part of this equation. It is the world's third-largest economy, after the two big rivals, and the United States' largest partner in the region. Clashes between Beijing and Tokyo over wartime history are no longer arcane matters limited to the participants; they can now have profound implications for the stability of the entire Asia Pacific.

Japan has built important bilateral relationships with both the United States and China, and its security alliance with the United States continues to be the cornerstone of peace and stability in the Asia Pacific region. Japan's alliance with the United States and its relationship with China are more than just bilateral relationships. They shape the future of the entire region. This is a significant difference from the Cold War, when Asia was relegated to a peripheral role. With the Asia Pacific now front and center, the United States–Japan alliance will continue to determine the flow of global public goods—trade, rule of law, peace and security—in the world's most important region.

At the same time, the rise of new powers is ending the West's dominance of the global economy and creating new challenges to the established international political order. Sometimes these calls for change can be violent, as seen in the terror attacks in Paris, New York, and elsewhere. A backlash in developed democracies has brought a new wave of protectionism, xenophobic nationalism, and angry, one-country populism. The liberal international order that took shape after World War II based on the Bretton Woods system of commercial and financial rules has been shaken.

In this increasingly uncertain global environment, just maintaining the postwar order's commitment to free and open international cooperation has become a major challenge. As a major beneficiary of this order, Japan has tried to step into the gaps. It is departing from its post-1945 passive pacifism as never before to seek a more active role on the global stage in support of the postwar liberal framework.

To promote peace and stability in the Asia Pacific, Japan has sought to turn itself into an indispensable regional player. While shouldering a heavier burden in its own backyard, the nation has also tried to become a larger contributor to the international community outside its own region. The backbone of these efforts has been its strategic alliance with the United States. Tokyo has stepped up cooperation with Washington, giving its military a larger role regionally and as far afield as the U.S.-led antipiracy operations off the Horn of Africa. At the same time, Japan has also seen a need to pursue a more multilateral foreign policy, reaching out to other democracies, like Australia, India, and nations in Southeast Asia, while also placing more weight on ties with China and Russia.

It is also time to update Japan's broader vision of itself and its place in the world. The strategy of the global civilian power must be revised to fit the realities of the early 21st century. Adapting the concept to current challenges requires the addition of three new initiatives: human security, rule of law, and capacity building for maritime peace.

Human Security

When he launched the 21st Century Japan Initiative, then prime minister Obuchi also put forth the then still untried concept of human security as a new pillar of Japanese foreign policy. Embraced by the United Nations Development Program in 1994, this concept was a move away from the traditional views of national security, which emphasize protecting the state with military action, in favor of a more people-centered approach. Human security is a much broader approach that includes protecting individuals from poverty and economic dislocation ("freedom from want") as well as from all forms of political violence and oppression ("freedom from fear"), not only war.

Obuchi tried to make this a new core concept of Japanese diplomacy. At a speech in Hanoi in December 1998, he defined human security as addressing "all threats to survival, life, and dignity" of individuals. To respond to the Asian financial crisis in 1997, he pledged ¥500 million, or about $4.2 million, to establish a United Nations Trust Fund for Human Security to finance related projects in the Asia Pacific region.

"We need urgently to implement measures for the socially vulnerable who are affected by the Asian economic crisis," he said in Hanoi. "Japan will continue to address this area utilizing its official development assistance and multilateral frameworks such as APEC."[13]

This was a clear signal that Japan was seeking a more active role in regional affairs while also pursuing a new approach that promoted economic cooperation, not military power. Obuchi's successor, Yoshiro Mori, continued the new focus on human security, pushing for the establishment at the United Nations in 2001 of a Commission on Human Security to serve as a forum for advancing the concept. Cochaired by Sadako Ogata, the Japanese diplomat and former UN high commissioner on refugees, and Amartya Sen, the first Asian to be awarded the Nobel Prize for Economics, the commission published a report two years later, *Human Security Now*. The report called human security a more appropriate response to "a new wave of dramatic crises at the turn of the millennium related to terrorist attacks, ethnic violence, epidemics and sudden economic downturns."[14]

"There is also a fear that existing institutions and policies are not able to cope," the report continued, "with weakening multilateralism, falling respect for human rights, eroding commitments to eradicate poverty and deprivation, outdated sectarian perspectives in education systems and the tendency to neglect global responsibilities in an increasingly interrelated world."

Mori also increased financial support of the human security initiatives, announcing on September 7, 2000, at the Millennium Summit at UN headquarters that Japan would add another $100 million to the Human Security Fund.

Mori also gave Japan's efforts a more global scope. Where Obuchi embraced human security in response to the Asian financial crisis, Mori carried the concept far beyond Japan's own region. He used a 2001 visit to South Africa, Kenya, and Nigeria, the first trip by a Japanese prime minister to Sub-Saharan Africa, to promote a diplomatic vision that called for advancing human security. During his trip, "Prime Minister Mori stated in the strongest terms that all measures aimed at human security are based on the premise that each individual human should be valued, and that Japan's peace diplomacy for the 21st century places human security at its core."[15]

By promoting human security in Africa, Mori was elevating Japan to the position of a global actor, and one that was advocating the nonmilitary goals of health and development. In other words, the vision of Japan as a global civilian power, first promoted by Obuchi in the late 1990s, was beginning to take form by the start of the next decade. And this more global Japan enjoyed some early successes. Thanks in part to Japan's advocacy, the UN General Assembly embraced the term "human security" for the first time in 2005. The Human Security Fund has since dispensed more than $390 million to projects including reconstruction in war-torn Kosovo and East Timor.[16]

Of course, Japan is not the only country to advocate the concept of human security. Both the European Union and Canada have used it to promote peace efforts. However, the EU and Canada appear to view human security as part of a broader paradigm of humanitarian intervention that also advocates the use of military force as a means to end human-rights violations. In contrast to Canada's advocacy of a "human security network" that embraces as its mission "the responsibility to protect," Japan's version of human security eschews coercive action, says Ambassador Takahiro Shinyo, the head of Japan's mission at the United Nations.

"The Japanese concept is one of non-compulsion," said Shinyo, who was also a specialist in the Ministry of Foreign Affairs on human security. Japan is "trying to achieve human rights and fundamental freedoms only with the consent of the parties involved and by non-military means."[17]

Japan's promotion of the Human Security Fund also coincided with the launching of wars in Afghanistan and Iraq by the U.S. administration of President George W. Bush. This should make clear Japan's very different approach to security, despite its strong alliance with the United States. Looking at the results, it would not be unreasonable to say that Japan's approach proved able to bring results at far lower cost in both money and lives. In an era when advanced democracies face increased financial constraints, as well as growing public fatigue with overseas military intervention, a nonmilitary approach may offer a more sustainable, and thus politically acceptable, alternative.

Rule of Law

More recently, Japan has placed growing emphasis on strengthening the rule of law, and seeking peaceful settlements to disputes, as part of its response to China's increasingly assertive claims to surrounding territory.

Japan does this for two reasons: to win support of its position in global public opinion and to secure a voice for itself in creating international laws and norms. In December 2013, the Japanese government released its first National Security Strategy, which said Japan should promote rule of law as one of its key strategies:

> Japan will continue to faithfully comply with international law as a guardian of the rule of law. In addition, in order to establish the rule of law in the international community, Japan will participate proactively in international rule-making from the planning stage, so that Japan's principles and positions based on fairness, transparency and reciprocity are duly reflected.[18]

Japan has specifically called for fortifying the rule of law on the sea and in both outer space and cyberspace. Of these, the sea is the highest priority. The vast majority of Japan's imports of energy, food, and raw materials, and also its exports of manufactured goods, must travel by ship, often passing through chokepoints like the Straits of Malacca. Rather than try to secure these strategic straits through military means, Japan has taken the lead in creating a shared international recognition that secure sea lanes advance the entire world's peace and prosperity. One way it has done this is by promoting antipiracy and other multinational maritime initiatives aimed at keeping those lanes open.

This new approach was most forcefully expressed by Prime Minister Shinzo Abe at the 13th Asia Security Council—better known as the Shangri-La Dialogue—in Singapore in May 2014. In his keynote speech, optimistically entitled "Peace and Prosperity in Asia, Forevermore," Abe called on nations to find "common benefit in keeping our oceans and skies as global commons, where the rule of law is respected throughout, to the merit of the world and humankind." He went on to express three principles related to the rule of law at sea that he said will ensure peace and prosperity in Asia.[19]

"The first principle is that states shall make and clarify their claims based on international law," Abe said. "The second is that states shall not use force or coercion in trying to drive their claims. The third principle is that states shall seek to settle disputes by peaceful means."

Advocating the rule of law does not come without costs. It means that Japan must commit to respecting that law, even in rulings that prove disadvantageous for Japan itself. One such example was Australia's successful suit in the International Court of Justice to stop Japan's Antarctic research whaling, which is widely condemned abroad but enjoys strong domestic support from cultural conservatives. In 2014, the court ruled against Japan, withdrawing a permit for the second phase of its annual Antarctic Ocean research hunt. Japan issued a statement saying that in accordance with the ruling, it had decided to cancel Antarctic whaling, though it has since resumed in a way that it believes satisfies the court ruling.[20]

As China's strength grows, the rule of law approach is likely to become an even more important strategy for maintaining peace in the Asia Pacific, not just for Japan but other nations in the region as well.

In July 2016, on the basis of the United Nations Convention on the Law of the Sea, the Permanent Court of Arbitration in The Hague ruled on a suit filed by the Philippines in its territorial dispute with China over islands in the South China Sea. In a widely watched case, the court ruled against China, concluding that "there was no historical basis" for China's exclusive claims to the island, or the nine-dash line invoked by China to claim control over much of the South China Sea.

Almost immediately, Japanese prime minister Abe expressed support for the ruling, in this case directly to his Chinese counterpart. Abe, who was visiting Ulaanbaatar in Mongolia for a summit of Asian and European leaders, happened to have a scheduled meeting with the Chinese prime minister, Li Keqiang. Abe used the meeting to tell Li, "Japan has always advocated the importance of peacefully resolving disputes based on the 'rule of law,'" and he urged China to abide by the judgment. Prime Minister Li showed his strong dissatisfaction with this, countering that Japan "should exercise caution in its own words and deeds, and stop hyping up and interfering."[21]

As China's response shows, the rule of law approach has its limits, especially if one side feels "core interests" are at stake. Nevertheless, Japan's advocacy of the approach is a chance to display its commitment to peace and stability and to being a global civilian power that follows its own path of addressing regional and global disputes through nonmilitary means.

Capacity Building

China has been stepping up its maritime activities in the East China Sea and South China Sea and has been rapidly modernizing its naval and air power. It unilaterally declared the establishment of an air defense identification zone, or ADIZ, in the East China Sea on November 23, 2013. These claims of exclusive rights, and the challenge they represent to existing international conventions, have contributed to growing tensions in the region.

A clear example has been the Senkaku Islands, which are controlled by Japan as part of Okinawa but which China also claims using the name Diaoyu Islands. In recent years, China has been dispatching coast guard and other government-agency vessels, some of them armed, into waters near the islands in an attempt to erode Japan's claims to administrative control and create a new, more ambiguous status quo.

While relying primarily on calls for peaceful dialogue and negotiation, Japan sees a need to prevent a further militarization and expansion of Chinese efforts to establish their own claims of control over this area. The urgency to do so has only grown as China has ratcheted up its activities, a trend that is evident in the growing number of warnings issued to Chinese fishing vessels to stay away from waters around the islands. In 2011, the Japan Coast Guard issued eight such warnings; in 2014, the number had soared to 208.[22]

As tensions have risen, Japan has been careful to avoid actions that could lead to a potentially dangerous escalation. It has primarily done this by relying on the Japan Coast Guard, and not its military, to intercept Chinese vessels. This sends a clear signal that Japan's moves are a limited law-enforcement action, not a challenge directed at the Chinese state. There are fears that introducing Self-Defense Force ships or aircraft would invite a response in kind by China, which would greatly increase the risk of an accidental military conflict. Doubtlessly for the same reasons, China has also been careful to rely on civilian vessels from its coast guard and also its fisheries agency in its efforts to challenge Japan's control of the islands.

At the same time, the stepped-up Chinese activities near the islands have forced Japanese policy makers to plan for the possibility that China may make even more forceful efforts to subvert the status quo. These could include so-called gray-zone situations, in which, say, a group of Chinese citizens or even armed activists land on the islands to claim them without the overt backing of Beijing. Another scenario might be an attack on a Japanese fishing craft or other nongovernment vessel, also by some sort of armed group.

Such an attack could be very difficult to respond to effectively. While subduing an armed group may surpass the abilities of the coast guard and other law enforcement agencies, sending in the Self-Defense Forces brings the risk of a dangerous escalation, especially with Chinese military assets lurking just over the horizon.

Leaders may find themselves facing another, very different hurdle in contemplating use of the Self-Defense Forces: the tight legal restrictions that Japan has placed on the use of its postwar armed forces. There have been growing calls to work out in advance the changes in laws and procedures that Japan needs in order to respond to a crisis in the Senkakus. These would include clarifying the steps to allow the prime minister to authorize a use of lethal force. Such moves are evident in the government's *Maritime Safety Report 2015*, a planning document that says that Japan will "put in place a framework for building a seamless maritime security system in the waters around the Senkaku Islands and throughout the country."[23]

For the moment, Japan and China have avoided a military clash in the East China Sea, though just barely. This has required Japan to not only rely on its coast guard but also to show self-restraint at dangerous moments, such as when a Chinese frigate aimed its weapons radar at a Japanese destroyer in January 2013. China has also used its coast guard to press its claims, though the warships of its People's Liberation Army Navy are never far away. One result of this standoff has been a mini arms race between the two nations' coast guards, which compete to add ever-faster and larger cutters around the islands. The potential volatility of this situation has also added urgency to Japan's efforts to create "a seamless maritime security system" that would allow the Self-Defense Forces to step in quickly during an emergency, increasing their ability to serve as a deterrent to maintain the uneasy balance of peace.

The lessons of the East China Sea inform Japan's response to another, equally dangerous flash point with China, far from its own borders in the South China Sea. To help its allies in the region offset China's increasingly aggressive claims to that sea, Japan has embraced a security strategy that also relies on the use of coast guards and other law-enforcement capabilities. This strategy, known as capacity building, calls on Japan to help other nations, mostly in Southeast Asia, build up nonmilitary forces so that they can police their territorial claims, much as Japan does in the Senkaku Islands.

This strategy of capacity building was made possible by Japan's recent lifting of self-imposed restrictions on the transfer of its defense hardware abroad. The biggest changes came in 2014, when the government of Prime Minister Abe lifted a half-century ban on the export of Japanese-made weapons that had been a pillar of Japan's postwar pacifism. That same year, the administration also made legal changes that allowed Japan for the first time to provide defense-related equipment as part of its foreign aid. (There are still tight restrictions on recipient countries, which must promise not to use the Japanese-provided equipment beyond their own borders.) These changes allowed Japan to announce in May 2016 that it will lease the Philippines up to five unarmed surveillance aircraft, taken secondhand from Japan's own navy, to patrol the South China Sea. Since 2014, Japan has also pledged to provide used coast guard vessels and other patrol ships to Vietnam, Malaysia, and the Philippines to help those nations strengthen their early warning and surveillance capability.

Japan has been able to offer not only ships and equipment but also training and advisors to help less-developed Asian nations build up their coast guards and nonmilitary security capabilities. Much of this training is offered as foreign aid conducted jointly by Japan Coast Guard and Japan's main aid agency, the Japan International Cooperation Agency, or JICA. According to the Japan Coast Guard, Japan has brought 1,700 trainees from 79 countries and three regions to train with Japan Coast Guard, while also sending some 600 instructors from the Japan Coast Guard and other agencies to 24 countries.[24] Southeast Asian nations, which have been intimidated by China's growing capabilities, have been a key focus of these efforts. One such aid effort, the Maritime Safety and Security Policy Program, established in 2015 by JICA and the coast guard, offers advanced-level education in maritime security policy by inviting trainees from Asia to study at the National Graduate Institute for Policy Studies, a graduate school in Tokyo.[25]

The region's need for nonmilitary responses to China has given Japan an opportunity to expand its influence by playing to its strengths. Japan benefits from possessing one of Asia's oldest and most capable coast guards, created in 1948. By contrast, many Southeast Asian nations are only now building up their nonmilitary maritime security capabilities in response to China. The nations that have established unified coast guards and maritime security agencies independent of the navy only in the past decade or so include Malaysia (2005), Vietnam (2013), and Indonesia (2014).

The Japan Coast Guard is particularly well suited to this mission of peacefully counterbalancing China because of its unique history and organization. It was created under the postwar constitution as a means to defend Japanese territory without resorting to military force. In this way, it differs from the United States Coast Guard, which is a full-fledged military service. Other established coast guards around the world also typically have military or paramilitary roles. "The strength of the Japan Coast Guard is that it is not paramilitary," says Yuji Sato, a former commandant of the Japan Coast Guard. "That's what Asian countries are looking to."[26]

According to Sato, the Japan Coast Guard's nonmilitary character is fundamental to accomplishing its mission near the Senkaku Islands. He said the coast guard is not seeking to offer an armed challenge to the Chinese so much as "calmly" keep the status quo. In this regard, Japan's use of its coast guard illustrates the essence of the global civilian power approach: to be strong enough to counter China in the East China Sea, and help partner nations do the same in the South China Sea, by deploying a nonmilitary, law enforcement force whose ultimate goal is maintaining peace and stability.

Global Civilian Power 2.0

Today, we are seeing unprecedented threats to the principles of free and open commerce and communication that have undergirded the world's peace and growing prosperity since 1945. Many of the advanced democracies that led the postwar liberal order have now taken an inward turn toward one-country nationalism, as seen in the UK's vote for "Brexit" withdrawal from the European Union and the electoral victory of Donald Trump. At the same time, undemocratic nations have mounted challenges to the established order that include efforts to rewrite international norms. Russia and China have led efforts to disrupt the status quo by flouting the rule of law in Ukraine and the South China Sea.

In the face of this reality, Japan must step forward to contribute more to international peace and stability and uphold the liberal international order from which it has benefited so much. But it must do so in a way that is consistent with its postwar identity.

In particular, Article 9 of the constitution continues to place tight restrictions on Japan's ability to use its military, even after the Abe government's recent moves to ease some of those restraints. These include the Abe government's adoption in 2014 of collective self-defense, a reinterpretation of the constitution that allows the Self-Defense Forces to come to the aid of allies under attack. While this has been seen as opening the way for joint military actions with allies such as the United States, the fact is that collective self-defense only permits Japan to act in a crisis that is deemed to threaten the nation's existence.

Despite the reinterpretation, and a raft of new security laws passed in 2015 that drew huge popular opposition as "war legislation," Japan remains far from a "normal country" capable of relatively unfettered military action. Its military remains legally unable to participate in most multinational security efforts, whether led by the United States or organized under the auspices of the United Nations, despite the recent changes. One example of Japan's self-imposed limits came in March 2017, when Japan suddenly announced the withdrawal of its 350 peacekeepers from a UN mission in the South Sudan, apparently out of fear that the deteriorating security situation may force its soldiers to actually fire their weapons.

But this nonmilitary approach, seen in Japan's positioning of itself as a global civilian power, remains the wisest and arguably most effective strategy for the nation to pursue. Its three pillars—international cooperation for human security, advocacy of rule of law, and promotion of regional capacity building—draw no resistance from most nations, and in fact have been widely welcomed. By contrast, the other alternative, becoming a "normal" military power, faces enormous barriers that are not limited just to legal and constitutional restrictions. The hurdles would also include fiscal realities, not to mention the huge emotional pushback that could be expected from neighboring countries where memories of the war remain raw.

This is not to say that Japan should go back to the passive pacifism of the pre-1990s, either. For one, there are many vitally important areas in which the boundary between "military" and "nonmilitary" is growing increasingly hazy, such as cyberspace, gray-zone conflicts, or even China's use of its One Belt, One Road economic development initiative to build a sphere of influence. A blanket rejection of all military action could actually hurt Japan by binding its hands during an unforeseeable future crisis. Rather, the more prudent strategy would be to keep a military option available, but only as a last resort, to be used in extreme cases such as Japan coming under attack. In all other cases, Japan would insist on adhering to a strictly nonmilitary approach. This paradigm does not seem dissimilar to the stance of "proactive contributor to peace" promoted by the current government.

Maintaining a commitment to nonmilitary action, while acquiring the ability to defend oneself, represents a modification of the existing global civilian power idea. This updated version, which I shall call Global Civilian Power 2.0., is a necessary response to the realities of Asia Pacific's changing strategic environment while also remaining consistent with Japan's postwar identity. This identity, with its insistence on seeking peaceful resolutions to conflicts, and using military force only when attacked, can actually empower Japan and enable it to step out onto the global stage and take a more proactive diplomatic role in maintaining and strengthening the liberal international order. By acting as a civilian power, working on behalf of the global good, Japan can gain the support and goodwill of other nations. In other words, remaining true to its postwar ideals can be a successful formula for Japan to win greater international respect and admiration, and perhaps even become a model for emulation by other nations.

Notes

1. "Report of the Special Committee on the Role of Japan in the International Community," *Monthly Liberal Democracy* (in Japanese) 480 (1993): 279–304.

2. Ichiro Ozawa, *Blueprint for a New Japan* (in Japanese) (Tokyo: Kodansha, 1993).

3. Yoichi Funabashi, "Japan and the New World Order," *Foreign Affairs*, 70 (5, 1991/2): 58–72.

4. Toshiki Kaifu, *Politics and Money: Memoirs of Toshiki Kaifu* (in Japanese) (Tokyo: Shinchosha, 2010), p. 123.

5. Michael Green and Akira Igata, "The Gulf War and Japan's National Security Identity," in Yoichi Funabashi and Barak Kushner, eds., *Examining Japan's Lost Decades* (Abingdon, UK: Routledge, 2015), pp. 158–173.

6. Yoichi Funabashi, "The Post-Cold War World and Japan," in Yoichi Funabashi, ed., *Japanese Strategy Declaration—Towards a Civilian Superpower* (in Japanese) (Tokyo: Kodansha, 1991), p. 45.

7. The Prime Minister's Commission on Japan's Goals in the 21st Century, "The Frontier Within: Individual Empowerment and Better Governance in the New Millennium," posted January 2000, http://www.kantei.go.jp/jp/21century/report/pdfs/index.html.

8. Ibid., p. 58.

9. Ibid., p. 59.

10. Ibid., p. 199.

11. Ibid., p. 204.

12. Private conversation between a Chinese intellectual and a member of the 21st Century Commission during a trip to China after the report was released, as recounted to the author.

13. Keizo Obuchi, "Towards a Bright Asian Future," speech given in Hanoi on December 16, 1998, http://www.mofa.go.jp/region/asia-paci/asean/pmv9812/policyspeech.html.

14. "Human Security Now," Commission on Human Security, accessed July 21, 2017, http://www.un.org/humansecurity/sites/www.un.org.humansecurity/files/chs_final_report_-_english.pdf.

15. Keizo Takemi, "Presentation for Session 1: Evolution of the Human Security Concept," in Pamela J. Noda, ed., *Health and Human Security: Moving from Concept to Action—Fourth Intellectual Dialogue on Building Asia's Tomorrow* (Tokyo: Japan Center for International Exchange, 2002), p. 45.

16. Ministry of Foreign Affairs, "Support Projects by the Trust Fund for Human Security" (in Japanese), posted February 8, 2016, http://www.mofa.go.jp/mofaj/gaiko/oda/bunya/security/ah_list.html.

17. Takahiro Shinyo, "Japan's Human Security Policy and Its Diplomatic Practice" (in Japanese), *International Public Policy Research*, 13 (1, 2008): 40–41.

18. National Security Council, National Security Strategy, posted December 17, 2003, http://www.cas.go.jp/jp/siryou/131217anzenhoshou/nss-e.pdf.

19. Shinzo Abe, "Peace and Prosperity in Asia, Forevermore: Japan for the Rule of Law, Asia for the Rule of Law, and the Rule of Law for All of Us," keynote speech at the 13th IISS Asia Security Summit (Shangri-La Dialogue), May 30, 2014, http://www.mofa.go.jp/fp/nsp/page4e_000086.html.

20. Ministry of Foreign Affairs, "International Court of Justice (ICJ)—Whaling in the Antarctic," remarks by the representative of Japan, Koji Tsuruoka, posted March 31, 2014, http://www.mofa.go.jp/ecm/fsh/page2e_000012.html.

21. Ministry of Foreign Affairs, "Japan-China Summit Meeting," posted July 15, 2016, http://www.mofa.go.jp/a_o/c_m1/cn/page3e_000509.html. Also, "Clear Difference in Sino-Japanese Positions," *Asahi Shimbun* (in Japanese), July 16, 2016.

22. Japan Coast Guard, "The Current Situation and Importance of Maritime Law Enforcement Agencies," handout by Yuji Sato at Asia Pacific Initiative, May 17, 2016.

23. Japan Coast Guard and Ministry of Land, Infrastructure, Transport and Tourism, Maritime Safety Report 2015 (in Japanese), accessed July 21, 2017, http://www.kaiho.mlit.go.jp/info/books/report2015/html/tokushu/toku15 _02-5.html.

24. Sato handout.

25. "Maritime Safety and Security Policy Program at the GRIPS," National Graduate Institute for Policy Studies, accessed July 21, 2017, https://www.jcga .ac.jp/shisetu/center/pamphlet(en).pdf.

26. Yuji Sato, speaking at Asia Pacific Initiative, May 17, 2016.

CHAPTER ELEVEN

Obama in Hiroshima: A Model for Historical Reconciliation?

Jennifer Lind

Crowds lined the streets of Hiroshima, reaching out with cell phones or waving at the passing motorcade and the famous visitor within. The day was historic: Barack Obama was the first sitting American president to come to the site of the 1945 U.S. atomic bombing. His visit alongside Japanese prime minister Shinzo Abe was one of the most celebrated moments not only that year but also in the history of United States–Japan relations.

At the ceremony at the Peace Park, in short but emotional speeches, the two leaders noted how far relations between their countries had come since World War II. "Seventy years later, enemies who fought each other so fiercely have become friends, bonded in spirit, and have become allies, bound in trust and friendship, deep between us," Abe said as the American president watched. "The Japan–US alliance, which came into the world this way, has to be an alliance of hope for the world."[1]

Echoing the sentiment, Obama said, "The United States and Japan have forged not only an alliance but a friendship that has won far more for our people than we could ever claim through war." After the speech, the president stepped over to shake hands with *hibakusha*, the aging survivors of the atomic bombing, many of whom said they had thought they would never live to see this day. Sunao Tsuboi, 91, grasped the president's hand for minutes while speaking with him. A memorable image of the visit came when the president embraced Shigeaki Mori, who had been eight years old at the time of the attack and who had spent much of his life trying to uncover the fate of 12 American prisoners of war killed in the bombing.

Most media and academic commentary declared Obama's May 27, 2016, visit to Hiroshima a resounding diplomatic success. A *Kyodo News* poll reported that fully 98 percent of Japanese approved of the visit.[2] The *Mainichi Shimbun* lauded it as "a step toward true post–World War II reconciliation" between Japan and the United States.[3] It was, some commentators proclaimed, "a foothold for Japan and the US to overcome a negative chapter in their common history," a chance to remove a "thorn that has continued to hinder postwar reconciliation between Japan and the United States."[4] The two countries made history again in December, when Abe visited Pearl Harbor and mourned the "precious souls of the fallen." At the ceremony, Abe laid a wreath in honor of the "brave men and women whose lives were taken by a war that commenced in this very place, and also to the souls of the countless innocent people who became victims of the war."[5]

Some commentators went further, declaring that the United States and Japanese rapprochement gestures a model for Japan's rapprochement with the rest of Asia—particularly with estranged neighbors China and South Korea, whose relations with Japan seem permanently mired in disputes over history and territory. After all, if the United States and Japan, who had fought so bitterly during the war, can bury the hatchet, could not Japan do the same with the former victims of its early-20th-century empire building in Asia? "If Japan and the U.S., which clashed head-on with each other in the war, can move forward with their reconciliation and further deepen their friendship, Japan and other Asian countries should be able to do the same thing," wrote the *Nikkei Asian Review* in one representative article.[6]

Obama's visit to Hiroshima and Abe's visit to Pearl Harbor were indeed historic. But to argue that they can serve as a model for mending fences with the rest of Asia over history is to oversimplify their lessons and risk drawing the wrong conclusions. First, the twin visits did not bring about a rapprochement over history between the United States and Japan. In fact, they occurred decades after the countries had set their differences behind them in forging a new postwar relationship. Thus, calling these visits the cause of reconciliation—suggesting that reconciliation had previously been lacking—is misleading. It obscures the true causes, timing, and significance of one of the most striking cases of international reconciliation the world has ever seen.

While the visits were unquestionably watershed events in the United States–Japan relationship, the claim that they had finally healed the war wounds between the two countries is an assessment that mixes up cause and effect. The visits did not bring about reconciliation between the United States and Japan. Rather, they were the *result* of decades of healing and building of trust between the two former foes. This was a lengthy process in which the United States and Japan discovered new common ground; created close economic, political, and military bonds; and established one of the most enduring and important alliances of the postwar era. The visit was the product of these efforts.

Because the visits did not create the reconciliation between the United States and Japan, they cannot by themselves serve as a model for other nations. Rather, the fact that the visits were the *product* of reconciliation shows how such acts can only be the result of a deep commitment to cooperation that brings with it a willingness to compromise and find common ground. One can thus imagine Japan holding similarly meaningful visits with a number of other Asia Pacific countries—Australia, India, and the Philippines, for example—with which it has common strategic interests. But such an Obama-in-Hiroshima or Abe-in-Pearl Harbor moment remains a long way away between Japan and South Korea, and it would not be possible between Japan and China without an extraordinary reordering of regional politics.

Model for the World

The Hiroshima and Pearl Harbor visits demonstrated the ability of the United States and Japan to move beyond the past and build a durable alliance. The significance of this accomplishment becomes all the more apparent when compared with other cases in history, which show that such reconciliation after war is difficult and rare. Countries that fight wars often fall into relationships of enduring and often bitter rivalry. By the same token, alliances between countries also tend to be driven by narrow self-interest, with the partners cooperating only with respect to a particular shared challenge. Once that challenge disappears, the impetus for working together is also lost, and the alliance itself can dissolve. To paraphrase Lord Palmerston's famous observation, countries have "no permanent friends, only permanent interests." This all goes to underscore just how truly remarkable the reconciliation was between Japan and the United States after World War II—*prior* to the historic visits of 2016.

How did the United States and Japan achieve this? The first step, made in the 1950s, was the two countries' initial decision to align. Given their shared history, this move was itself striking. Their soldiers had faced each other in brutal combat, fighting not just each other but unforgiving climates, disease, hunger, and fear of death, capture, and execution. Japan had attacked Pearl Harbor, killing and wounding more than 3,500 Americans. American prisoners of war held by the Japanese suffered and starved as forced laborers. The United States pulverized not only Hiroshima and Nagasaki but 67 other Japanese cities, including Tokyo, which had been laid waste by fire bombs. At home, choked by the U.S. naval blockade, Japan's people starved and mourned. As John Dower has shown, soldiers and civilians on both sides were fed a steady fare of hateful, racist propaganda about the savagery of the enemy.[7]

In this context, postwar cooperation between Tokyo and Washington was in itself remarkable. The victorious United States abandoned the idea of a punitive peace in favor of rebuilding Japan and creating a prosperous democracy as a bulwark in East Asia against communism. For their part, the Japanese people chose not to resist the occupiers. As Dower writes, the Americans "encountered a populace sick of war, contemptuous of the militarists who had led them to disaster, and all but overwhelmed by the difficulties of their present circumstances in a ruined land."[8] Japan's total defeat certainly narrowed its choices. But after the devastating war they had just fought, the decision of most Japanese people not to resist the U.S. occupation, and the decision on both sides to cooperate, was historic.

Their cooperation was all the more remarkable because of the plethora of other differences that the two countries had to bridge, including culture, language, religion, and geography. Edwin O. Reischauer recognized the historic nature of the reconciliation early on: in 1960, the Harvard professor (and later ambassador to Japan) called the United States–Japan relationship a model for relations "across cultural and racial lines for the whole world." For the United States and Japan, Reischauer argued, enjoyed "the closest relations that had ever been developed between a Western country and a major nation of non-Western background."[9]

That said, the alliance in those early postwar years was in no way an equal partnership. The American occupiers, particularly those in the military, remained bitter and distrustful of the Japanese. The American and other Allied presence in Japan was neocolonial. The Americans took over areas of Tokyo that had withstood the aerial bombings, requisitioned grand houses from their owners, and filled those houses with Japanese maids, laundresses, gardeners, and cooks.[10] The hub of social life in Japan was the American Club, where the only Japanese allowed were waiters and bartenders.[11] Scavenging for food in the ruins of Tokyo, the Japanese saw American wives shopping at U.S. military stores and commissaries, whose shelves were filled with huge steaks and sacks of rice and impossible luxuries like chocolate. The Yanks reclined in rickshaws pulled by trotting Japanese; desperate Japanese women turned to prostitution to service the occupiers. "I and nearly all the Occupation people I knew," recalled official Faubion Bowers, "were extremely conceited and extremely arrogant and used our power every inch of the way."[12]

After Japan began its economic recovery in the 1950s, doubts grew there about the wisdom of alignment with the United States. Some leaders, even within the governing Liberal Democratic Party, advocated a more equidistant policy toward Washington, Beijing, and Moscow in a desire to keep Japan neutral and disarmed in East Asia's emerging political competition. Many Japanese doubted whether the Soviet Union or any other country actually posed a threat. As John Emmerson wrote at the time, "the Japanese in general feel no immediate threat to the security of their country."[13]

Many Japanese worried that siding with the United States could entangle Japan in Cold War conflicts, such as the American standoffs with the Soviet Union over Berlin and later Cuba. Soviet foreign minister Andrei Gromyko left nothing to Japan's imagination when he told Japan's ambassador in Moscow that if war were to occur, "all Japan with her small and thickly populated territory, dotted . . . with foreign war bases, risks sharing the tragic fate of Hiroshima and Nagasaki in the very first minutes of hostilities."[14] Japanese critics of the alliance also saw it as corrosive to Japan's young democracy because of American support for conservatives in Japan, such as Prime Minister Nobusuke Kishi, who had been a member of the Imperial cabinet. (Later evidence has shown that the Central Intelligence Agency did indeed support right-wing Japanese leaders while undermining and infiltrating the opposition left).[15]

During the 1950s, as the two countries discussed an upcoming revision of the security treaty, Tokyo sought to change what many viewed as a highly unequal relationship. The original 1951 treaty provided no constraints on the United States' use of its Japanese bases and no rules about the stationing of nuclear weapons there. The treaty even empowered the U.S. military to use force to quell domestic disturbances within Japan. Another sore spot was Okinawa, which remained under American military control. The United States governed Okinawa "like a colony," noted Reischauer's aide Ernest Young, as the island's military administrators enjoyed large mansions filled with servants and private golf courses.[16] Okinawan farmers protested what they saw as inadequate compensation for their lands used for military bases; people on the island resented the thundering planes and the debauched and sometimes violent American troops.

In 1960, as the treaty revision deadline loomed, more and more Japanese opposed the alliance, and protests spread. Dwight Eisenhower had planned to be the first American president ever to visit Japan; he was forced to cancel after his advance team was surrounded by angry protestors and had to be airlifted away. When Prime Minister Kishi engaged in extralegal measures to pass legislation to renew the treaty, hundreds of thousands of marching protestors filled Tokyo's streets. The demonstrators, wrote Reischauer, "wanted the treaty killed and the present military link with the United States, together with the existing American bases in Japan, either eliminated at once or else ended in stages."[17]

Despite such resistance from the political left, Kishi and U.S. secretary of state Christian Herter signed the new treaty on January 19, 1960. It obligated the United States to help defend Japan if Japan came under attack in exchange for allowing the U.S. military to use bases and ports in Japan. Given its turbulent beginnings, the treaty has proven remarkably resilient, as George R. Packard, president of the United States–Japan Foundation, wrote in *Foreign Affairs*:

> The agreement has endured through half a century of dramatic changes in world politics—the Vietnam War, the collapse of the Soviet Union, the spread of nuclear weapons to North Korea, the rise of China—and in spite of fierce trade disputes, exchanges of insults, and deep cultural and historical differences between the United States and Japan. This treaty has lasted longer than any other alliance between two great powers since the 1648 Peace of Westphalia.[18]

Forging Reconciliation

How did the United States and Japan build such an enduring alliance? While the initial decision to align had rested on a perception of a shared security threat, in the turbulence of the early 1960s, leaders in Tokyo and Washington realized that narrow national interests alone would not be enough to sustain the relationship. Not just the Japanese leadership but the people had to be convinced that close ties with the United States were desirable, and not solely for security reasons. As Reischauer observed, the alliance had to be reimagined and broadened. "I saw Japan rapidly catching up with the United States in most matters and felt that a relationship of full equality was a necessity for the future," he wrote.[19] Japanese historian Makoto Saito noted "a keen feeling in Japan today of the need for 'diplomacy in depth' between our two countries . . . it is no longer sufficient to do business merely with the government in power."[20]

Furthermore, the Americans realized that they had to resolve the problem of Okinawa. Reischauer, who became ambassador to Japan under John F. Kennedy, argued that Japanese resentment over continued American control of the island could potentially break the alliance. Shuttling tirelessly between Tokyo and Okinawa, Reischauer mediated between U.S. military commanders and the Japanese to build understanding. In March 1962, the Kennedy administration announced a series of reforms in Okinawa and the United States' intention to eventually return Okinawa to Japanese sovereignty. The reversion was delayed by President Kennedy's assassination but finally took place in 1972.

American and Japanese leaders realized that they had to build wider and deeper support for the alliance within their societies by expanding dialogue and cooperation. They set out to do just that, making the 1960s pivotal in the creation of a new kind of United States–Japan relationship. This goal became explicit at a 1961 summit between President Kennedy and Prime Minister Hayao Ikeda, who sought to broaden United States–Japan relations beyond a politico-military alliance by creating a program of cabinet-level exchanges to foster economic and scientific cooperation. The two leaders created the United States–Japan Conference on Cultural and Educational Interchange, or CULCON, to encourage interactions outside of government in the realms of arts and education. The inaugural meeting in Tokyo in 1962 included such participants as composer Aaron Copeland and novelist Robert Penn Warren and proclaimed a goal of bridging two countries "widely separated by differences of thought, manners, and tradition."[21] CULCON urged increases in the teaching of the English language in Japan and of Japanese in the United States; interactions between artists, sculptors, writers, and musicians; and fellowships and exchange programs for students and scholars. It also sought to broaden its programs by including women as well as intellectuals critical of the alliance. CULCON continues today, alternating meetings in both countries.

Leaders also used official visits to strengthen bilateral ties. The Kennedy administration, assisted by officials and private citizens in Japan, began planning what would have been a historic first visit to Japan by an American president. In 1962, President Kennedy dispatched his brother, Robert Kennedy, to Japan to lay the groundwork for the trip. Though the planning was cut short by the president's tragic assassination, Robert Kennedy's visit itself served as a milestone in the bilateral relationship.[22] Before he arrived, the Japanese had formed an RK Committee to manage the visit, which included pro-alliance Japanese officials. Many of them, such as Yasuhiro Nakasone, the future prime minister, went on to have long careers as alliance managers. After the visit, the RK Committee spawned numerous activities and institutions designed to strengthen the two nations' partnership. One was a forum for bilateral dialogue called the Shimoda Conference, which was first convened in 1967 at the Japanese seaside town of that name and has been held periodically ever since (most recently in 2011). At the 1967 meeting, over 70 Japanese and American politicians, industrialists, and academics discussed bilateral relations; delegates from the Japanese side expressed frank views that the continued delay in the reversion of Okinawa to Japan would threaten the future of the bilateral relationship.

Over the next half century, these efforts paid off to an astonishing degree. What had begun as a narrow military alliance evolved into a broad relationship between the two nations and their people. Washington embraced Tokyo as a partner in global governance, welcoming it into the myriad of multilateral economic and political institutions created after World War II. Japan emerged as a leader in international development with its creation of the Asian Development Bank and other institutions. Bilateral economic ties flourished: today, Japan is the fourth-largest trading partner of the United States, and the United States is Japan's second-largest partner. Tourists and students flow back and forth. Cooperation in the arts, education, science, and sports has proliferated, seen in everything from shared Nobel Prizes to Hollywood soundtracks composed by Japanese musicians and Major League Baseball records set by Japanese athletes.

Political and military cooperation between the two countries has also deepened and broadened. Despite continuing opposition within Japan, Tokyo has gradually accepted the need to widen the scope of the United States–Japan alliance beyond the narrow interest of defending the Japanese home islands. Legislation passed by Japan in 2015 acknowledges that conflict elsewhere in Asia could be deeply consequential for Japan's security and authorizes broader action beyond its borders than has ever been allowed in the postwar period. While still constrained by a constitution that eschews war as a means of resolving disputes, Japan has eased the institutional inhibitions on its military activity and in the process empowered itself to contribute more to both the alliance with the United States and regional security.

Today, both countries increasingly speak not just of a bilateral alliance but of shared efforts toward the larger goal of sustaining and broadening the world order based on democracy and market economics. Liberal internationalists in Tokyo and Washington reject Lord Palmerston's dictum about no "permanent friends" and view one another as essential partners in upholding this global liberal order. "It is my belief," declared Prime Minister Abe in 2013, "that Japan and the U.S. together should lead the Indo-Pacific Century to make it one that cherishes freedom, democracy, human rights, and rules-based order."[23] Japan is cultivating partnerships with other democratic states as well; for example, Abe and India's Narendra Modi pledged to work for a "peaceful, open, equitable, stable and rule-based order in the Indo-Pacific region and beyond."[24]

Obama's visit to Hiroshima was indeed a historic moment in the United States–Japan alliance. But it was a moment made possible by a myriad of earlier decisions and actions over the previous decades that had built remarkably deep and enduring bonds between the two wartime foes.

Hiroshima Visit as Model?

Obama's visit to Hiroshima raised expectations that it could serve as a model for how Japan and its closest neighbors could move forward after their long inability to reconcile. The White House, quoted by *The Washington Post*, asserted this view, saying that one goal of the president's trip was to "perhaps open the door to more symbolic, trust-building gestures among leaders in the region."[25]

While no one could object to encouraging greater empathy among Japan and its neighbors, these expectations confuse cause and effect. As shown, grand gestures such as Obama's visit to Hiroshima are in fact the *result* of a long process of reconciliation—not the starting point. Acts of shared remembrance, including also Abe's visit to Pearl Harbor, are only possible between countries that strongly value cooperation and that can show a level of frankness, trust, and willingness to compromise. Japan and its neighbors China and South Korea lack the shared strategic need that drives such cooperation. In other words, Prime Minister Abe cannot "go to Nanjing" in the same way that he went to Pearl Harbor or Obama went to Hiroshima. The underlying conditions for such a visit are absent.

In the aftermath of war, bitter memories can remain for years, decades, even generations. Former adversaries paint each other as the aggressor while emphasizing their own suffering. Tales of the rival's abuses— "Japanese devils," "Yankee wolves," "the Huns"—are remembered through government propaganda, political cartoons, song lyrics, art, novels, and history books. As people become convinced of the rival's dishonest and dangerous nature, cooperation becomes politically harder to achieve.

Sometimes, however, former adversaries find themselves in a position of needing each other. This can happen when they face a shared security threat. For cooperation to succeed, they cannot continue to dwell on the traumatic past and to vilify each other. Instead, they must convince their people why the other side qualifies as a reliable partner. So countries find a way to frame the past that supports this goal; they "harmonize" their narratives.[26]

Witness the French and the West Germans in the decades after World War II, when a shared fear of the Soviet Union and a superpower war fought on their territory led them to overcome vastly different interpretations of the war. The French abandoned the narrative, prevalent in the 1950s, of an inherently violent German national character. Leaders in the two countries crafted a new, joint narrative: that democracy and pan-European unity were the only ways to bring peace to a continent torn apart by centuries of conflict. French and German leaders have encouraged this narrative with staged, shared remembrances at Reims Cathedral in 1962, Verdun in 1984, and elsewhere.[27]

The same willingness to compromise that led French and West German leaders to clasp hands at Verdun brought Obama to Hiroshima. Like the Europeans, the United States and Japan were pushed together by strategic necessity. The alliance was created in the days of the Soviet threat and in recent years has been given new life in the face of rising Chinese power and assertiveness. The United States sees Japan as a key regional military ally and like-minded partner in a host of other issues. Japan wants to maintain regional influence, deter Chinese claims to the Japanese-controlled islands, and preserve the existing trade and financial order from which it has benefited. The alliance therefore rests on a foundation of shared interests, and both governments are committed to preserving and strengthening it.[28]

Partners who value each other show empathy toward one another—and Obama's decision to visit Hiroshima reflected this. Tomohiko Taniguchi, a speechwriter and special advisor to the prime minister, wrote of the "deep grief and sorrow many in the country feel every year in August, on the anniversaries of the atomic bombings of Hiroshima and Nagasaki, and of Japan's surrender which ended World War Two." Though Japan's people "silently buried the pain," he wrote, they felt pain nonetheless.[29]

In fact, expectations had been building within Japan that Obama, who had won a Nobel Peace Prize in 2009 for his call to abolish nuclear weapons, would become the first American president to visit either Hiroshima or Nagasaki. This hope was expressed by Hiroshima mayor Kazumi Matsui a year before the visit: "President Obama and other policymakers, please come to the A-bombed cities . . . and encounter the reality of the atomic bombings."[30] Hiroshima TV conducted a "Letters to Obama" campaign in which it solicited expressions of support for a visit, which it forwarded to the White House: "letters written by governors, members of economic organizations, university professors, professional baseball team owners, atomic bomb survivors, students and housewives."[31]

During the ceremony at Hiroshima, Abe and Obama presented a shared narrative of the lessons of the bombing and of World War II. To be sure, the two countries' memories of the war diverge in many ways. However, at Hiroshima that day, the two leaders sought common ground by expressing messages that both countries could support: a call for abolition of nuclear weapons, remembrance of the war's suffering, and celebration of postwar reconciliation.

From the visit's planning stages, the White House had described the president's purpose as seeking "to highlight his continued commitment to pursuing the peace and security of a world without nuclear weapons."[32] Once in Hiroshima, Obama emphasized the terrible destruction of nuclear weapons, writing in the A-bomb memorial's guest book: "We have known the agony of war. Let us now find the courage, together, to spread peace, and pursue a world without nuclear weapons."[33] Abe used the same language in his speech, proclaiming that "we are determined to realize a world free of nuclear weapons" and that Japan, as the only country to have come under atomic attack, has a special responsibility "to make sure that terrible experience is never repeated anywhere."[34]

The leaders jointly warned of the horrors of war by speaking in moving terms about the other side's losses. Abe echoed remarks he had made the previous year in Washington, in which he honored the American war dead: "That war deprived many American youngsters of their dreams and futures." In his speech, Obama memorably lamented Japanese loss of life:

> We come to mourn the dead. We stand here in the middle of this city and force ourselves to imagine the moment the bomb fell. We force ourselves to feel the dread of children confused by what they see. We listen to a silent cry. Mere words cannot give voice to such suffering. But we have a shared responsibility to look directly into the eye of history and ask what we must do differently to curb such suffering again.[35]

Obama also sought to draw a universal lesson from Hiroshima's suffering, saying that he had come to "reflect on the nature of war" and "recognize that innocent people caught in war can suffer tremendously." He referred to the 60 million who died worldwide during the war, a gesture that, as Council on Foreign Relations scholar Sheila Smith put it, served to "remind us of the expanse that was World War II and the catastrophe that was World War II that was culminated in the dropping of the bombs."[36]

Both leaders also echoed each other in celebrating the reconciliation that their countries had achieved following the horrors of war. This message came through clearly when Abe declared the United States–Japan relationship an "alliance of hope for the world" and when Obama embraced Japan's aging *hibakusha.*

Shared narratives require concessions by both sides, and the remembrance at Hiroshima reflected significant compromises, especially by Tokyo. This was evident during the ceremony, when the Japanese audience accepted without a murmur Obama's bluntly critical description of their country's wartime behavior as reflecting a "base instinct for domination or conquest."

More importantly, the Japanese accepted what was *not* in the speech. Before his arrival, the president and his administration made it clear that, despite the deaths of hundreds of thousands of civilians, he would not be offering an apology. "The president is not going to revisit the decision to use the atomic bomb" was the phrasing offered by both the principal deputy press secretary, Eric Schultz, and the deputy national security advisor, Ben Rhodes.[37] When asked in an NHK interview if he would apologize, Obama was blunt and frank in explaining why he would not: "I think that it's important to recognize that in the midst of war, leaders make all kinds of decisions. It's a job of historians to ask questions and examine them, but I know as somebody who has now sat in this position for the last seven and a half years, that every leader makes very difficult decisions, particularly during war time."[38]

Obama's visit was only possible because of Tokyo's decision to accept it on these terms.[39] Japanese leaders showed a keen sensitivity to American domestic sensibilities, especially in an era of increasing political polarization and extreme rhetoric in the United States. Obama had previously given multiple speeches, including in Strasbourg and Cairo, that American conservatives had derided as part of an "apology tour." The Japanese understood that a presidential visit to Hiroshima made Obama vulnerable again to such criticism from the American right.[40] They had seen opinion polls showing 73 percent of the U.S. public opposed an apology for the atomic bombings. One Japanese official told me, "Given the domestic political climate in the United States at the moment, the Japanese government is sensitive to the impact such a visit could have on US-Japan relations."

Japan's own highly fraught experiences with official apologies toward its neighbors also made Tokyo all too aware of the political complexities that the administration faced. Indeed, regional sensitivities about Obama's visit were another concern for not pushing the Americans: Japan wanted to avoid criticism among its neighbors that Obama was reinforcing a Japanese "victim narrative" in which Japan casts itself as receiving, and not inflicting, the bulk of suffering during the war.[41]

Thus, the Japan–United States remembrance at Hiroshima would not have been possible without an extraordinary willingness to compromise on Tokyo's part. From the calls by local mayors and citizens groups that inspired the visit, to the careful consultations with the White House in the delicate planning stages, to allowing Secretary of State John Kerry to test the water by visiting Hiroshima on the sidelines of a Group of Seven meeting, to the moment when Obama and Abe stood shoulder to shoulder in front of the cenotaph to lay two—not one—wreaths before it, Tokyo showed the flexibility necessary to make Obama's visit a reality. From start to finish, the event was a negotiated, bilateral event.

Could Abe "Go to Nanjing"?

Could the Hiroshima and Pearl Harbor visits serve as models for Japan to reconcile with its neighbors in East Asia? As described above, such symbolic gestures are the culmination of a long process of compromise and cooperation that usually starts with recognition of a shared strategic need.

In Japan's relations with China, the necessary conditions are absent. Not only do the two countries lack a shared threat, they have conflicting strategic interests, seen in the standoff over the Senkaku/Diaoyu islands, which Japan administers but both nations claim. China's potentially volatile mixture of authoritarianism and nationalism also adds to tensions, as when an angry mob attacked the Japanese consulate in Shanghai in 2005. The growing rivalry encourages not empathy but hostility, pushing China's and Japan's national historical narratives even further apart, not closer together.

The prospects for reconciliation are only slightly more promising between Japan and South Korea. Americans often argue that Tokyo and Seoul, their two biggest East Asian allies, need to cooperate against North Korea. The two countries also share much more than that: both are liberal democracies bound by thriving economic ties and a shared interest in upholding the liberal international order. However, South Korea clearly sees itself as lacking the strategic need to cooperate with Japan. Against the North Korean threat, South Korea relies almost exclusively on the United States. While Tokyo could offer some support, as recognized by those South Koreans who urge intelligence sharing and other forms of cooperation, the additional security benefit that Japan offers South Korea is marginal.

The countries' interests also appear to diverge with respect to China. Seoul has not usually shared Tokyo's anxious view of China as its most pressing strategic threat. In fact, growing economic ties and lack of a significant territorial dispute have tended to make Beijing's ties with Seoul less troubled than those with Tokyo. (There have been exceptions, such as a 2017 standoff between China and South Korea over deployment of a U.S. antimissile system.) South Korea has stayed out of the new efforts by not just Japan and the United States but other states in the region, including Australia and Vietnam, to counterbalance China's territorial assertiveness in maritime East Asia. South Korea's security concerns remain focused on its own peninsula and the threat from the North and not on the East or South China Seas.

With a lack of a strategic imperative to reconcile, Japan and South Korea maintain divergent narratives about the war and Japan's early-20th-century colonization of the Korean peninsula. These differences, which also include conflicting claims to the Dokdo/Takeshima islands, grow so emotionally charged that the two countries' leaders can appear unable to even have a conversation, much less engage in a shared contemplation of history. Despite past pledges to look toward the future rather than the past, South Koreans have continued to insist on their own victimhood, demanding apologies and criticizing Japan for what they call a failure to atone for wartime atrocities. These demands have been met with "apology fatigue" in Japan, where conservatives push back by disputing the narratives put forth by the Koreans and promoting more "patriotic" depictions of Japan's past behavior.[42]

Given these constant clashes over history, the governments of Abe and his South Korean counterpart at the time, Park Geun-hye, surprised everyone in December 2015 by reaching a landmark deal on one of the most contentious historical issues dividing the two nations. The deal was intended to put to rest once and for all a festering, decades-old dispute over so-called "comfort women" forced to work in Japanese wartime military brothels. In the agreement, the Abe government admitted the Imperial army's involvement in coercing the women, overruling objections by Japanese conservatives—including many of the prime minister's own supporters—that the military played no role. In no uncertain terms, Japan declared that the abuses constituted "a grave affront to the honor and dignity of large numbers of women" and acknowledged "the Government of Japan is painfully aware of responsibilities from this perspective."[43] Abe also expressed his "most sincere apologies and remorse to all the women who underwent immeasurable and painful experiences," and Japan agreed to pay ¥1 billion, or about $10 million, to the surviving comfort women, now in their 80s and 90s. In return, South Korea agreed to regard the matter as resolved.

That agreement was groundbreaking because it suggested that, after years of acrimony, the two countries were moving closer to a shared narrative of their troubled past.[44] The deal required substantial compromise on both sides. Abe had to end his government's previous evasion and backtracking about official culpability by acknowledging that the Japanese government bore responsibility. He apologized to the women and offered compensation, reversing the Japanese government's position that all claims to compensation had been settled by a 1965 treaty establishing diplomatic relations with South Korea. The agreement also rejected the claims by Japan's right that the comfort women were nothing more than camp-following prostitutes who had worked voluntarily.

Nor would the deal have been possible without compromise by South Korea. President Park agreed to accept Abe's apology and admission of responsibility as the final word on the issue, a bold move for a government under enormous domestic pressure to take a harder line against Japan on history. By making the deal, the Park government showed a willingness to move past a particularly divisive historical issue, agreeing that both countries would "refrain from accusing or criticizing each other regarding this issue in the international community." In a nod to Japanese feelings, Seoul also acknowledged that Tokyo perceived the comfort woman statue outside its embassy in Seoul as an affront to Japan's "dignity."

However, there are signs that South Korea, at least, may not be ready for a shared new narrative on the comfort women. In May 2017, South Korean voters elected as their president Moon Jae-in, a liberal human rights lawyer who had criticized the comfort women deal. In a June 2017 interview with *The Washington Post*, Moon said his predecessor may have gotten ahead of the South Korean people, who were not ready for such reconciliation, at least on the current deal's terms. "The reality is the majority of our people cannot emotionally accept the comfort women agreement," Moon said. He said Japan must go further by offering an official government apology in addition to the personal one offered by Abe. However, Moon also stopped short of saying that the deal needed to be renegotiated, adding that he did not want this issue to block all ties with Tokyo: "But we should not block the advancement of Korea-Japan bilateral relations just because of this one issue."[45]

Officially, Japan has reacted in measured tones. "This agreement, which is highly evaluated by international society, is being steadily implemented," said the government's top spokesperson, Chief Cabinet Secretary Yoshihide Suga.[46] However, Japanese diplomats warn privately of a potential backlash in Japan, where many describe frustration with yet more South Korean demands.

It remains unclear whether or not the 2015 deal will actually unravel. Much will depend on South Korea's evolving views of China and whether ties with Beijing continue to sour, as they did during the 2017 antimissile system dispute. A change in South Korea's threat perception about China may push Seoul to seek deeper cooperation with Tokyo. Perhaps someday the two countries can eventually hold their own versions of Obama's visit to Hiroshima and Abe's visit to Pearl Harbor. However, the postwar experience of the United States and Japan suggests that a significant shift in perceptions is needed before Japanese and South Korean leaders can stand side by side at a site of past suffering.

Meanwhile, Japan has other former adversaries in the region with whom it has already reconciled, including Australia, India, and the Philippines. These and other countries found common ground with Japan as a result of the Cold War or due to shared alarm about Chinese encroachments. Bound by shared strategic interests, many of these nations have already held their own ceremonies with Japan to jointly mourn the past. In 2015, Japan's Emperor Akihito and Empress Michiko visited the Pacific Ocean battlefield of Peleliu, an island in the Republic of Palau, where they prayed not only for the fallen Japanese and American soldiers but also noted the suffering of islanders caught in between.[47] In 2016, the Imperial couple also paid a similarly moving visit to the Philippines.[48] In cases like these, where the countries share strategic interests, Obama's visit to Hiroshima, and Abe's reciprocal visit to Pearl Harbor, can provide a useful template.

The extraordinary acts of shared remembrance at Hiroshima and Pearl Harbor do provide hope for countries divided by a violent past. However, they can only serve as a model for countries that are strongly committed to reconciliation and have spent years carefully building domestic support. Only such countries will be motivated to find a shared narrative with which to discuss history; only such countries will find the necessary empathy and willingness to compromise that such gestures require. To date, an absence of shared strategic need has prevented such cooperation between Japan and its closest neighbors. There are signs that such conditions may one day appear with South Korea, but reconciliation with China will continue to be elusive.

Notes

1. "Remarks by President Obama and Prime Minister Abe of Japan at Hiroshima Peace Memorial," The White House, posted May 27, 2016, https://obama

whitehouse.archives.gov/the-press-office/2016/05/27/remarks-president-obama
-and-prime-minister-abe-japan-hiroshima-peace.

2. "Majority of Japanese View Obama's Visit to Hiroshima Positively," *Sputnik News*, posted on May 26, 2016, https://sputniknews.com/asia/201605291040
444402-japan-obama-hiroshima/.

3. "Obama's Hiroshima Visit Can Open Way to Broader Reconciliation," *Mainichi Shimbun*, May 28, 2016.

4. Curt Mills, "Obama's Hiroshima Visit a Historic Milestone," *U.S. News & World Report*, May 27, 2016; see also "US-Japan Reconciliation Process over Hiroshima and Nagasaki," Nippon.com, September 19, 2014.

5. "Shinzo Abe at Pearl Harbor: 'Rest in Peace, Precious Souls of the Fallen,'" *The New York Times*, December 27, 2016.

6. "Obama's Hiroshima Visit Can Inspire Steps toward Asian Stability," *Nikkei Asian Review*, June 2, 2016.

7. John W. Dower, *War Without Mercy: Race and Power in the Pacific War* (New York: Pantheon, 1993).

8. John W. Dower, *Embracing Defeat: Japan in the Wake of World War II* (New York: Norton, 1999), p. 24.

9. Edwin O. Reischauer, "The Broken Dialogue with Japan," *Foreign Affairs*, 39 (1, October 1960): 12.

10. Dower, 1999, p. 216.

11. George R. Packard, *Edwin O. Reischauer and the American Discovery of Japan* (New York: Columbia University Press, 2010), p. 157.

12. Eiji Takemae, *The Allied Occupation of Japan* (New York: Continuum, 2003), p. 76.

13. John K. Emmerson, "Japan: Eye on 1970," *Foreign Affairs*, 47 (2, 1969): 356–357.

14. Quoted in Michael Schaller, *Altered States: The US and Japan Since the Occupation* (Oxford, UK: Oxford University Press, 1997), p. 145.

15. Tim Weiner, *Legacy of Ashes: the History of the CIA* (New York: Knopf Doubleday, 2007).

16. Jennifer Lind, "When Camelot Went to Japan," *National Interest*, July/August 2013.

17. Reischauer, 1960, p. 12.

18. George R. Packard, "The United States-Japan Security Treaty at 50," *Foreign Affairs*, March/April 2010, p. 89.

19. Edwin O. Reischauer, *My Life Between Japan and America* (New York: HarperCollins, 1986).

20. Makoto Saito, "Reflections on American-Japanese Relations," *Far Eastern Survey*, 29 (10, 1960): 151–153.

21. Douglas Overton, "US and Japan Probe Cultures," *Christian Science Monitor*, March 22, 1962, p. 3.

22. Lind, 2013.

23. "Remarks by Prime Minister Shinzo Abe on the Occasion of Accepting Hudson Institute's 2013 Herman Kahn Award," Cabinet Public Relations Office,

posted September 25, 2013, http://japan.kantei.go.jp/96_abe/statement/201309
/25hudson_e.html.

24. Natalie Obiko Pearson, "Abe-Modi Deals Shows Asia's Top Powers Moving to Keep Rising China in Check," *The Japan Times*, December 14, 2015.

25. David Nakamura, "In Hiroshima, Obama Will Offer a Chance for Reconciliation that Is Fraught on All Sides," *The Washington Post*, May 26, 2016.

26. Charles Kupchan, *How Enemies Become Friends: The Sources of Stable Peace* (Princeton, CT: Princeton University Press, 2010); Yinan He, *The Search for Reconciliation: Sino-Japanese and German-Polish Relations Since World War II* (Cambridge, UK: Cambridge University Press, 2009).

27. Jennifer Lind, *Sorry States: Apologies in International Politics* (Ithaca, NY: Cornell University Press, 2008).

28. Many Japanese and other observers feared the weakening of the relationship after Donald Trump's election, but the Trump administration remained committed to the United States–Japan relationship. See Jennifer Lind, "The Art of the Bluff: The US-Japan Alliance Under the Trump Administration," essay for The H-Diplo/ISSF Policy Series: "America and the World—2017 and Beyond," April 25, 2017.

29. Tomohiko Taniguchi, "Why Even No Apology Was Welcome in Hiroshima," *Nikkei Asian Review*, May 31, 2016.

30. Scott Neuman, "70 Years After Atomic Bombs, Japan Still Struggles with Wartime Past," NPR, posted August 6, 2015, http://www.npr.org/sections/thetwo
-way/2015/08/06/429989339/70-years-after-atomic-bombs-japan-still-struggles
-with-war-past.

31. Hideaki Miyama, "An Obama Visit to Hiroshima Would Send the Right Message," *The Japan Times*, September 15, 2015.

32. "Statement by the Press Secretary on the President's Travel to Vietnam and Japan," The White House, posted May 10, 2016, https://www.whitehouse
.gov/the-press-office/2016/05/10/statement-press-secretary-presidents-travel
-vietnam-and-japan.

33. Motoko Rich, "President Obama Visits Hiroshima," *The New York Times*, posted May 27, 2016, http://www.nytimes.com/live/president-obama-hiroshima
-japan/obama-greets-survivors/.

34. Quoted in Gardiner Harris et al., "Obama to Be First Sitting President to Visit Hiroshima," *The New York Times*, May 10, 2016.

35. "Text of President Obama's Speech in Hiroshima, Japan," *The New York Times*, May 27, 2016.

36. "Obama Visits Hiroshima, Which Symbolizes Atomic Age Horrors," *Morning Edition*, National Public Radio, May 27, 2016, accessed November 28, 2017, https://www-s1.npr.org/templates/transcript/transcript.php?storyId=4796
96617.

37. "Press Briefing by the Principal Deputy Press Secretary Eric Schultz," The White House, posted May 20, 2016, https://www.whitehouse.gov/the-press
-office/2016/05/20/press-briefing-principal-deputy-press-secretary-eric-schultz
-52016.

38. "Exclusive Interview with President Obama," *NHK News*, posted May 22, 2016, http://www3.nhk.or.jp/nhkworld/en/news/editors/5/20160522/.

39. Japan adopted this model—acknowledgement without apology—for Abe's subsequent visit to Pearl Harbor. On the benefits of the model, see Lind, 2008. On the Pearl Harbor visit, see Steve Herman, "Japan: Abe Will Not Apologize at Pearl Harbor," *VOA News*, December 6, 2016, and Jennifer Lind, "It Took Years of Diplomacy for Abe and Obama to Stand Together at Pearl Harbor," *Quartz*, December 27, 2016.

40. See, for example, John Bolton, "Obama's Shameful Apology Tour Lands in Hiroshima," *New York Post*, May 26, 2016.

41. Emma Chanlett-Avery, "A Presidential Visit to Hiroshima," Congressional Research Service, April 21, 2016.

42. Yoshiko Nozaki, *War Memory, Nationalism and Education in Postwar Japan: the Japanese History Textbook Controversy and Ienaga Saburo's Court Challenges* (London: Routledge, 2008); also Koichi Nakano, "Political Dynamics of Contemporary Japanese Nationalism," in Jeff Kingston, ed., *Asian Nationalisms Reconsidered* (London: Routledge, 2016), pp. 160–171.

43. "Full Text: Japan-South Korea Statement on Comfort Women," *The Wall Street Journal*, December 28, 2015.

44. Anna Fifield, "Japan, South Korea Reach Settlement on Wartime Korean Sex Slaves," *The Washington Post*, December 28, 2015.

45. Lally Weymouth, "South Korea's New President: 'Trump and I Have a Common Goal,'" *The Washington Post*, June 20, 2017.

46. Christine Kim, "South Korea's Moon Asking for Japan's Patience in Resolving 'Past History,'" *Reuters*, June 12, 2017.

47. Martin Fackler, "Ahead of World War II Anniversary, Questions Linger Over Stance of Japan's Premier," *The New York Times*, April 9, 2015.

48. Yuki Tatsumi, "Japan's Emperor Visits Philippines: Major Takeaways," *The Diplomat*, February 6, 2016; Alan Rix, *The Australia-Japan Political Alignment: 1952 to the Present* (London: Routledge, 1999), p. 33.

Conclusion: Japan's Frontiers Are Global Frontiers

Yoichi Funabashi

An Age without Models

The twin forces of the digital revolution and globalization have brought exhilarating changes to our world but also a growing popular backlash. Millions in developing nations have been lifted from poverty and given opportunities that were unimaginable just a generation earlier. At the same time, an increasingly homogenous global culture is creating new sources of income disparity, unemployment, and industrial hollowing. People feel that not only their economic livelihoods but also their communities and even their very belief systems are under threat.

There has also been growing anxiety about the future. Industrialized countries face protracted economic stagnation, sluggish or declining wages, and the rise of protectionist sentiments. Low birth rates have led to "silver democracies" dominated by aging voters, creating new challenges in the form of intergenerational inequalities and the question of how to manage societies of citizens with ever longer life spans. Geopolitically, the rise of new powers and the emergence of a more multipolar world have strained the rule of law in global affairs. Cracks have emerged in the free and open liberal international order forged at Bretton Woods in 1944 to bring peace and prosperity to a world torn by war.

One result has been a resurgence of nationalism and populism. Across the world, moderate politics have come under assault from political parties and demagogues catering to the passions of the discontented. Both Europe and the United States face dysfunction in their political and economic systems. One way to look at this situation is as a crisis in models: with so many leading nations facing the same problems, and so far proving unable to come up with convincing solutions, the world has no obvious place to go for answers.

The world stands at a new frontier, but who will point the way forward? It is hard to identify a nation that provides a new and suitable model for this era of greater uncertainty. But perhaps we are looking for the wrong thing. Perhaps such a model nation does not need to be clearly ahead of other countries, forcing them to catch up. Perhaps, instead, we can learn to navigate this new frontier by gleaning the lessons to be found in the efforts of fellow travelers who are also working to find a new way forward.

It is precisely at such a time, when no model exists, that Japan's ideas and experiences can provide meaningful hints to the world. Japan has been a frontrunner in many of the problems now faced by other nations: deflation, depopulation, stagnation, natural disasters, shrinking budgets, massive national debt, diminished horizons. This is not to say that Japan has the right answers for all or even most of these issues. In fact, many still view Japan as a negative example of how not to respond to these problems, as seen in the nation's inability to escape its own Lost Decades of low to no growth after the 1990s.

Yet, Japan's efforts to overcome its challenges do have much to offer the world despite these difficulties—or perhaps because of them. In Japan, the Lost Decades have been a spur to innovation, a push to create new ideas, new ways of doing things, even new values that better suit the country's changed reality. During this time, Japan has become more aware of its own place in the world and of its own core competencies, sifting through its experiences to discern what may be of real value.

It is this process of identifying those things with global appeal—of finding the uniqueness within Japan that can be made universal—that may provide the most compelling answers to this volume's overarching question: Why does Japan matter? Finding the value locked within itself is the task facing Japan in the early 21st century. In a sense, this is Japan's frontier—an internal frontier.

To succeed, Japan needs to recognize that its frontier is also the world's frontier. For Japan does offer answers, or at least point a way forward, for many of the most pressing problems facing all nations.

Globalizing Japan's Galapagos

Historically, Japan's appeal has been its perceived uniqueness. Japan was seen as exotic, different, and strange, a topsy-turvy world where all the assumptions had been turned upside down.

In the 16th century, the Portuguese Jesuit missionary Luís Fróis came to Japan, where he befriended the warlord Nobunaga Oda. He collected some 600 cases in which Japan appeared vastly different, even the mirror image of cultures in Western Europe:

"Women in Western Europe polish their teeth white, while Japanese women make their teeth black."

"The door of a Western European house is closed with a hinge, but Japanese doors slide shut."

"A man will look feminine when using a fan, but if a Japanese man doesn't use one, he is considered low in status and poor."[1]

This celebration of the singularity of Japanese culture became so common that the 19th-century French coined a word for it: *Japonisme*. The idea was that this island country in the Far East, cut off from the centers of the world, had followed its own unique path of cultural evolution.

In the early 20th century, Japan became an industrial and military power rivaling the United States and Europe. This made Japan unique for a different reason: as the only non-Western society to join the ranks of advanced, modern nations. Japan became the object of the West's hopes and fears about the ability of the non-Western world to follow in its footsteps. It is undeniable that before and after World War II, it was this uniqueness that lay at the core of the world's interest in Japan, as Western scholars searched for the sources of Japan's successful economic development.

However, the world's view of Japan changed once again after the end of the Cold War, as Japan seemed to fade as a challenge to the global economic order. And that order itself underwent enormous changes due to the forces of globalization, homogenization, and interconnectedness. As the world pulled closer together and embraced common standards and values, Japan seemed to fall out of synch. Japan was slow to adopt the new shared standards and to nurture companies and people who could thrive in this new, globalized environment.

As the world drew closer together, Japan seemed to once again be following its own separate evolutionary course. Japan became known as a Galapagos, after the isolated islands that fascinated Charles Darwin for evolving their own unique ecosystem. In Japan's case, it was an economic isolation in which Japanese companies grew comfortable dominating their still-huge domestic market and producing products and services tailored just to Japanese consumers. A new term was coined for this inward turn: Galapagosization.[2] Moreover, Galapagosization was not limited to products and services; Japan drifted away from the rest of the world not only in cell phone networks and other technological standards but also in rules and regulations and even in the realms of research and intellectual inquiry.

According to Tadashi Maeda, chief executive officer of the Japan Bank for International Cooperation, Japanese companies still believe in the myth of their own technological superiority, formed a generation ago in the era of the Sony Walkman and Datsun Z. These days, he said, the results are less compelling: overly complex, Galapagos-style products that are well engineered but in which the sum is somehow less than the parts and as a result fall flat with global consumers. Japanese companies are no longer able to make the same impact on the world that they once did, seen in Apple's usurpation of Sony as leader in consumer electronics.[3]

Japan's Galapagosization is rooted in domestic politics and the dictates of powerful vested interests that oppose outside competition and changes to the status quo. It also resonates with *nihonjinron* theories of cultural exceptionalism and the desire of many Japanese to believe that they are different and special, which can lead to navel gazing and a shutting of the mind to foreign ideas. This Galapagos syndrome was even a root cause of the devastating accident at the Fukushima Daiichi Nuclear Power Plant. Japan's nuclear industry had created its own safety myth: the belief that nuclear safety in Japan was the best in the world and thus did not need outside peer review. The industry became aloof, oblivious to the changes and improvements in global best practices, while feeling satisfied with Japan's own nuclear safety regulations. This created a blind spot in the safety culture that allowed the plant to be inadequately prepared for the huge earthquake and tsunami that struck on March 11, 2011, causing three reactors to melt down.

However, Galapagosization also has its advantages. In a globalized world, where shoppers in New York and New Delhi increasingly find the same products at the same branded stores, there is a huge appeal in having something different to offer. In this sense, not only Japan's unique products and services but also the methods and practices that have evolved separately from the rest of the world should actually be seen as a precious resource. Used properly, these unique offerings can be an opportunity for Japan to take a bigger global role. They can offer fresh insights to a world that seems to have exhausted its old models and to be in search of a new direction. As the distinctive ecosystem that had been shut off within the borders of Japan's Galapagos comes in contact with the outside world, it can add to the global community's intellectual and cultural diversity by contributing Japan's ideas, approaches, and experiences.

It is at these points, where Japan's Galapagos and the outside world interact, that the mixing of cultures and ideas will occur. Out of them may spring something new and exciting. In Japan, chefs say the most delicious part of the puffer fish is the roe that sits dangerously close to the liver, which contains lethal toxins. So, too, might Japan's offerings with the richest potential for the rest of the world lie in its most closed, inwardly focused, Galapagos-like areas. In short, the question is whether or not we have the clarity of mind and certitude of hand to slice away these tastiest of parts and give them universal appeal by rendering them in a way that satisfies global palates. This is why it is necessary for Japan to open more to the world, to grasp and share its standards and expectations.

By engaging with the world, Japan can rediscover itself. By identifying its own individuality and diversity, Japan can create fresh narratives that allow it to offer more to other nations. This is the new challenge—the new frontier—that Japan faces in the era of globalization.

The Real Thing

As of 2016, the number of Nobel Prize winners from Japan in the natural sciences totaled 22—11 in physics, 7 in chemistry, and 4 in medicine. Japan's number has been increasing rapidly; it has the second-highest tally after the United States since the beginning of the 21st century.[4]

This flies in the face of the reputation that Japan had up until recently as a nation of conformists unable to think outside the box. As recently as 2012, *The Economist* wrote that "young Japanese scientists tend to stick with the theories of the past," while in the West "careers were built tearing down old theories."[5] In a measure of how much Japan's image has changed, when Yoshinori Ohsumi won the Nobel Prize in medicine in 2016, a vigorous debate erupted on the Chinese Web site Sina Weibo on why China was lagging so far behind its neighbor. In an article entitled "Why Japan Can Win So Many Nobel Prizes," a professor of neurobiology at Peking University praised Japan for "cultivating children's independent spirit of exploration while at school and learning from developed countries." The Chinese newspaper *Global Times* noted that there were over 1.23 million views for this article.[6]

In fact, Japan's strength lies in many years of emphasizing basic research and precise measurements, high-quality materials, and accurate experimental equipment that make productive theoretical studies possible. This experimental infrastructure is supported by the quality of engineering education and the fact that the wall separating engineering from theoretical sciences tends to be relatively low at Japanese universities. At the same time, it should be pointed out that many of the Nobel laureates in Japan have research experience in the United States. This sort of intellectual exchange between different fields and different countries is an important spur to creative discovery.

Traditionally, Japan has promoted outbound dialogue and exchanges, usually in the form of sending students and researchers abroad. Such efforts are all the more necessary in an era of globalization. But this era also requires Japan to nurture dialogue and exchange in the other direction, by attracting the world to come here. With the upcoming Tokyo Olympic Games in 2020, Japan has made inbound tourism a national strategic industry. An enormous potential lies in opening the country not just to tourists but to global talent and investment.

This is not to undervalue tourism, which has become a growth industry that has forced Japan to evolve beyond the conventional notions of "sightseeing." Japan is learning to offer visitors not just a location or products but something broader and more rewarding: an experience. This is rooted in the customer satisfaction that comes from the tradition of *omotenashi*, or "hospitality," that anticipates the customers' needs and desires even before the customers themselves are aware of them. This culture of service comes from practice and hard work, an attention to etiquette, and a virtuous cycle in which a commitment to detail teaches diligence, which in turn makes such commitment possible.

It was this spirit of diligence that was the driving force behind the relative economic prosperity and cultural sophistication of Japan's premodern Edo era, from 1603 to 1868. According to Professor Emeritus Akira Hayami of Keio University, an authority on historical demography, if Western Europe experienced the Industrial Revolution, Japan saw its own "Industrious Revolution," a preindustrial period in which households worked harder to earn more money and buy more goods. This era of increasing diligence most likely encouraged Japan's commitment to detail and was in turn also nurtured by it.[7]

Of course, diligence is far from a Japanese monopoly, and hospitality can be found around the world. Indeed, much of what we now view as Japanese culture actually originated abroad. One feature of Japan is the innovation that takes place here through a process of adaptive evolution, in which culture from the outside is brought in and then refined independently into something new and unique. Japan has a tradition of creating added value through this process of importing and improving. It begins with an original raw material that it consciously breaks down over the course of years and then reshapes into a new form.

An example is American fashion. In the early 1960s, many young Japanese embraced the collegiate, Ivy League style of the time: button-down shirts, blazers with ties, penny loafers, and chino pants. But after American students moved on into the bell-bottom jeans and T-shirts of the more casual late 1960s, the preppy fashions lived on in Japan, where they were adapted, modified, and in some cases radically transformed into something new and more refined. They became the so-called Take Ivy trend, also known as American Trad, or *Ametora*.

In a historical twist, these Japanese versions are now gaining fans back in the United States, where brands like A Bathing Ape and Uniqlo are popular. As some Americans have tired of casual wear, they have gone back to a more dapper, vintage look, often via styles and brands that now come from Japan, as writer W. David Marx described in his book *Ametora: How Japan Saved American Style*. In this cycle, the United States was the originator but proved unwilling or unable to maintain its original style. Having imported, maintained, and developed these American-born fashion styles, Japan is now reverse exporting them back to the United States. It is also selling them to other countries as well, creating a global fashion trend. Marx wrote that this process reflects a desire in Japan to find the essence—what he called the Real Thing—of the object of desire, in this case American fashion.[8]

Japan's appeal also lies in its diversity. In general, Japan is regarded as a homogeneous culture lacking in variety, but, in reality, its culture is highly diversified. Just as the charm of Italian cuisine lies in the differing regional styles of Milan, Venice, and Tuscany, so, too, does Japanese food, or *washoku*, offer a great variety of tastes.

This diversity is not limited to regional differences. It is also seen in the ability of Japan to allow the new and the old to exist side by side, even in ancient times. A millennium ago, when control of Japan shifted from the Imperial court to the newly emerging warrior class, the court and its florid culture did not disappear. Rather, the elaborate, colorful costumes of the imperial courtiers continued alongside the drab, spartan kimonos of samurai, with their starkly minimalist ethos. The coexistence of different layers of history is itself a form of diversity. As David Atkinson, an author and former financial analyst who advocates a new tourism strategy for Japan, points out, "the strata of ancient times, medieval times, and modern times still exist" in Japan.[9]

Japan's uniqueness, in other words, lies in its accumulated cultural and historical diversity. However, Japanese themselves often fail to see these layers and recognize their potential. Inbound tourism can be a tool with "the power to awaken" the Japanese people to their nation's diversity, which can be a new frontier for still more creation and innovation.[10]

The Beautiful Foolishness of Things

Japan's ecosystem of the Real Thing, with its commitment to detail and craftsmanship, is supported by the accumulated know-how and dedication to perfection of Japan's producers. But it also depends on Japanese consumers, who are very demanding, refusing to wink at even the smallest flaw.

One of Japan's underappreciated sources of strength is its sophisticated and vigorous consumer culture, which sets a high bar for its manufacturers and retailers. Japanese consumers' refined taste and discerning eye are not the monopoly of a handful of fashionable elite but evident more broadly in the choices of the general populace. An essential part of this consumer culture is its playful spirit. This was already evident in the early 20th century, when thinker Kakuzo Okakura introduced "the spirit of the tea ceremony" to the world as the framework for Japanese culture. Okakura, who also went by the name Tenshin, called this spirit "Teaism," which he described in his classic, *The Book of Tea*:

> It is essentially a worship of the Imperfect, as it is a tender attempt to accomplish something possible in this impossible thing we know as life.
>
> For Teaism is the art of concealing beauty that you may discover, of suggesting what you dare not reveal. It is the noble secret of laughing at yourself, calmly yet thoroughly, and is thus humour itself—the smile of philosophy.
>
> Meanwhile, let us have a sip of tea . . . Let us dream of evanescence, and linger in the beautiful foolish of things.[11]

Okakura first published *The Book of Tea* in English, so the phrase "beautiful foolishness of things" is his, in the original. By it, I think he meant a sort of almost whimsical playfulness. Whether it is a cute character added to the design of wrapping paper, high-tech artificial intelligence packaged up in Sony's new adorable Aibo robot dog, or an emoji on a smartphone, the addition of such playful touches adds color to Japan's consumer culture.

Monocle, a British magazine that explores world lifestyles, frequently carries articles that plumb the depths of Japan's appeal: the popularity of Ichiro's Malt, made by a nearly four-century-old sake brewery that reinvented itself as a whiskey distillery; the understated wooden displays at Tsutaya, "the most attractive electronic products store in the world"; the Isetan department store in Shinjuku, whose staff includes a professional pillow fitter, a towel "sommelier," and the everything-you-want-to-know-about-ceremonial-occasions consultant.[12]

According to Kenji Hall, a Tokyo-based reporter for *Monocle*, one appeal of Japan—its people, shops, objects, designs—lies in its authenticity, in "a culture supported by an unstudied truth and sure craftsmanship." Put another way, this is a union of the Real Thing and the beautiful foolishness of things.

"Every product, every piece has a particular attention to detail," Hall said. "This can be seen all the way through from a piece of packaging. It is quite beautiful, and yet it doesn't show off, that kind of commitment to detail."[13]

Japan's Frontiers Are the World's Frontiers

In January 2000, an advisory body created by then prime minister Keizo Obuchi called the Prime Minister's Commission on Japan's Goals in the 21st Century released a report entitled "The Frontier Within."[14] As the title suggests, the commission's goal was to point a way for Japan to graduate from its postwar focus on catching up with the West, and emulating external models, to becoming a leading nation in its own right, capable of finding the way forward within itself.

Looking within oneself does not mean closing one's borders—far from it. In an era of globalization, the need is greater than ever for citizens who are capable of communicating in real time with the world and in languages that the world can understand, be they English or computer code. It is only by knowing the world's common standards and lingua franca that a nation can tap the enormous opportunities to be found in the connectivity and economies of scale that globalism makes possible.

However, this does not mean that cultural homogenization is desirable. In fact, diversity acquires a new importance, not only from the viewpoint of maintaining identity but also as a means of both finding competitive advantage and contributing more to the world. Globalization is therefore also a process of self-discovery of both one's own individuality and the diversity that one has to offer. Identifying one's own differences makes it possible to utilize them, heighten their value, and build strategies around them.

"If the 20th century was the 'century of the organization,' the 21st century will be the 'century of the individual,'" the commission concluded in its report. "The driving force for the 21st century will be individuals and their pioneering spirit."[15]

Put differently, the source of Japan's future potential lies in unleashing the possibilities created by its internal diversity and particularly the diversity of its individuals. This requires broadening the choices of individuals and their freedom to realize their own potential. It is this freedom that creates what is unique and valuable not only in individuals but also in society as a whole.

This is the frontier within Japan that may hold the key to many of its challenges. With Japan's declining population, falling birthrate, demographic aging, and decline of regional economies, we can no longer rely on economic expansion to simply grow our way out of our problems. We must look for different solutions by making innovations in technology and also social systems. Such steps are needed for Japan to maintain its competitive advantage and avoid being engulfed by globalization or left behind by technological change. Opening up the frontiers is not only a way for Japan to compete but to remain relevant.

At the same time, Japan's problems are increasingly the world's problems. What kind of economic growth should we seek in an era of globalization and long-term stagnation? How do we offer quality health care and medical services to a shrinking and aging population? How do we build resilient societies in the face of global climate change and large-scale natural disasters? What are the peaceful actions that nations can take to shore up or replace the crumbling postwar liberal order? Japan, like other countries, is still grappling with these issues. But in many, Japan may actually have a head start, with ideas, experiences, and innovations to contribute to the rest of the world. In this sense, Japan's frontiers are increasingly the world's frontiers.

Muji Growth

With the rise of China and India, it is the emerging nations that are leading the world economy into the 21st century. Japan must also learn to grow and compete in this new world. Indeed, one of Japan's greatest strengths, its ability to offer the quality and authenticity of the Real Thing, is itself a product of competition.

Why are Japan's three-star restaurants, its architecture and design, and its automobile industry all so strong? Not because the Japanese are special but because of fierce competition. Each is part of an ecosystem within Japan that is intensely competitive and therefore innovative.

Take the automobile industry. Subaru sells 1 million vehicles a year. This may sound like a lot, but it is only about a tenth of Toyota's annual sales. However, the company has been enormously profitable, and demand is so high that there is a waiting list for its automobiles. Subaru's success is based on its image as a maker of rugged, high-performance vehicles with the highest levels of safety. This image is reinforced by Subaru's exemplary performance in crash safety tests: its models have won gold awards for five consecutive years from the Insurance Institute for Highway Safety, an American insurance industry group.[16]

Yasuyuki Yoshinaga, Subaru's chief executive officer, says he decided to focus the company on becoming a "high-quality company that is not big in size but has distinctive strengths" with commitment to higher quality and higher profit margins, rather than trying to compete with bigger rivals on volume of output. "We cannot fight when quantity is the game decider," Yoshinaga said. "How are we unique? Where are our strengths?" His decision was to invest more heavily in safety measures, including the development of new technologies like EyeSight, computer-assisted visual sensors that help drivers avoid accidents.

He called this a natural step for Subaru, which was originally Naka-jima Aircraft Company, a manufacturer of fighter planes and bombers for the Imperial Japanese military until 1945. After the war, it was dismantled by the Allies and reborn as Fuji Heavy Industries. However, Yoshi-naga says the company remains an aircraft maker at heart, an identity that includes the aviation industry's deep commitment to safety.[17]

Like Subaru, Japan itself cannot fight when quantity is the game decider, especially versus competitors with huge domestic markets such as China and India. Rather, Japan must borrow a page from Yoshinaga's playbook and focus its efforts more selectively on differentiating itself and creating products and services with high added value.

These lessons apply not just to autos but also to areas in which Japan has been far less competitive. Take agriculture. Japanese farming has long been seen as an economic backwater, populated by inefficiently small farms shielded behind a wall of tariffs. But with rural villages disappearing due to demographic trends, efforts are afoot to make Japanese farming competitive.

Shinjiro Koizumi, a member of the House of Representatives and rising star in the governing Liberal Democratic Party, goes so far as to say farming could be a growth industry for Japan. This is a radical notion in a nation that currently imports more than half of its food. "Japanese agricultural policy has long focused on agri-Culture," or preserving rural communities, said Koizumi, who is on the party's agricultural subcommittee. "What we need now is to create agri-Business," or a farming industry more oriented toward profits and growth.[18]

Like Yoshinaga at Subaru, Koizumi wants Japan's farmers to compete through differentiation and by offering higher quality. Koizumi said that many Japanese agricultural products, such as beef, green tea, and scallops, are already popular in nearby markets like China, where food safety has become a paramount concern. Some, like Suntory whiskey or high-end *wagyu* beef, have found success in Europe and the United States. By improving global competitiveness through a process of "selection, concentration, differentiation, and added value," Koizumi said Japan's farming exports could even become a big earner in the 21st century.

Each of the frontiers opened up by Japan embodies its own values and cultural appeal. Nowhere is this more apparent than in the success of

Muji, a retailer of household items known for their minimalist, eco-friendly designs. However, Muji's appeal is not limited to the appearance of its products. The company has won a foothold abroad by offering its customers something more, a philosophical reflection on the spirit of the times and values that challenge the homogenizing forces of globalization. According to Muji's first designer, Ikko Tanaka, Muji is an ongoing exploration of how to coexist in a world facing dwindling energy resources, climate change, growing gaps between rich and poor, and the limits of conventional growth models.[19]

What we find here is a story not of a company emphasizing numerical growth but something that makes customers feel more ethical and responsible, what we might call Muji-style growth. Like Subaru, Muji's success is not a simple battle for ever-greater quantity or output. Rather, it is based on the customers' empathy for Muji's message of a calm, thoughtful existence, as expressed in the items that fill their living space.[20] This message can take new meanings in developing countries. Upon Muji's entry into the Chinese market, young customers are said to have tweeted "Muji is fair." In other words, by selling thoughtful, elegantly designed products at affordable prices, Muji appeared not only ethical but egalitarian to young Chinese living in an era of rising income disparities and ostentatious displays of wealth.

A challenge in the 21st century will be finding a way to achieve economic growth without widening the gap between rich and poor. The world's most populated nations—China, India, the United States, Brazil, Russia—all have severe inequalities in wealth.[21] While these gaps were once smaller in Japan, its disparity between the rich and poor is also expanding. Curbing this expansion will be key for walking the path of Muji-style growth.

The Power of Longevity

Japan is an aging society whose citizens enjoy the longest life spans in the world. According to the World Health Organization, Japan ranked No. 1 out of 183 nations in 2015, with a life expectancy of 83.7 years.[22]

Long lives bring special care requirements, some of which Japan is starting to meet with new technologies. One is the HAL suit, a mechanical exoskeleton developed by robotics company Cyberdyne and Tsukuba University. Short for Hybrid Assistive Limb, HAL is essentially a robot that fastens to the user, using motors to assist his or her movements. The suit can be worn by elderly or disabled people to help them walk and use their limbs. It can also be used by caregivers to augment their strength, allowing them to pick up and carry disabled patients. Cyberdyne chief executive officer Yoshiyuki Sankai says HAL's aim is to reduce "severe elder care to zero" by helping the weakened and infirm move without assistance from other people.[23]

The challenges of aging must be met with more than just technology. Preventing an aging society from becoming a collection of old people devoid of energy requires exploring the possibilities of seniors' participation in both society and the economy. This will also have economic benefits, turning the elderly into both a productive part of the workforce and a new source of demand. Kenya Hara, an art director at Muji, says the elderly are consumers who bring not youth or age but purchasing power, experience, and discerning taste. He says that as society ages, it may have to rethink its notions of participation and "activeness," a shift that could allow "hitherto unseen markets to emerge."[24] So an aging society is yet another frontier.

Japan leads the world in not only human life spans but also corporate longevity. In the world, there are some 5,600 companies that are known to be at least two centuries old; more than half of those—3,100 firms—are in Japan. This is far more than the second-ranked country, Germany, which has 840 such long-lived firms.[25]

Not only Japan's companies are long-lived. Horyuji, a Buddhist temple in Nara, was founded in 607. Every 400 years, Horyuji undergoes large-scale repairs, while smaller renovations take place once every century. Each renovation allows the master carpenters, or *miyadaiku*, to engage in a sort of dialogue with predecessors from more than 1,300 years ago. This is how tradition is handed down.

There are many shrines and temples in Japan that are at least a millennium old. In Kyoto alone, the number exceeds 50.[26] This is more than in all of China, the country that originally transmitted Buddhism to Japan but that destroyed much of its ancient history in its 20th-century political paroxysms. One unexpected result is that a growing number of Chinese tourists come to Japan seeking glimmers of their own nation's lost past. According to Mao Danqing, one of the contributors in this volume, Chinese travelers are fond of saying: "If you want to see Tang and Song, go to Japan," referring to the two Chinese Imperial dynasties that existed more than seven centuries ago.[27]

"Only the officially approved remains in China," Mao said. "In Japan, it is the private sector that has maintained these things. Japan's appeal is this endurance of the people."[28]

Social Resilience

In Japan's long history, there have been few shocks as huge as the magnitude 9.0 earthquake that struck on March 11, 2011. Known in Japan as the Great East Japan Earthquake, the temblor triggered a towering tsu-nami that left more than 18,000 people in northeastern Japan dead or missing. The waves also knocked out vital cooling systems at the Fuku-shima Daiichi nuclear plant, causing a triple meltdown that threatened the very survival of the Japanese nation-state. While desperate workers finally regained control of the runaway plant, the disaster made the Japa-nese people acutely aware of their country's vulnerability.

This included fiscal vulnerability. The trade deficit soared as Japan's 50 undamaged commercial reactors were taken offline, creating an energy shortfall that had to be filled by increasing imports of fossil fuels. This raised the specter of Japan, long one of the world's largest creditor nations, falling into a current account deficit, meaning that more money flows out of the country than into it. In the worst-case scenario, this could cause a Greek-style fiscal crisis, since Japan relies on its current account surpluses to self-finance its huge national debt, now worth more than 200 percent of gross domestic product.

Japan has entered an era in which "the twin issues of geopolitical vul-nerability and fiscal vulnerability will continue to be the biggest chal-lenges," said Kathy Matsui, vice chair of Goldman Sachs Japan.[29]

At the same time, popular solidarity in the face of the earthquake, nuclear disaster, and long reconstruction helped tide Japan through the darkest days of the crisis, raising awareness about the importance of social resilience. Japan saw an outpouring of volunteerism that included social entrepreneurs and even companies that sought to contribute to disaster relief and recovery.

The Japanese people's ability to pull together and to help each other in times of need drew wide praise overseas. None less than Henry Kissinger spoke out to commend Japan's solidarity and willingness to work for the national good after the 2011 disaster, saying that these are exactly the qualities that Japan will need as it faces an increasingly uncertain future.[30]

It is these social aspects that explain Japan's remarkable resilience to natural disaster. Cohesion and mutual aid are forms of social capital that are created when local communities encourage participation and a sense of involvement. Rather than physical infrastructure, such as roads and wave walls, it is the strength of community along with good governance and leadership that are essential for surviving disaster and recovering.

Global Civilian Power

I mentioned above how, when Western Europe discovered Japan, it was fascinated by what it saw as a land of the topsy-turvy. However,

European interest also had an ulterior motive, of using Japan as a point of comparison with China.

In 1857, Lord Elgin, a former governor of Canada, was appointed the British Empire's high commissioner in the Far East. He is best known for leading the British to victory during the Second Opium War, but he also negotiated Britain's first treaty of commerce with Japan. Elgin wrote about both countries, often by contrasting orderly Japan's charms with his undisguised dislike of the chaos that he saw in China. In Elgin's writings, Japan served as a foil, used to highlight the problems in its larger Asian neighbor. Elgin even extended these comparisons into the aesthetic realm, contrasting what he saw as a hideously gaudy China with a more understated, refined Japan. This image of a sophisticated and elegant Japan has remained locked in the Western imagination ever since.[31]

It is unfortunate that the West used Japan to belittle China, but the comparison reflects a deeper perception that Japan and China represented fundamentally different cultures, even civilizations.[32]

With China's reemergence in the 21st century as a challenge to both the regional geopolitical power balance and global rules and norms, Japan is forced to reconsider its own position. Like it or not, Japan must reexamine its own identity, determine where it stands in the world, and engage in its own differentiation of itself from the values and vision of China.

So what are the values that Japan can put forth to the world? These might be dedication to peaceful resolutions of diplomatic disputes, freedom of navigation, liberal democracy, and a vibrant civil society. Japan's values can also include some of the characteristics mentioned above: authenticity, the beautiful foolishness of things, the importance of quality and detail, and above all, the nurturing of individuality and diversity.

Differentiating itself from China does not mean competing with China. Rather, it is a means of maintaining Japan's cultural autonomy and values even in the shadow of its far larger neighbor. What is required is a dual task. Japan must rediscover Asia, including China. At the same time, China, the rest of Asia, and the entire world must be allowed to rediscover what is different in Japan. Japan is now faced with such a historical opportunity and mission.

This will require Japan to reinvent itself.

After 1945, Japan embraced a new model, one that focused on catching up economically and technologically with the West while also recasting itself as a nonmilitaristic nation. Eventually, Japan came to see itself as what can be called a "global civilian power," a nation with influence in world affairs but that did not practice the might-based diplomacy of the

Cold War military superpowers. This fit well with Japan's national security strategy at the time, which was defined by its alliance with the United States, awareness of regional sensitivities to its imperialist past, and a domestic rejection of anything smacking of the earlier militarism that had led it to catastrophic defeat.

But the global civilian power was also a proactive vision, one that sought to turn Japan's postwar embrace of peace to its own advantage. It said Japan should play a constructive role in the international community as a nonmilitary, or "civilian," power by embracing three pillars: supporting regional security in peaceful ways, participating in global institutions centered on economic objectives, and helping developing countries mainly via official development assistance, or ODA.[33] Postwar Japan's focus on ODA has been a concrete expression of its desire to be a global civilian power and continues to be a central feature of Japanese diplomacy. Japan's post-1945 renunciation of war, pacifist constitution, and dedication to its alliance with the United States—in short, its strategy of being a global civilian power—have won praise for providing an important anchor to regional stability and global peace and prosperity.[34]

However, in the 21st century, this strategy is in need of a reboot. The postwar liberal international order is under pressure on many fronts. The United States is no longer the sole superpower that it was after the Cold War, due to the rise of China, India, and a more multipolar world. A series of financial crises, resurgent nationalism, and the rise of a new populism have challenged the American-led order's central tenets. This changing new environment calls on Japan to do more to uphold the postwar system from which it has benefited so much. To do this, Japan needs a new strategy, one that keeps its identity as a pacifist actor for peace and stability while also assuming a larger and more proactive role in ensuring stability. This revised version of Japan's postwar strategy might be called Global Civilian Power 2.0.

This vision of civilian power pursuing peaceful solutions can be a new model for not only Japan, with its constitutional constraints, but other nations as well.

Before 1945, Japan descended down a path of invasion and war that brought it to the brink of national suicide. Its postwar rehabilitation began first and foremost with remorse for its wartime actions, a negative historical legacy that has hung over Japan for decades. Reconciliation with a former foe, the United States, has progressed to the point that Prime Minister Shinzo Abe could welcome then president Barack Obama to Hiroshima, the site of the world's first atomic attack, and Obama could reciprocate by welcoming Abe to Pearl Harbor. But reconciliation with Japan's closest neighbors, China and South Korea, lags far behind. To advance this, Japan needs to share more openly with the world the lessons that we have learned from our failures.

The need to recognize our mistakes is not just limited to the war. The architects Kengo Kuma and Toyo Ito did precisely that when they put forth new plans for the main stadium of the 2020 Tokyo Olympics after the city scrapped the bold but increasingly expensive design of Iraqi-British architect Zaha Hadid.

Kuma said he recognized the need for a more affordable and modestly scaled design at a time when fiscal pressures are putting increasing scrutiny on public projects. In chapter 2, he and Dana Buntrock wrote about how Japanese politicians and citizens have come to publicly reject the use of large sums of money for constructing historical commemorative monuments. "More than anything else so far, this decision seemed to mark the end of a postwar era that had been so generous to architects," they wrote.

For his part, Ito described the rejection of Hadid's design as a move away from what he called a modernist mind-set, with its assumption that "the same architecture can be built anywhere in the world," toward something different that places more value on local setting and culture. He said the original design "ignored historical, sacred grounds, such as those in Meiji Shrine's inner and outer gardens," referring to a large, forested shrine of Japan's native Shinto religion that sits near the construction site in central Tokyo.[35]

Think Big

This is not to say that Japan should stop trying to "think big," to use the expression of James Higa, a designer who worked closely with Steve Jobs at Apple.[36] Rather, the lesson may be that there are different ways to do so. Thinking big does not have to be the creation of gigantic monuments. It can also be taking the raw materials that one has at hand—that which is local—and using them to create something with universal appeal.

This can take many forms. Director Makoto Shinkai turned *Your Name*, an animated film in which a high school girl in rural Japan swaps bodies with a high school boy in Tokyo, into a global blockbuster. Since premiering at the Anime Expo 2016 in Los Angeles, the film has quickly become the top-grossing anime film of all time outside Japan, earning more than $330 million.[37]

Critics abroad raved about the film's use of plot twists and vivid detail. But it is also a very Japanese tale, one in which the comical situations faced by the two characters take place in a nation still grieving over the deadly 2011 earthquake and tsunami.

Japan has always been poor at sharing its experiences with other countries, preferring instead to emphasize its differences from the rest of the world. Kenneth Pyle, a professor of modern Japanese history at the University of Washington, says that "Japan has never once tried to universalize its own experience. Instead, it has of its own accord wrapped up its beliefs into the conviction that they are special." This inward focus prevents us from appreciating the value of what Japan has to offer, and offering it to the world.[38]

Atkinson has pointed out that a major complaint by overseas tourists with Japanese museums is their lack of an overarching narrative to give displays meaning.[39] Perhaps the Japanese are poor at telling their own stories. Perhaps the Japanese lack the courage to put forth the world view that lies within them. Just as the Prime Minister's Commission on Japan's Goals in the 21st Century suggested, perhaps Japan's undeveloped frontiers lie within.

However, Japan's frontiers cannot be opened by Japan alone. Japan needs the world to help it explore its frontiers and tell its stories. To do this, Japan needs a recognition that its stories are not unique and inscrutable to outsiders but a precious asset that can offer inspiration and diversity to all humanity. Japan needs to recognize that its frontiers are also the world's frontiers.

By inviting in the world, Japan can rediscover itself. This dynamic allows Japan to recognize its own unique products, experiences, and values that have worth to the rest of the world—what we might call the appeal of Galapagos Cool. This opening also helps Japan avoid the biggest danger of Galapagosization, an inward turn in which Japan is content only looking at itself. I like to call this the mind-set of the Galapagos Fool.

Galapagos Cool and the Galapagos Fool share the same starting point. But their outcomes are vastly different. One is an engagement with the world, the other a rejection of it. To escape the fate of the Fool, Japan must recognize that it cannot pioneer its internal frontiers on its own. It needs to invite in the world to help it do so. And that requires a recognition that its frontiers also have much, in turn, to offer the world.

In that sense, Japan's real frontier is the outside world itself—is that not thinking big?

Notes

1. Ian Littlewood, *The Idea of Japan: Western Images, Western Myths* (Boulder, CO: Ivan R. Dee, 1996), p. 9.

2. Kenji Takada, *A Textbook on Overseas Web Marketing Expanding Marketing Destinations throughout the World* (Tokyo: Nippon Jitsugyo Publishing), 2016.

3. Maeda Masahiro, speaking at Asia Pacific Initiative, February 29, 2016.

4. The Nobel Foundation, "Nobel Laureates and Country of Birth," accessed July 19, 2017, www.nobelprize.org/nobel_prizes/lists/countries.html.

5. The Economist, *The World in 2050 World—The Economist Forecasts* (Tokyo: Bungei Shunju, 2012), p. 346.

6. Liu Xin, "Japan's Nobel Harvest Spurs Reflection," *Global Times*, October 9, 2016.

7. Akira Hayami, *Japan's Industrious Revolution* (Tokyo: Springer Japan, 2015), pp. 95–98.

8. W. David Marx, *Ametora: How Japan Saved American Style* (New York: Basic Books, 2015), pp. 236–237.

9. David Atkinson, *New Theory of a Tourism Nation* (Tokyo: Toyo Keizai, 2015), p. 69.

10. Kenya Hara, speaking at Asia Pacific Initiative, January 18, 2016.

11. Kakuzo Okakura, *Book of Tea* (Tokyo: Iwanami Bunko, 2015), pp. 21, 29, 31.

12. Kenji Hall, "Eastern Promise," *Monocle*, September 2013; Fiona Wilson, "Lifestyle Technique," *Monocle*, October 2015; Kenji Hall, "Expo 92: What's in Store," *Monocle*, April 2016.

13. Kenji Hall, speaking at Asia Pacific Initiative, June 10, 2016.

14. The Prime Minister's Commission on Japan's Goals in the 21st Century, "The Frontier Within: Individual Empowerment and Better Governance in the New Millennium," posted January 2000, http://www.kantei.go.jp/jp/21century /report/pdfs/index.html.

15. 21st Century Commission, "Frontier Within," pp. 37, 40, 45.

16. Insurance Institute for Highway Safety, "Top Safety Picks By Year," accessed July 19, 2017, www.iihs.org/iihs/ratings/TSP-List.

17. Yasuyuki Yoshinaga, interviewed by the author, July 5, 2016.

18. Shinjiro Koizumi, speaking at Asia Pacific Initiative, December 9, 2015.

19. Masaaki Kanai, interviewed by the author, June 8, 2016.

20. Masaaki Kanai, speaking at Asia Pacific Initiative, September 28, 2016.

21. Parag Khanna, *Connectography: Mapping the Global Network Revolution* (London: Weidenfeld & Nicolson, 2016), pp. 47–48.

22. World Health Organization, World Health Statistics 2016, June 2016.

23. Yoshiyuki Sankai, speaking at Asia Pacific Initiative, May 12, 2016.

24. Kenya Hara, *Japanese Design* (Tokyo: Iwanami Shoten, 2011), p. 226.

25. "Why So Many Longstanding Firms in Japan? A Bank of Korea Analysis," *Yonhap News Agency*, posted May 14, 2008, http://japanese.yonhapnews.co.kr /economy/2008/05/14/0500000000 AJP20080514003900882.HTML.

26. "Kyoto Walk Navigation, a List of Temple and Shrine Building Dates," Kyoto Sanpo Nabi, accessed July 19, 2017, http://kyoto-sampo.jp/list/konryu.html.

27. Mao Danqing, speaking at Asia Pacific Initiative, March 2, 2016.

28. Mao Danqing, interviewed by the author, February 9, 2016.

29. Kathy Matsui, speaking at Asia Pacific Initiative, February 9, 2016.

30. Henry Kissinger, *World Order* (London: Penguin Press, 2014), p. 190.

31. Littlewood, *The Idea of Japan,* pp. 74–75.

32. For example, Arnold J. Toynbee, *A Study of History, Volume 1: Abridgement of Volumes 1-6* (Oxford, UK: Oxford University Press, 1987), p. 103; Samuel P. Huntington, *The Clash of Civilizations and the Remaking of World Order* (London: Penguin Books, 1997), p. 45.

33. 21st Century Commission, "Frontier Within," p. 204.

34. Kissinger, 2014, p. 189.

35. Toyo Ito, *Change Japan with "Architecture"* (Tokyo: Shueisha, 2016), pp. 16, 38.

36. James Higa, speaking at Asia Pacific Initiative, November 11, 2015.

37. Jack Shepherd, "*Your Name* Beats *Spirited Away* to Become Highest-Grossing Anime Ever," *The Independent*, January 17, 2017.

38. Kenneth B. Pyle, *Japan Rising: The Resurgence of Japanese Power and Purpose* (New York: Public Affairs, 2008), p. 206.

39. David Atkinson, speaking at Asia Pacific Initiative, April 28, 2016.

About the Editors and Contributors

Editors

Martin Fackler was journalist in residence and research fellow at Asia Pacific Initiative from 2015 to 2017. He is currently Assistant Asia Editor for *The New York Times*, where he also worked as Tokyo bureau chief from 2009 to 2015, covering Japan and the Korean peninsula. He is the author (in Japanese) of the best seller *Credibility Lost: The Crisis in Japanese Newspaper Journalism after Fukushima*, a critical look at Japanese media coverage of the 2011 earthquake and nuclear disaster. Prior to becoming bureau chief, he was Tokyo economics correspondent for *The New York Times*. He has also worked in Tokyo for *The Wall Street Journal*, the *Far Eastern Economic Review*, the *Associated Press*, and *Bloomberg News*, and in Beijing, Shanghai, and New York for *AP*.

Yoichi Funabashi is the cofounder and chairman of Tokyo-based think tank Asia Pacific Initiative (formerly Rebuild Japan Initiative Foundation) and the former editor in chief of the *Asahi Shimbun* (2007–2010). He is an award-winning Japanese journalist, columnist, and author. He has written extensively on foreign affairs, the United States–Japan Alliance, economics, and historical issues in the Asia Pacific. He served as correspondent for the *Asahi* in Beijing (1980–1981) and Washington (1984–1987) and as American general bureau chief (1993–1997). His books in English include *Meltdown* (Brookings Institution, forthcoming), *The Peninsula Question* (Brookings Institution, 2007), *Reconciliation in the Asia-Pacific*, ed. (USIP, 2003), and *Alliance Adrift* (Council on Foreign Relations Press, 1998), among others.

Contributors

Daniel P. Aldrich (chapter 8) is professor and director of security and resilience studies at Northeastern University. He researches postdisaster recovery and the interaction between civil society and the state. He contributes to *The New York Times*, *CNN*, and the *Asahi Shimbun*, among other media. His publications include *Building Resilience* (University of Chicago Press, 2012) and *Site Fights* (Cornell University Press, 2010).

Matt Alt (chapter 1) is vice president of AltJapan. He has been working as a professional translator and freelance writer since the early 1990s. He is the coauthor of numerous books about Japan and is a contributor to *The New Yorker*, *CNN*, *Wired* magazine, *Slate* magazine, the *Independent*, *Newsweek Japan*, *The Japan Times*, and many other publications.

Dana Buntrock (chapter 2) is professor of architecture and chair of the Center for Japanese Studies at the University of California, Berkeley. Her work focuses on interdisciplinary collaborations in Japanese architecture and construction practices. She has authored three books and is currently working on a book provisionally titled *Untapped Social and Economic Opportunities in Japanese Architecture*.

David Cyranoski (chapter 6) is the Asia Pacific correspondent for the scientific journal *Nature*. Currently based in Shanghai, he held that position in Japan for nearly a decade and a half. He has a master's degree in the history of science and the history of Japan from the University of California, Berkeley. The views and opinions expressed in his chapter are his own.

Mao Danqing (chapter 7) is a professor at Kobe International University. After working at the Chinese Academy of Social Sciences Institute of Philosophy, he came to Japan for further studies at Mie University. In 2011, he launched *Zhiri* (Know Japan), a monthly Chinese-language magazine that introduces Japanese culture to readers in China, and he is editor in chief of a new Shanghai-based magazine called *Zai Riben* (In Japan).

Yuichi Hosoya (chapter 10) is a professor in the faculty of law at Keio University. His areas of expertise are international history, contemporary East Asian security, and Japanese foreign and security policy. His recent articles featured in books include "Japan's National Identity in Postwar Diplomacy" and "The Atlantic Community and the Restoration of the Global Balance of Power."

Hiromi Inami (chapter 9) is an assistant professor at the College of International Relations at Ritsumeikan University. She was an economist at the World Bank and was involved in education projects and poverty assessments in the Africa Region and the Europe and Central Asia Region. Since 2011, she has worked for JICA Research Institute and management consulting firms in Japan.

Yoshiki Ishikawa (chapter 5) earned a bachelor's degree in health science from the University of Tokyo, a master's of science in health policy and management from Harvard School of Public Health, and a PhD in medicine from Jichi Medical School. As a public-health researcher and science journalist, he specializes in health policy and management, behavioral science, and computational creativity.

Fumiko Kato (chapter 3) is the founder of WAmazing, a smartphone app for tourists from outside of Japan. She was chief researcher at the Jalan Research Center, where she focused on the Japanese domestic travel market and tourism's impact on regional revitalization. She joined Recruit Holdings in 1998 and was involved in establishing Jalan.net and Hot Pepper Gourmet.

Kengo Kuma (chapter 2) is the founder of Kengo Kuma & Associates and is a world-renowned architect. He has received several awards, including Architectural Institute of Japan Award for *Noh Stage in the Forest* (1997), Decoration Officer de L'Ordre des Arts et des Lettres (2009), and MEXT's Art Encouragement Prize (2011). His wooden lattice design was chosen for the Tokyo 2020 Olympic/Paralympic National Stadium.

Kenji E. Kushida (chapter 4) is a research scholar at the Shorenstein Asia-Pacific Research Center Japan Program at Stanford University. His research interests range widely, including international comparative politics, information technology, Silicon Valley, and the Fukushima nuclear accident. He is also an affiliated researcher at the Berkeley Roundtable on the International Economy.

Jennifer Lind (chapter 11) is associate professor of government at Dartmouth College. Her area of expertise is international relations in East Asia. She is the author of *Sorry States: Apologies in International Politics* (Cornell University Press, 2008) among others. She regularly contributes articles to publications such as *Foreign Affairs* and *The Wall Street Journal*.

Lully Miura (introduction) is a lecturer at the Policy Alternatives Research Institute of the University of Tokyo. Her Japanese books include *Civilian's War* (Iwanami, 2012), *Understanding Contemporary Japanese Politics and Diplomacy* (in Japanese, Bunshunshinsho, 2015) and *Dilemma of the State* (in Japanese, Shincho, 2017) among others.

Index